MICHAEL JACKSON

THE LAST DANCE

How Harlem Remembered Michael Jackson

FREDERICK MONDERSON

SUMON PUBLISHERS

SuMon Publishers
PO Box 160347
Brooklyn, New York 11216

sumonpublishers.com@sumonpublishers.com
blackfolksbooks.com@blackfolksbooks.com
fredsegypt.com@fredsegypt.com blackegyptbooks.com@blackegyptbooks.com

ISBN – 978-1-61023-014-8
LCCN - 2010918494

In the Tribute to Professor George Simmonds, "Unsung Hero," Dr. Fred Monderson sat at the feet of his heroes, Brother X, Michael Carter, Dr. Leonard Jeffries, El Hombre Brath, Dr. Lewis, Prof. George Simmonds, Dr. ben-Jochannan, Sister Camille Yarbrough, among others.

Michael Jackson's quintessential and immortalized dancing pose displayed on the "Altar of Remembrance" among other memorabilia fans displayed in paying tribute to the musical great.

MICHAEL JACKSON'S LAST DANCE

TABLE OF CONTENTS

	Preface	3
1.	Michael! Song Divine	7
2.	Michael Jackson Archangel	14
3.	Beating Back Wolves at the Door	22
4.	Joseph Jackson	32
5.	The Body of Work	42
6.	Michael Jackson Timeline	62
7.	President to Prisoners Salute MJ	74
8.	Staples Center Memorial to Michael Jackson on July 7, 2009	84
9.	Michael Jackson Beloved	94
10.	Expressing the Voice of the People	103
11.	Commentators on Michael Jackson	120

FREDERICK MONDERSON

12. Michael Jackson
    In Retrospect   129
13. Conclusions   138
14. Visceral Concern   147
15. The Legacy of
    Michael Jackson   193
16. Michael Jackson Postscript 202
17. Michael Jackson Post,
    Postscript   213
18. Michael Jackson:
    Final Word   220
19. Thoughts on the
    Funeral   236
20. Periodical Bibliographical
    Reference for Further
    Research   241

MICHAEL JACKSON'S LAST DANCE

Michael Jackson's Last Dance Photo 1. The Legendary Nat King Cole has his name officially recognized beside the Marquee of the legendary Apollo Theater.

Michael Jackson's Last Dance Photo 2. Another close-up view of the Marquee with the lights beneath all indicating the purpose of the Memorial.

PREFACE

Michael Jackson's Last Dance, is an attempt to capture photographically the essence and philosophic outpouring of love and affection offered for Michael Jackson, a truly incredible legend and wonderful product of the Apollo Theater, where so many have gotten their start. Upon Michael's passing, Rev. Al Sharpton, incisively avant-garde as he always is, called

3

FREDERICK MONDERSON

for the celebration not simply to honor this great artiste but also to help shape the overall response that would ensue in wake of Michael's public and private persona. Naturally, because of Michael's great talents that have serenaded so many for so long, the community from far and wide thought it fitting that this magnanimous hero should be remembered Harlem, New York, style. This is reflected in fact that the Apollo theater is one of Harlem, New York City's and America's most enduring cultural institutions. In that vein, Michael's fans came to give him the thunderous "Wake" or "Home Going Celebration" fitting for the charismatic megastar that Michael really was. In retrospect, with Sharpton stewarding the tribute, the "wolves" were forced to tow the line and with that the show beautifully unfolded with thunderous spirituality hovering, musically and mystically, while financially rewarding local merchants. All this notwithstanding, the photographs especially reflect on the fact, the Apollo Theater of Harlem, New York, celebrating its 75th year in 2009, certainly knows how to throw a party, especially for one of its greats which in turn reinforces the utility of that institution!

To complement the photographs presented in this work, texts praising Mr. Jackson in a positive manner offer different perspectives that constructively chronicle the originality of his life and work as well as seeking to counter negative sentiments expressed regarding the gentleman's personal life. This work of praise highlights some aspects of the mystical, spiritual, divine essence of a man who describes himself as "a slave to the rhythm" and as "a perfectionist" also confessed "I am blessed to be an instrument of nature." He had an exceptional work ethic. This was clearly manifest and through his extraordinary talents he was able to touch the esoteric metaphysical and spiritual inner core of so many, eschewing a healing potency that speaks to a heavenly endowed mission of human transformation brought about in wonderful expressions of love, love, love! In addition, as far as possible, paying attention to the significant body of work he has produced and recounting sentiments expressed by the people, this effort has sought to paint as positive a picture of a man whom Elizabeth Taylor dubbed "King of Pop, Rock, Soul, Entertainment." Equally a child star in the public eye just as Michael, she described him as "highly intelligent, intuitive, understanding, sympathetic and generous" even "larger than life."

Finally, a bibliography has been appended to encourage further research into the life of this incredible entertainer who knew so many in all walks of life and touched so many more offering sentiments of love, healing and compassion through his magical aura, charitable and humanitarian spirit, and extraordinary

4

creativity that now seems timeless. It equally casts a stern and critical view of the role Media has played in hounding Mr. Jackson with a seeming predetermined intent. While the insidious name calling and negativity is renown, an equally good example is also seen for, in the days after his death word circulated on the Internet that Evan Chandler, the young man who accused Mr. Jackson of child molestation, staining his career and persona, has reportedly confessed that his dad made him falsely swear to those allegations. How sad and even more important, the media has chosen to ignore this revelation unmindful it may make Mr. Jackson rest peacefully knowing the truth has finally and really set him free of that horrible experience; and to those who have so bitterly excoriated him over the years, make them realize how wrong they were in their harsh treatment of this wonderful soul who only had good intentions in his crusade to help and heal mankind, while gushing them with extraordinary joy of music and dance. This issue has been debated unending, however, no independent confirmation has been made that Mr. Chandler actually uttered the words attributed to him. Yet, it's believed if he did make such a confirmed confession it would probably open any number of possibilities of not just public moral condemnation but also possible legal ramifications. Still, the statue of limitations may have expired regarding the incident and therefore he could not be prosecuted. Nevertheless, conscience is a powerful prosecutor and only time will tell if this whole incident is really true or fabricated. Nonetheless, we should always be mindful of a powerful Michael's saying: "No one wants to be mortal. Everybody wants immortality. I know the creator will die, but his work will live on."

The Photographs for the most part, speak for themselves, even though they carry a caption, for they give the reader an opportunity to observe, ponder, reflect and connect to Michael through their own personal experiences which were shared with and through him. Afterall, hardly anyone over the last decades has not heard and participated in the enjoyment of some song or concert, video, etc., associated with Michael Jackson.

The Memorial was designed to celebrate a true Apollo legend, as the theater historian Billy Mitchell indicated; because Michael was someone who went forth and conquered the world through his work ethic, the sensational gracefulness of his dance routines and the ingenuity of his lyrics and angelic and melodic voice. Putting all of this together, we are convinced there was something special about Michael Jackson, something spiritual, mystical, even magical. He was a sort of mythical figure imbued and guided by divine inspiration and heavenly grace. Deepak Chopra described Michael as "one of the great iconic artists of our time." He was an "artistic genius of immense stature and though not formally trained he read classics and listened to Beethoven and Mozart." Even further, he added, Michael Jackson "will be remembered for the agony of what he experienced and the ecstasy he gave people." Equally his son, Gotham Chopra, a friend of Michael for many years added, "The same people who scandalized him turned around to

5

praise him. This is part of the mythical process." That is to say, Michael ascended from mortal to immortal to mystical, mythical stature.

All of this is sought to be captured in this volume in Tribute to a man of extraordinary artistry who worked tremendously hard to optimize his talents and become the very best in his profession, setting the bar above the rainbow and daring others to even attempt to reach or scale it. Nevertheless, in process of his unspoken challenge, he dared others to do what he did through love, charity and his trust of humanity, all within the philosophical constructs of the fatherhood of god and the brotherhood of man.

Michael Jackson's Last Dance Photo 3. View from the Seventh Avenue side of the Marquee.

MICHAEL JACKSON'S LAST DANCE

1.   MICHAEL! SONG DIVINE
By

Dr. Fred Monderson

"A wonderful song of praise to a gem of entertainment!"

Beautiful soul, man of love blest with the angelic voice, piece of divinity rests within you

For decades you created an inspiration with a delightful and elegant refinement of sweet musical poetry, seemingly guided by the highest spiritual authority, heart of a gentle lion

Ground breaking entertainer, the sweet melody of your wonderful craft was superhuman, spiritual, divine, and incandescent, master purveyor of a universal lyrical language

Your inspired music reached across cultures and nations to harmoniously soothe souls of young and old; genius, your innocence is divinely beautiful with a soothing potency

Michael Jackson's Last Dance Photo 4. An early view of the entranceway to the Apollo where well-wishers began to pay tribute to their idol on the "Altar of Remembrance" that would later blossom with flowers, hats, illustrations, all in love for MJ.

FREDERICK MONDERSON

Adorable and mystical spirit, Michael, archangel, child of exorbitant talent, maker of sweet music of happiness and healing, you are a master commander of musical arenas where your rhythm is classic and explosive, thunderous entertainer extraordinary

Man of boundless vision and magical creativity, how well you play those delectable keys of enchanting music, seeming whatever the poet writes is divinely inspired, professional

Cultural icon, though never echoing black is beautiful with your euphonic voice, existing above mundane issues of blackness, your light is illuminating

Your life and legacy is a manifestation of that forcefully creative shibboleth and the god of music, Thoth, is pleased with your iconic cultural contribution

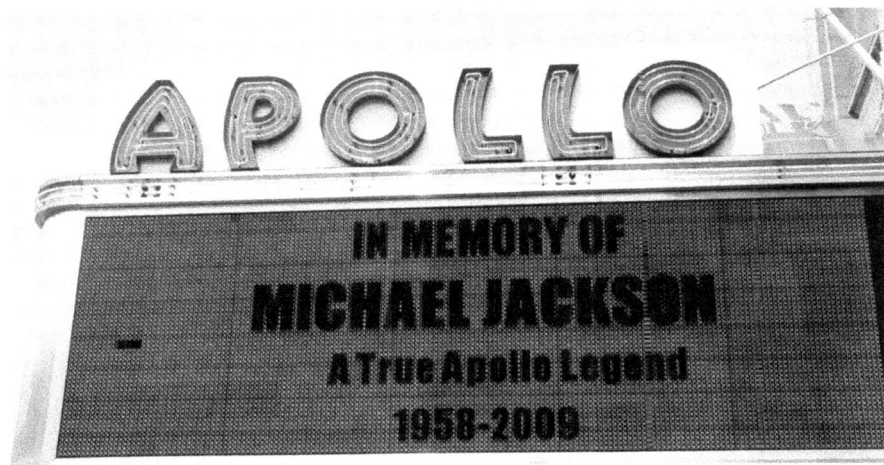

Michael Jackson's Last Dance Photo 5. A close-up of the Apollo Marquee, from the Seventh Avenue side.

Purveyor of happiness through sweet music, imbued with spiritual creativity to create, virtuoso you are a giver of merriment to fans worldwide, your influence is unmatched

Possessing great spiritual grace, merry-maker, your vivid melody charms the soul, engulfs and makes the heart flutter, all wonderfully pleasing to the ear and bosom

Joy maker, your immortal lyrics awaken the dawn, salivates the sun, illuminates the heavens, and soothes evening bloom dressed in gleaming stars of your

8

MICHAEL JACKSON'S LAST DANCE

picturesque attires manifested in colorful garbs, zippers, glasses, white sox, gloves, glitter

Possessing great spiritual vitality, Moonwalker, the best of your superabundant musical charm is pleasing and joyful to the hearing with an original healing potency, unmatched, representing the joy of all humanity

Cultural celebrity phenomenon, your melodic dancing waves and musical expression is poetry in motion, exalting in its chants, everlasting in its blissful exuberance, classical

Great one blest with originality, your spirituality is incredible, your earned immortality is enshrined in photos, images, film, cards, race, music, entertainment, and much more since your talent was before and above your time

Very complicated, yet never racially or culturally controversial, you espoused godliness in your genius, gentle disposition and soft-spoken mannerism, yet endowed with powerful creative talents you are beyond legend, barrier breaker possessing a loving heart and wonderful disposition, philanthropist who cared for the poor across the globe

Forcefulness of you as symbol advanced the cause of blackness through culture, music and exquisite harmony that charmed the great mystical beauty and light of the universe

Not just a crossover artiste by any means, your intelligence, stature and persona, global in its consummate perfection, is a testimonial of impressive proportions, soul of genius, existing above our earthly concerns

Michael Jackson's Last Dance Photo 6. View of the Apollo from across the streets, with people who gathered to pay their respects after the passing of their Icon Michael Jackson.

FREDERICK MONDERSON

Brilliant creator of exquisite sounds, you harmoniously impregnated cultural salt in the earth's consciousness, to rejoice and celebrate an enlightening symphony through an amazing body of music, the greatest testament to your extraordinary persona
Extolling love, brotherhood, and cultural syncretism, exalted in your delightful chants
You help others to see,
We are the world, where so many aspire to be

Michael Jackson's Last Dance Photo 7. View of people gathered, from directly across the street.

Cherubim transcending the realms of the most high, beautiful ornament, wonderful addition to the heavenly choir, your well-mannered, soft spoken nature is unique
The euphoric melody of your elegant and graceful dancing footsteps partnering with the heavenly and dignified Alvin Ailey
Will forever virtuously echo, Michael, music maker, with the magnificent majesty of Marvin, Miriam, and Marley
As the sweet harmony of your lyrics resonate thunderously in the many mansions of the almighty's silvery universe, an audience of angels will welcome you into divine bosom

MICHAEL JACKSON'S LAST DANCE

Michael Jackson's Last Dance Photo 8. Another view of bystanders who gathered.

Michael Jackson's Last Dance Photo 9. Still another view from across the street.

We mortals continue to sing you praises delightful one, you're more than a crossover star, you were beloved by all
So we can never say goodbye, uniqueness
We will forever be grateful you provided intangible food for the human soul and spirit through your boundless and harmonious musical chords

FREDERICK MONDERSON

Michael Jackson's Last Dance Photo 10. Another view of the Marquee from the east.

Trumpeter of splendid chimes, the sweet resonance of your lyrics is like bells chiming musically in the heavenly Milky Way, all resonating into eternity without ending
Hounded in life because of envy, betrayed, yet not guilty, triumphant and martyred for pursuit of creative merriment that pleases the hearts of many cultures, your blessed talent is powerful and everlasting in the celestial firmaments you sang under unending

Today we mourn
Yet thankful for your sojourn,

MICHAEL JACKSON'S LAST DANCE

Knowing your sweet fire will forever burn in your comfortable global domain, soul man

King of Pop, talented creator with exceptional artistic charisma, disciplined and a gentle person, man of love in search of love, the deathlessness of your silver sounds and golden harmony will live in musical remembrance for eons to come as the heavens proclaim the mystical and magical genius of your offers to aid humanity

Gifted beyond comparison, beyond legend, yours is music while music lasts, unrivaled, supreme

Because your mind is a musical instrument of great and melodious refinement, you're considered a universal pop culture icon, born to perform

Thus, songbird, we give thanks you blest humanity's existence with creative expressions of joyousness, civility and soulful inspiration possessing a tremendously spectacular potency

Your musical and human contributions will echo for generations to come, because your chords reached deep into the universe helping create and echoing the food of divine love

Blessed as an angelic light your magic shined wonderfully bright as a young vigorous sun

Bells of heaven chimes as you are called home to embellish the heavenly orchestra

Sorrowfully, we know humanity is deprived when such a soft creative voice of love dies.

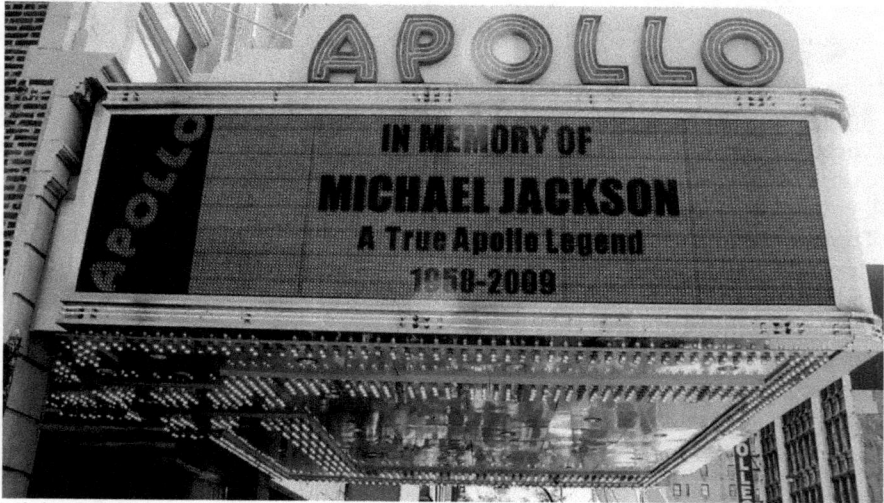

Michael Jackson's Last Dance Photo 11. Another close up of the Marquee's sign.

FREDERICK MONDERSON

Michael Jackson's Last Dance Photo 12. Still another close up of the Marquee.

2. MICHAEL JACKSON ARCHANGEL
By

Dr. Fred Monderson

This inquiry and exposition is a rebuttal of the negativity that has attempted to drown the celebration of the life and work of the gifted and wonderful light Michael Jackson manifested and represented as an African American cultural phenomenon. In the continuum of attempting to degrade black people one has to wonder whether the Media, obsession with the flaws of this talented young man, really reflects the toxic stream that runs in the American psycho-cultural consciousness. Rev. Al Sharpton once remarked, the Media focused too much on Michael Jackson's few imperfections and not sufficient on his extraordinary talent and compassionate humanitarianism. Even before allegations of misconduct with children surfaced, Michael Jackson was under the Media gun for his artistic creativity. Let's face it, when "Thriller" was first released he was criticized, yet the song and video kept making record sales. Nearly three decades later, "Thriller"

14

MICHAEL JACKSON'S LAST DANCE

seems to have become the national anthem for Halloween, attesting not only to Mr. Jackson's talent as an artiste, but also indicating how well ahead of his time and critics he really was.

The unfolding Media onslaught that has sought to tear down Mr. Jackson in life and now again in death, we saw in Byron Styron's depiction of Nat Turner, the revolutionary leader in 1831; with the attention paid the early heavyweight champion Jack Johnson; in the case against Marcus Garvey who founded the Universal Negro Improvement Association and who gave us the powerful symbol of the Red, Black and Green; and again with Paul Robeson, whose talents were on stage and screen, particularly on the international scene. Also, let us not forget what J. Edgar Hoover did to Dr. Martin Luther King, Jr., as he waged the Civil Rights Struggle to help transform American society. Such Media assault efforts set out to upset the psychic equilibrium of these black leaders and yet, after the sensational hounding, their names still remained positively and indelibly imbedded in the collective consciousness of the African America community. This is so because, as Malcolm X instructed, "No matter what the man says, you better look into it." Therefore, and upon close inspection, it was revealed the full extent of the envy and vindictiveness contained in the Media onslaught. The only difference with Michael Jackson is that he was extraordinarily creative, yet tough, strong, and manifested and encapsulated himself in tremendous good. Even more, he was bigger than all these leaders in that his contributions were national and international, in diverse fields. Still more, his giftedness was of a divinely inspired, magical, mystically spiritual nature so his creations soared heavenwards. Yet, in death, no compassion was shown in the Media frenzy now playing.

Nonetheless, those with the vision of consciousness realize Michael Jackson possessed and manifested the continuum of the artistic beauty of our people, the spiritual power, and the mysticism of the African, who from days of the plantation would sing:

"My lord what a morning when the stars begin to fall,
I've been buked and I've been scorned,
But I ain't going to lay my religion down."

When questioned about his religion Michael responded without hesitation "I believe in god, absolutely!"

Heaping buke and scorn on Brother Michael, not being mindful of his genius, in aid of sensationalism is simply shallow; still we will hold him high for beyond his many talents; he was an extraordinary humanitarian who sought to help and heal humanity. We must stand positively in solidarity with Michael Jackson! The Media held Michael to a different standard, because they did not know him. And so, we will hold him high because there was much good in his actions. He changed

15

FREDERICK MONDERSON

popular culture by setting standards for people to come after him. He mirrored a sentiment of Malcolm X; 'The Man in the Mirror' is a powerful force for change. He is the leader we waited for; he encouraged us to empower ourselves wanting us to be compassionate towards humanity.

In all this, we cannot lose sight of the ancestral words of potent wisdom that has meant so much for, according to Dr. Leonard James of Stone Mountain, Georgia:

"Don't look for the flaws as you go through life
And even when you find them, it is wise
And it is kind to be somewhat blind
And look for the virtue behind them."

Therefore, the virtues of Brother Jackson far outweigh the flaws. This literary effort is therefore a humble attempt to help correct a long unfolding wrong, that is, to correct distortions and omissions systematically implanted and designed to continue destroying the name and legacy of Michael Jackson, because of his greatness, and his unending attempts to more creatively express himself. We know he was bigger than Elvis Presley and Frank Sinatra, perhaps better than both combined. Also, let's not forget Sammy Davis was better than most, but did not get the recognition he deserved.

A legitimate question therefore is, 'how does Katherine Jackson in this time of grief feel about the negative publicity being showered on her beloved son?' This is a time of empathy and compassion for this gifted family, yet the Media, viz., print, radio and television, fall tremendously short in this department. Reverend Sharpton reminded us: "We all owe a debt to Michael, that family, for the joy he brought the world." As such, when we consider this shoddy treatment, we are being reminded Michael Jackson and by extension the Jacksons are members of the American household; some believe not members of the American family! Such a mindset is a throwback to the plantation mentality that wrecked so much psycho-social havoc on the African American family structure both physically and literally. Nevertheless, in assessing this malady, 'let us not forget, all our dignity lies in thought, not in time and space which we cannot fill, therefore, let us endeavor to think well for that is the meaning of morality and spiritual power.'

In that universal humanistic outlook, we must remember John Dunn's immortal words:

16

MICHAEL JACKSON'S LAST DANCE

Michael Jackson's Last Dance Photo 13. Gentlemen delivering the famous image.

"The death of any man diminishes me
For I am involved with humanity
Send not then for whom the bell tolls
For it tolls for thee!"

Thus, it must be pointed out, in the psychic consciousness of African Americans the climb and the journey of Michael Jackson mirrors our climb and journey on that steep hill in life. We must give Michael peace; he gave us peace, but did not get peace here on earth! Thank you Michael, rest peacefully, and may God bless your everlasting soul!

FREDERICK MONDERSON

Michael Jackson's Last Dance Photo 14. Beautiful hands gently rest the tribute on the "Altar of Remembrance."

Michael Jackson's Last Dance Photo 15. Flowers can say so much as they adorn the "Altar of Remembrance."

MICHAEL JACKSON'S LAST DANCE

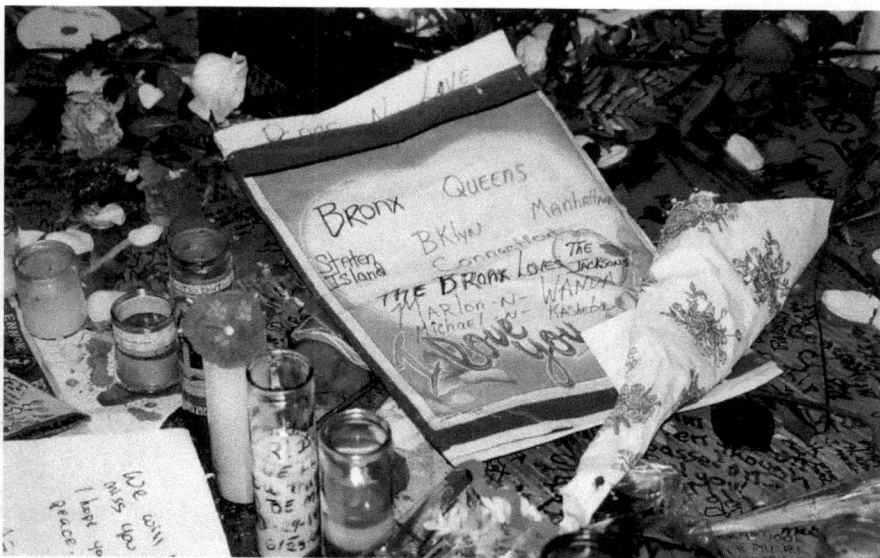

Michael Jackson's Last Dance Photo 16. All Boroughs are represented in this photo, resting gently on the "Altar of Remembrance."

Michael Jackson's Last Dance Photo 17. The space begins to fill up with goodwill greetings on the "Altar of Remembrance" including the hat, candles and flowers in tribute to a very special entertainer and human being.

FREDERICK MONDERSON

Michael Jackson's Last Dance Photo 18. Now the field gets crowded with tribute on the "Altar of Remembrance."

Michael Jackson's Last Dance Photo 19. Balloons of love with bouquets of flowers for King of Pop, Michael Jackson, all adorn the "Altar of Remembrance."

MICHAEL JACKSON'S LAST DANCE

Michael Jackson's Last Dance Photo 20. Another close up of the loving tribute. See Michael peeping out from the rear in a famous photo and to the right another such photo on the "Altar of Remembrance."

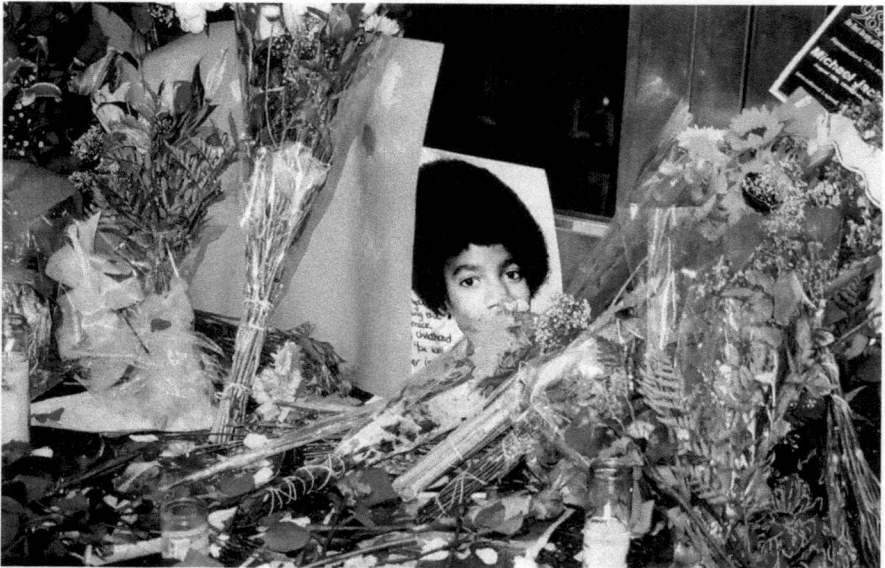

Michael Jackson's Last Dance Photo 21. A close up of the now crowded "Altar of Remembrance" adorned with flowers as Michael peeps out from the rear.

3. BEATING BACK WOLVES AT THE DOOR
By

Dr. Fred Monderson

In death as in life, Michael Jackson's image remains tarnished in the Media as it appears, which cannot say a positive word, for as Rev. Al Sharpton said, "Why harp on the negative, why not ask questions about the positive things the man has done?"

The Media's obsession with whether Michael Joseph Jackson used prescription drugs or harping on claims of sexual misconduct seems to underscore, at this historically important time, going 'up the down staircase' or 'driving in the wrong direction on a one way street.' The people whom Michael Jackson reached, those touched by his music, his adorable fans, people in the music industry-influenced by him and are carrying forth his legacy, are determined at this time that "good will triumph over evil," and Michael Jackson will get his due!

When questioned about burials in the African American tradition, Professor John Henrik Clarke replied, "We put them away nicely!" This is what those who love him in the Civil Rights Movement, entertainment, the clergy and adoring fans worldwide are striving sternly to accomplish!

Now, as I stumble through the morass of allegations against Michael Jackson following his death, I remained convinced this wonderful soul is a victim of innuendos, speculations, lies, ignorance, and "matchstick men mentalities" and those who tried to swindle the entertainer. We are all familiar with the role of the Media in the constant replay of innuendos and false claims to nauseating proportions, while not paying attention to activities of peace, justice and humanitarianism he was so greatly involved in.

MICHAEL JACKSON'S LAST DANCE

The Cable station CNN reported on July 6th, 2009, on Wolf Blitzer's *Situation Room* Ticker that Rep. King of Queens, New York, said "There is nothing good about this guy!" Imagine! Michael Jackson holds the *Guinness Book World Record* for charity giving somewhere between $300-500 million US Dollars. This man only bears the name King which he was born with. Through hard work, dedication and creativity Michael Jackson earned the title "King of Popular Culture Music." This is a global acclimation for one billion people worldwide watched the Staples Center memorial in Los Angeles! There is only one King of New York, that person is Rev. Al Sharpton. Instead of spending time saying scurrilous things about Mr. Michael Jackson, Mr. Peter King should be more concerned whether this is his last term as a Congressman from New York, since he is on the National Democratic Radar Screen to be defeated at the next Congressional election. His colleagues in the House of Representatives honored Michael Jackson with a moment of silence. One has to wonder what he was doing when they were so acting. He was probably texting, maybe to the *New York Post*. Equally, President Obama praised Mr. Jackson as "one of the greatest entertainers of our time." He was in good stead with American Presidents Nixon and Reagan, with foreign royalty and enjoyed a fan-base in every country across the globe. To this we could add the positive things said by Elizabeth Taylor and so many others who praised Michael and attested to his character.

This is why the attitude and posturing of Rep. King is exactly symptomatic of the adherents of "Jackson character assassination" based on rumors and innuendos fed by Media power and influence. As a result, the false claims against Mr. Jackson have taken on a life of their own. Another example of the perennial "black balling of Mr. Jackson" has to do with the claims of his prescription drug use. Rush Limbaugh is a reported drug addict, prescription drug addict, but no one is going after him, because he is not black! Imagine, news reporters were tracking down leads that Mr. Jackson had used such medication in 1996. Imagine! Again!

Wolf Blitzer on CNN's Situation Room, July 6, 2009, 4:00-7:00 pm, interviewed Mr. Tom Mesereau who defended Michael Jackson in the child molestation trial. Mr. Mesereau said, according to his research Mr. Jackson "was never a child molester; he was a wonderful person!" The attorney talked about how Michael was "acquitted 14 times, 10 felonies and 4 misdemeanors." Then he went into how the District Attorney brought 4 witnesses to testify against Michael, who in fact, said "He had never molested or done anything inappropriate with them." The Prosecution's witnesses became character witnesses for Michael! The millions of kids who passed through Neverland and they could only find 4, and they would not support the Prosecution's case. Mr. Mesereau discussed how the accuser and his brother were discredited through inconsistencies in their statements. Next Mr. Blitzer brought up the fact Mr. Jackson had settled a suit, in the past, for millions of dollars when the charge of child molestation was brought against him. This is

FREDERICK MONDERSON

when Mr. Mesereau pointed out Michael Jackson was surrounded by "mediocre people who did not have his best interest at heart."

When the money grab was made, these people whom we can generally equate with parasites, or hangers-on, are the ones who suggested such "accusations would not look good for Mr. Jackson's image." This is when they all agreed to pay the "go away money" in a settlement thinking the issue would go away. However, this was the first of the one-two punch to derail his creatively cultural express and destroy Mr. Jackson himself.

In the movie **Malcolm X**, directed by Spike Lee and starring Denzel Washington, the scene is in front of the police station after the Muslim brother was arrested and held in the Precinct. The Muslim brothers gathered, Malcolm arrived, with hand gestures he communicated with the phalanx of disciplined black men who appeared willing to do anything Minister Malcolm pronounced, even storming the Precinct. When the police Captain observed the unfolding phenomenon taking place in front of him he turned to one of his Lieutenants and confessed, "That Negro has too much power!" Therein lay the fear that motivates people to attempt to destroy people such as Michael Jackson, the successfully powerful black man!

While some have argued Malcolm X was radical, Michael Jackson's power was in his creative gentility and artistic genius ability. That artistic creativity, exceptional and original, was fueled and fired ostensibly by divine guidance and inspiration, his gentleness that caused his light to shine so brightly. This heavenly gift bred a consciousness to empathize with the sufferings of humanity and through the soothing potency of song and dance; Jackson hoped to impart a message of healing through expressions of love and giving. Let us not forget, two thousand years ago, another gentle soul, proponent of love, healing and giving was crucified by similar "wolves at the door," as the ones who hounded Michael Jackson in life and death.

Next, having beaten back the child molestation accusations as represented in the charges, Mr. Mesereau was questioned about drug use by Michael to which he responded, "Mr. Jackson never appeared impaired in any way during any time they were in contact." He was always consciously consistent. This was a man in complete control of his faculties. Finally, Wolf posed the money question, whether Mr. Jackson had paid for his services. Mr. Mesereau responded, "Michael was

MICHAEL JACKSON'S LAST DANCE

very good to us." This is why this is "a very, very sad moment" for those who loved and cared about him.

Such contentions are somewhat reminiscent of Rev. Al Sharpton's Apollo Theater and Post-Apollo Memorial pronouncement that "Michael's image was tarnished by the Media." "Wait a minute" he said, "people loved Michael. They knew him and respected him. Michael Jackson was a fore-runner for Tiger Woods, Oprah Winfrey, and Barack Obama. His fame was based on talent. He created a comfort level that expressed a positive view. Michael Jackson is a strong historic force being treated unfairly. We believe in him and that's why we stand up for Michael Jackson."

This gentle soul was an iconic figure. He was kind, well-spoken, well-read, giving, and a loving father as well as a global superstar. This loving, caring, transformational figure is, as Ossie Davis said of Malcolm X, "he was our Prince, Our Shining Black Prince!" That is why at 5:26 pm (EST) (2:26 PST) on Tuesday, June 30, 2009, inside the Apollo, five days to the minute after Michael passed, Al Sharpton, before calling for a moment of silence for Michael Jackson, said to the Media, "You can lie on him, we stand up for him. We are here to preserve his legacy with dignity. His work, his life, his dignity must be preserved, because he was a wonderful man who was smeared in life and death." There are many who will not stand for any form of assault on the character, creative intellectual abilities and giving nature of our heroes, and especially so when their lives are devoted to improving the good of humanity in general.

Michael Jackson's Last Dance Photo 22. Candles, a hat, bouquets, newspapers and inscribed tributes to the incomparable Michael Jackson on the "Altar of Remembrance" as visitors are reflected in the glass door.

FREDERICK MONDERSON

Michael Jackson's Last Dance Photo 23. Fans are letting their tributes be shown on the "Altar of Remembrance."

MICHAEL JACKSON'S LAST DANCE

Michael Jackson's Last Dance Photo 24.   Another view of the love left for Michael on the "Altar of Remembrance."

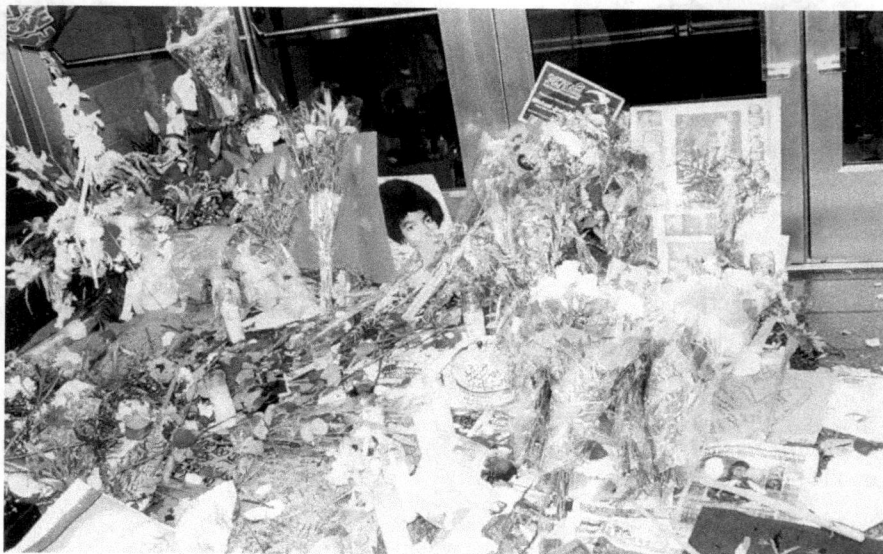

Michael Jackson's Last Dance Photo 25. The Apollo's "Altar of Remembrance" entrance is inundated with flowers and other forms of tribute for the angelic voice silenced but his music lives on.

FREDERICK MONDERSON

Michael Jackson's Last Dance Photo 26. Even more of the "Altar of Remembrance."

Michael Jackson's Last Dance Photo 27. The barrier separating the worshippers from the "Altar of Remembrance."

MICHAEL JACKSON'S LAST DANCE

Michael Jackson's Last Dance Photo 28. Stepping back to view visitors in the barrier paying respects to the "King of Pop," incomparable Michael Jackson.

Michael Jackson's Last Dance Photo 29. The crowd keeps coming and now police.

FREDERICK MONDERSON

Michael Jackson's Last Dance Photo 30. The Red, Black and Green flies directly across from the Apollo Theater in 125th Street in Harlem, New York City.

MICHAEL JACKSON'S LAST DANCE

Michael Jackson's Last Dance Photo 31. A "Little Green Belt" is among the many Jackson well-wishers standing beneath the Apollo Marquee.

FREDERICK MONDERSON

4.   JOSEPH "JOE" JACKSON
By

Dr. Fred Monderson

Mr. Joseph Jackson, father of Michael Jackson, is a parent reviled by the media because he did not fulfill their ideal of how a man should raise his children. Afterall, isn't the final product the best barometer of how well one has done in a particular task.   Take for instance, Mr. Williams, father of Venus and Serena Williams, tennis "phenoms" who have excelled in that sport.   He has come in for his share of criticisms because he does not fit the mold.   Yet, he produced two world class daughters and while not controversial, they were certainly successfully trained, driven and accomplished acclaimed heights. The same can be said for Earl Woods who pushed his son Tiger to the dominating position he now holds in the world of golf!   However, and importantly, Mr. Jackson's handiwork produced equally astonishing results, if not more so, in that all the members of his family became successful entertainers.

With the passing of Michael, Mr. Joe Jackson's presence at the Black Entertainment Television tribute was criticized and again in the news conference with Rev. Al Sharpton the critics continued their assault. Apparently, Mr. Jackson began pedaling on BET's red carpet a new record company he was forming and again with Rev. Al Sharpton he had to again explain he was grieving inside. The critics, both professional and lay, complained this was an inappropriate time for Mr. Jackson to be pitching his new company. However, objectively speaking, it was the appropriate time to make such an announcement.

When we consider how the entertainment and entrepreneurial wolves have swooped down and began exploiting the name, life's work and legacy of Michael Jackson for personal gain; Joe Jackson, as a seasoned musical campaign insider wanted to convey the unmistakable message that there would be no music vacuum created by Michael's passing. In fact, he wanted to establish continuity in his family remaining in the music business.

32

MICHAEL JACKSON'S LAST DANCE

We need to understand Mr. Joe Jackson's history, for at 80 years old, he is a child of the Great depression, too young to serve in World War II but certainly the Korean Conflict. Equally, as Mr. Joe Jackson matured in the pre-Civil Rights Age he had to confront American society's racism and challenges to the black family. Yet Mr. Joseph Jackson was lucky to find a job as a steel worker, meet the beautiful Katherine, marry and begin raising a family. Thus, the credible questions should surround what types of experiences he confronted in his many travels and travails and what shaped the determination his family would not share the same experiences.

Upon realizing he had talented kids, Joe began cultivating their musical skills and insisting hard work was essential. The old adage, 'How do you get to Carnegie Hall? You practice, practice, practice' became the watchword for the ultimate success Joe envisioned. Subsequently as the Jackson family became renowned for their musical talents, in an interview on Oprah Winfrey show, Michael Jackson was heard to say his father whipped him and forced him to practice unending. Therein lay the charges that Joe Jackson was an unfit father because he disciplined his child. Therefore, here lay the crux of the matter that perhaps painted an incorrect portrait of a father whose concerns were misunderstood. A friend, Lawrence Williams always boasted, "My father came home to beat me."

That interview in this enlightened age of corporal punishment and avoidance ought not to be applied to Joe Jackson for it undermines his parenting skills and also his concern for his family. The society condemns absentee fathers, which Mr. Jackson was not. Today we insist you not discipline your child, but with all the distractions and inducements children very easily are led astray. In those cases, law enforcement does discipline them and with behaviors bordering on brutality and a prison industrial complex that threatens and destroys their manhood, physically, emotionally and psychologically, one has to take a stand or lose one's children. All this notwithstanding, many older persons will gladly confess their parents took the rod to them and they came out pretty well. Now as the law emphasizes non-corporal punishment, seems those with limited education and resources are caught unprepared to be "good parents," then their children get into trouble.

Sure Mr. Jackson ran a tight ship, he was tough on his children; but, he was not absent, he was strict and lo and behold, when we consider the results of his insistence, Mr. Michael Jackson became a wonderful success as did many of his siblings. As an extension of the argument, an artist, a painter, sees, envisions and paints a picture, not as the viewing public sees it but as he envisioned the image he hopes to create. Joe Jackson, in vowing to make his son a superstar never envisioned the Oprah Winfrey interview. If his methods had been different, there probably would not have been such an interview that followed the trail of success leading to it.

33

FREDERICK MONDERSON

In an interesting article, George E. Curry's "Another side of the maligned Joe Jackson" in *Daily Challenge* Thursday, August 13, 2009, pp. 4-5, the author sheds light on this issue in an interesting way. Importantly, he recounts a fascinating speech Michael Jackson made at Oxford University on March 21, 2001 where he, in fact, contravened the Oprah interview, praising his father However, one has to wonder why the "Jim Morets" and other media people never recounted nor highlighted this confession rather than continuously harping on the Oprah interview.

George Curry relates how, in Oxford, Mr. Jackson told that gathering, "You probably weren't surprised to hear that I did not have an idyllic childhood. The strain and tension that exists in my relationship with my own father is well documented. My father is a tough man and he pushed my brothers and me hard, from the earliest age, to be the best performers we could be. He had great difficulty showing affection. He never really told me he loved me. And he never really complimented me either. If I did a great show, he would tell me it was a good show. And if I did an OK show, he told me it was a lousy show."

He seemed intent, above all else on making us a commercial success. And at that he was more than adept. My father was a managerial genius and my brothers and I owe our professional success, in no small measure, to the forceful way that he pushed us. He trained me as a showman and under his guidance I couldn't miss a step."

Now grown and looking back Michael seemed to see the wisdom in Joe's efforts, that as a child he could not really comprehend. He continued: "I have started reflecting on the fact that my father grew up in the South, in a very poor family. He came of age during the Depression and his own father, who struggled to feed his children, showed little affection towards his family and raised my father and his siblings with an iron fist. Who could have imagined what it was like to grow up a poor Black man in the South, robbed of dignity, bereft of hope, struggling to become a man in a world that saw my father as subordinate. I was the first Black artist to be played on MTV and I remember how big a deal it was even then. And that was in the 80s!"

"My father moved to Indiana and had a large family of his own, working long hours in the steel mills, work that kills the lungs and humbles the spirit, all to support his family. Is it any wonder that he found it difficult to expose his

34

MICHAEL JACKSON'S LAST DANCE

feelings? Is it any mystery that he hardened his heart, that he raised the emotional ramparts? And most of all is it any wonder why he pushed his sons so hard to succeed as performers, so that they could be saved from what he knew to be a life of indignity and poverty?" Even further, "I am forced to think of my own father and despite my earlier denials; I am forced to admit that he must have loved me. He did love me, and I know that. There were little things that showed it."

Curry believed, for his own healing, Michael had to forgive his father!

"I have begun to see that even my father's harshness was a kind of love, an imperfect love, to be sure, but love nonetheless. He pushed me because he loved me. Because he wanted no man ever to look down at his offspring. And now with time, rather than bitterness, I feel blessing. In the place of anger, I have found absolution. And in the place of revenge I have found reconciliation. And my initial fury has slowly given way to forgiveness."

Now, if only "honest media" would pick up on this acting unaware of its existence and equally ferret out the truth behind Evan Chandler's story, then perhaps Michael Jackson could truly rest undisturbed and the world would continue to remember what a great person he really was. Nevertheless, the true Michael Jackson fans never really believed, as Spike Lee said at the Apollo, "the negativity" associated with the man, the world came to recognize as the "King of Pop."

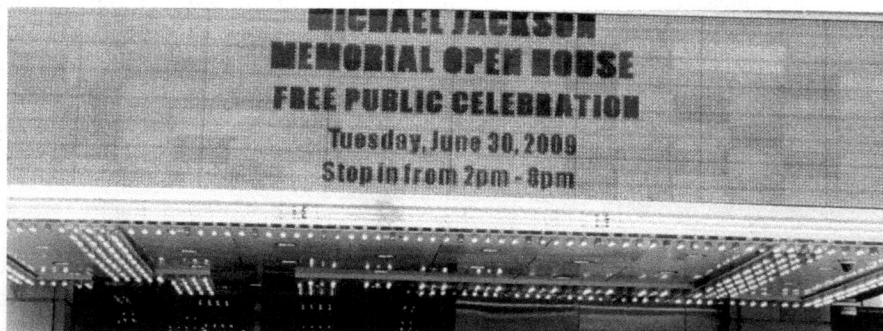

Michael Jackson's Last Dance Photo 32. Here's another Marquee's sign.

35

FREDERICK MONDERSON

Michael Jackson's Last Dance Photo 33. There's that "Little Green Belt" again signing "The Wall" for Michael.

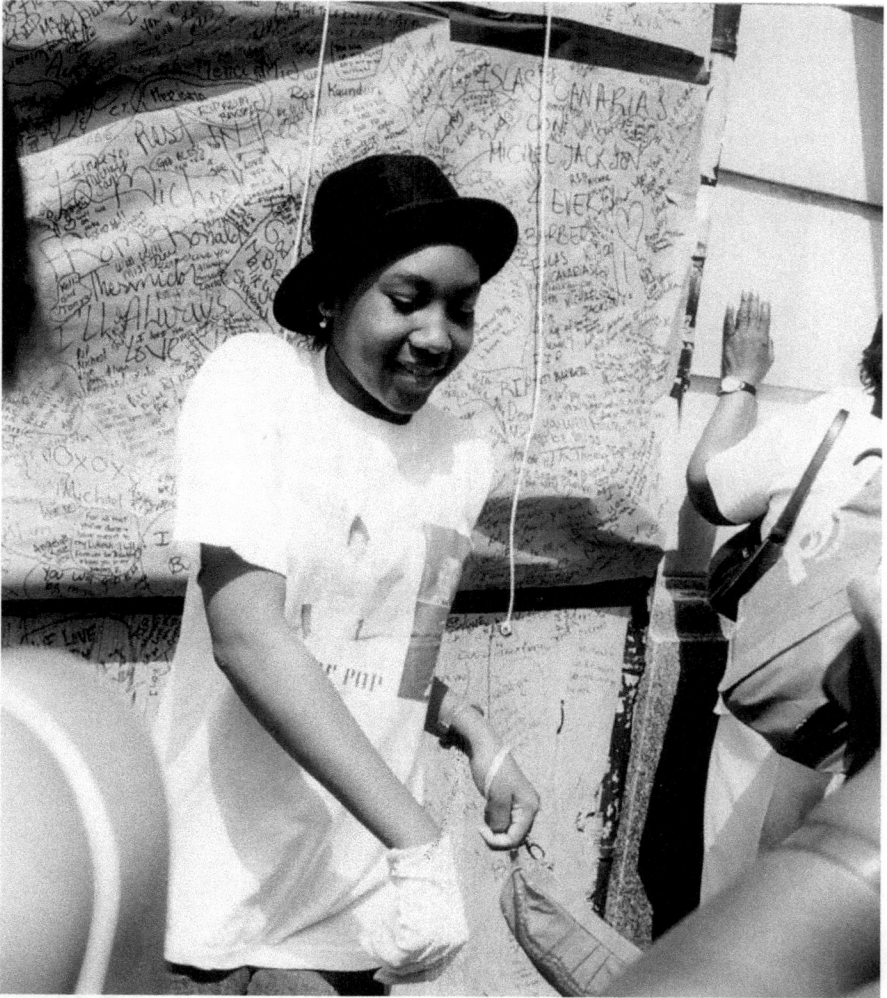

Michael Jackson's Last Dance 34. There are so many Michael Jackson "impersonators," this young lady tries her hand at being the "King of Pop."

FREDERICK MONDERSON

Michael Jackson's Last Dance Photo 35. Red, Black and Green again shining on Michael's tribute.

Michael Jackson's Last Dance Photo 35. Another look as people use cell phones to photograph the "Altar of Remembrance" in front of the Apollo's entrance.

MICHAEL JACKSON'S LAST DANCE

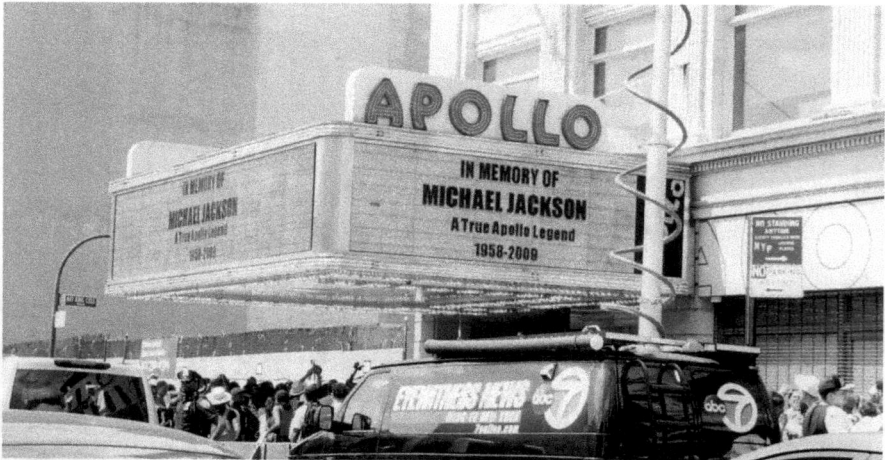

Michael Jackson's Last Dance Photo 37. All the News Media were there especially Channel 7, Eyewitness News, ABC, New York.

Michael Jackson's Last Dance Photo 38. Fans gather to take pictures of the "Altar of Remembrance."

FREDERICK MONDERSON

Michael Jackson's Last Dance Photo 40. Fan sports the "King of Pop" T-shirt.

MICHAEL JACKSON'S LAST DANCE

Michael Jackson's Last Dance Photo 41. Some of the throngs under the Marquee.

Michael Jackson's Last Dance Photo 39. More of the excitement to get that photo of the "Altar of Remembrance."

FREDERICK MONDERSON

5. THE BODY OF WORK
By

Dr. Fred Monderson

In every field of intellectual and artistic endeavor, the great ones create an enormous body of work, some of which their adoring fans admire tremendously. Oftentimes, after the artiste has passed, then "unpublished" creations stagger the imagination that this individual has been gainfully creative producing so prolifically. Johnny Cash and Tupak Shakur were two individuals who fit the bill, upon their passing it was revealed how much "unknown" work they had produced.

In a number of ways, Michael Joseph Jackson fits the above characterization but upon closer examination, he exceeds the "limitations" of the above named individuals. The Michael Jackson body of work is recognized and celebrated in a number of genres, principally in music as singer, song-writer, producer, choreographer, dancer and actor. He created numerous musical videos, called "short films" that highlighted his many songs. He was also an inventor who created a contraption that allowed him to lean forward during a performance that seemed out of the ordinary!

Michael Jackson is unlike any other entertainer in history in that he came early and stayed late, creating, innovating, and performing at the highest level of genius achievable.

I must admit, I did not expect to discover as much about the volume of production as has been released particularly from Michael Jackson's website, allMichaelJackson.com. The number of videos as indicated in the following albums was astonishing as this genius ventured to graphically immortalize his songs with visuals.

As so often happens when a popular singer passes, sales of his or her music skyrocket. In Michael's case according to *USA Today*, Wednesday, July 1, 2009, D1 "Jackson's music sees explosion in sales" is reporting "Despite inventory

MICHAEL JACKSON'S LAST DANCE

shortages nationwide, sales of Michael Jackson's music skyrocketed after his death. Total albums soared 4,000% to more than 400,000, up from 10,000 the week before, according to Nielsen Sound Scan. The 2003 compilation *Number Ones* topped the list, followed by 2005's *The Essential Michael Jackson* and 2008's *Thriller* re-issues; each sold more than 100,000 copies by Sunday. Fans downloaded 2.3 million tracks, up 6,100 % from the previous week. If Jackson 5 tracks are included, the figure climbs to 2.6 million. Of the 200 tracks in the digital chart, 36 are Jackson solo tunes; six are by the Jackson 5."

Pop Eater's "Tribute: Top Ten Michael Jackson Songs" are reported as:

ABC
I Want You Back
Rock With You
Don't Stop 'Til You Get Enough
Beat It
Billie Jean
Thriller
Wanna Be Startin' Something
The Way You Make Me Feel
Man in the Mirror

Leah Greenblatt provides "Michael Jackson's 10 Greatest Music Videos" as follows:

Rock With you
Billie Jean
Beat it
Thriller
Bad
Man in the Mirror
Smooth Criminal
Black or White
Remember the Time
Scream

Leah Greenblatt again provides "Michael Jackson, The Ultimate Playlist" featuring the tunes and the year of their release.

I Want You Back	1969
Who's Loving You	1969

FREDERICK MONDERSON

I'll Be There	1970
ABC	1970
Mama's Pearl	1971
Don't Stop 'Til You Get Enough	1979
Rock With You	1979
Billie Jean	1982
Wanna Be Startin' Something	1983
Human Nature	1983
Thriller	1984
The Way You Make Me Feel	1987
Smooth Criminal	1988
Man In The Mirror	1988
Black or White	1991
Scream	1995

The Jackson, later The Jacksons, produced several albums with Michael Jackson as lead vocalist. These songs are still favorites even to this day.

They first produced singles with Motown in 1970 included: "I Want You Back," "ABC," "The Love You Save," and "I'll Be there." They later left Motown Records which had produced much of their early records through "The Corporation," a group of writers including Berry Gordy, Freddie Perron, Alphonso Mizell and Deke Richards. And now the Jackson 5 wanted to be more in control of what they sang. Therefore, they moved to CBS Epic Records. With this move they had to change their name to The Jacksons. Two albums for their new label Epic Records were: "The Jacksons" and "Going Places."

Their first album **"Diana Ross Presents the Jackson 5"** was released in December 1969 and then **"ABC"** in April 1970. They were both big hits. Before the end of 1970 they produced their **"Third Album"** and **"The Jackson 5 Christmas Album."** Then they produced the following albums **"Destiny,"** (1978) **"Triumph,"** (1980) and **"Victory"** (1984) and then a Victory Tour in 1984, after which Michael left the group to become a solo artist. In March of 1983 they performed **"Motown: Yesterday, Today and Forever"** in which Michael Jackson, singing Billie Jean, first performed **"The Moonwalk."** In June of 1995 they produced **"Soulsations: The 25th**

MICHAEL JACKSON'S LAST DANCE

Anniversary Collection." On May 6, 1997, the Jackson 5 brothers were inducted into the Rock and Roll Hall of Fame.

The **Rock and Roll Hall of Fame Museum** lists the Jackson 5's Essential songs as:

I Want You Back
ABC
I'll Be There
Never Can Say Goodbye
The Love You Save
Mama's Pearl
Enjoy Yourself
Dancing Machine
Shake Your Body (Down to the Ground)
State of Shock

Jackson 5 Albums with Michael as a significant player.

Diana Ross Presents The Jackson 5

Zip A Dee Doo Dah
No Body
I Want You Back
Can You Remember
Standing In The Shadows Of Love
You've Changed
My Cherie Amour
Who's Loving You
Chained
I know I'm Losing You
Stand
Born To Love You
The Love You Save
One More Chance
ABC
2-4-6-8
(Come 'Round Here) I'm the One You Need
Don't Know Why I Love You
Never Had A Dream Come True

45

FREDERICK MONDERSON

True Love Can Be Beautiful
La La (Means I Love You)
I'll Bet You
I Found That Girl
The Young Folks
Oh, I've Been Bless'd

Looking Through The Windows

I Want You Back
Maybe Tomorrow
The Day Basketball Was Saved
Stand
I Want To Take You Higher
Feelin' Alright
Walk On/The Love You Save
Goin' Back To Indiana
Ain't Nothing Like The Real Thing
Looking Through The Windows
Don't let Your Baby Catch you
To Know
Doctor My Eyes
Little Bitty Pretty One
E-Ne-Me-Ne-Mi-Ne-Moe (The Choice Is Yours To Pull)
If I Have To Move A Mountain
Don't Want To See You Tomorrow
Children Of The Light
I Can Only Give You Love
Love Song
Who's Lovin' You

"Third Album"

I'll Be There
Ready or Not (Here I Come)
Oh How Happy

MICHAEL JACKSON'S LAST DANCE

Bridge Over Troubled Water
Can I See You In The Morning
Goin' Back To Indiana
How Funky Is Your Chicken
Mama's Pearl
Reach In
The Love I Saw In You Was Just A Mirage
Darling Dear
Maybe Tomorrow
She's Good
Never Can Say Goodbye
The Wall
Petals
Sixteen Candles
(We've Got Blue Skies)
My Little Baby
It's Great To Be Here
Honey Chile
I Will Find A Way
Sugar Daddy \I'm so happy

Skywriter/Get it Together

Skywriter
Hallelujah Day
The Boogie Man
Touch
Corner Of The Sky
I Can't Quit Your Love
Uppermost
World of Sunshine
Ooh, I Love To Be With You

You Make Me What I Am
Get It Together
Don't Say Good Bye Again
Reflections
Hum Along And Dance
Mama I Gotta Brand New Thing (Don't Say No)
It's Too Late To Change The Time
You Need Love Like I Do (Don't You)

47

FREDERICK MONDERSON

Dancing Machine
Pride And Joy
Love's Gone Bad
Love Is The Thing You Need

Dancing Machine/Moving Violation

I Am Love
Whatever You Got, I Want
She's A Rhythm Child
Dancing Machine
The Life Of The Party
What You Don't Know
If I Don't Love You This Way
It All Begins And Ends With Love
The Mirrors Of My Mind
Forever Came Today
Moving Violation
(You Were Made) Especially For Me
Honey Love
Body Language (Do The Love Dance)
All I Do Is Think Of You
Breezy
Call Of The Wild
Time Explosion
Through Thick And Thin
Forever Came Today

The Jacksons: An American Dream

Main Titles

Katherine And Joe Meet
Katherine's Heartbreak

48

MICHAEL JACKSON'S LAST DANCE

Katherine And Joe Meet Again
Trust In Me
Start Of The Family
The Falcons
Michael Enters The Family
1964 – Family Life
"Baby I Need Your Loving"
Joe's Idea
Michael Sings
Jackson 5 Beginnings
High School Talent Show
The First Gigs
First Recording Session
Family Tension
The Jackie Wilson Gift
Joe's Disapproval
The Apollo
Motown Auditions
Rebbie's Wedding
J5 Joins Motown
The Spotlight
The Jacksons Move to California
Being A Leader
Recording Session
The Early Years Credits

Disc 2

J5 Pandemonium
Tito And Dee Dee
J5 On Tour
Jermaine And Hazel
Adolescence
J5 New Deal
"Never Can Say Goodbye"
Michael Goes Solo
Joe's Big Mistake
Motown 25
"Billie Jean"
The Jackson 5 Reunion
Katherine Talks To Michael
Victory Tour

FREDERICK MONDERSON

The Success Years Credits

The Ultimate Collection

I Want You Back
ABC
The Love You Save
I'll Be there
It's Your Thing
Who's Lovin' You
Mama's Pearl
Never Can Say Goodbye
Maybe Tomorrow
Got To Be There
Sugar Daddy
Rockin' Robin
Daddy's Home
Lookin' Through The Windows
I Wanna Be Where You Are
Get It Together
Dancing Machine
The Life Of The Party
I Am Love – Pts I and II
Just A Little Bit Of You
It's Your Thing

THE JACKSONS

DESTINY

Blame It On The Boogie
Push Me Away
Things I Do For You

MICHAEL JACKSON'S LAST DANCE

Shake Your Body (Down To The Ground)
Destiny
Bless Her Soul
All Night Dancin'
That's What you Get (For Being Polite)
Shake Your Body

TRIUMPH

Can You Feel It
Lovely One
Your Ways
Everybody
This Place Hotel
Time Waits For No One
Walk Right Now
Give It Up
Wondering Who
Can You Feel It?

THE ESSENTIAL JACKSONS

Enjoy yourself
Show You The Way To Go
Goin' Places
Find Me A Girl
Blame It On The Boogie
Shake Your Body
Lovely One
This Place Hotel
Can You Feel It
Walk Right Now
State Of Shock
2300 Jackson Street
Nothin' (That Compares 2 U)
Don't Stop 'Til You Get Enough (Live From The 1981 US Tour)

FREDERICK MONDERSON

VICTORY

Torture
Wait
One More Chance
Be Not Always
State of Shock
We Can Change The World
The Hurt
Body

THE JACKSON 5

THE CHRISTMAS ALBUM

Have Yourself A Merry Little Christmas
Santa Claus Is Coming To Town
The Christmas Song
Up On The House Top
Frosty The Snow Man
Little Drummer Boy
Rudolph The Red Nose Reindeer
Christmas Won't Be The Same This Year
Give Love On Christmas Day
Someday At Christmas
I Saw Mommy Kissing Santa Claus

GOING BACK TO INDIANA

Released in August 1979 **"Off The Wall"** was Michael's first solo album as an adult artist and it sold nearly 20 million copies. There were there music videos with this album. These were: **Don't Stop 'til You Get Enough**, **Rock With You**, and **She's Out Of My Life**.

Don't Stop 'Til You Get Enough
Rock With You
Working Day And Night
Get On The Floor
Off The Wall
Girlfriend (McCartney)
She's Out of My Life (Tom Bahler)
I Can't Help It
It's The Falling In Love
Burn This Disco Out

"Thriller" was released in 1983. It won 8 Grammy Music Awards and 8 American Music Awards in 1984. Thriller had three music videos, **Billie Jean**, **Beat it** and **Thriller** itself.

Wanna Be Startin' Somethin'
Baby Be Mine (Temperton)
The Girl Is Mine
Thriller
Beat It
Billie Jean
Human Nature
P.Y.T. (Pretty Young Thing)
The Lady In My Life

"Bad" was released in August 1987. Michael had devoted two and a half years to recording the follow up to the Thriller Album, which at the time of the Bad album's release had sold nearly 50 million records and at that time was the world bestselling album. There were 7 music videos accompanying this album. These were: **Bad, The way you make me feel**, **Man in the Mirror**, **Dirty Diana**, **Another Part of** Me, **Smooth Criminal**, **Leave me alone** and **Liberian Girl**.

Bad
The Way You Make Me Feel
Speed Demon
Liberian Girl
Just Good Friends (Duet with Stevie Wonder)
Another Part of Me

FREDERICK MONDERSON

Man In The Mirror
I Just Can't Stop Loving You
Dirty Diana
Smooth Criminal

The **Dangerous** album was released on November 26, 1991. There were 10 music videos with this album. These were: **Black or White**, **Remember the Time**, **Come Together**, **In the Closet**, **Who is it**, **Jam**, **Heal the World**, **Give it to Me**, **Will You Be There**, and **Gone Too Soon**.

Jam
Why You Wanna Trip On Me
In The Closet
She Drives Me Wild
Remember The Time
Can't Let Her Get Away
Heal The World
Black Or White
Who Is It
Give In To Me
Will You Be There
Keep The Faith
Gone Too Soon
Dangerous

The **HIStory** album was released on June 20, 1995, and was Michael's two disc album with a total of 30 songs. The music videos accompanying this album are as follows: **Scream, You are Not Alone, Earth Song, They Don't Care about Us, Stranger in Moscow**, and **HIStory**.

Disk 1

Billie Jean
The Way You Make Me Feel
Black Or White
Rock With You

MICHAEL JACKSON'S LAST DANCE

She's Out Of My Life
Bad
I Just Can't Stop Loving You
Man In The Mirror
Thriller
Beat It
The Girl Is Mine
Remember The Time
Don't Stop 'Til You Get Enough
Wanna Be Startin' Somethin'
Heal The World

Disk 2

Scream (Duet with Janet Jackson)
They Don't Care About Us
Stranger In Moscow
This Time Around
Earth Song
D.S
Money
Come Together
You Are Not Alone
Childhood
Tabloid Junkie
2 Bad
HIStory
Little Susie
Smile

Blood on the Dance Floor – Released May, 1997,
sold 6 million copies. Music Videos accompanying this album are as follows: **Blood On the Dance Floor**, **HIStory**, and **Ghosts**.

Blood On The Dance Floor
Morphine
Superfly Sister
Is It Scary
Scream Louder - Flyte Time Remix
Money - Fire Island Radio Edit
2 Bad - Refugee Camp Mix
Stranger In Moscow – Tee's In-House Club Mix

FREDERICK MONDERSON

This Time Around - D.M Radio Mix
Earth Song – Hani's Club Experience
You Are Not Alone - Classic Club Mix
History - Tony Moran's History Less

Invincible

Invincible was released the end of October 2001, and featured 16 new tracks. This album sold 10 million copies. Music Videos accompanying this album are as follows: **You Rock My World** and **Cry**.

Unbreakable
Heartbreaker
Invincible
Break Of Dawn
Heaven Can Wait
You Rock My World
Butterflies
Speechless
2000 Watts
You Are My Life
Privacy
Don't Walk Away
Cry
The Lost Children
Whatever Happens
Threatened

Michael Jackson Number Ones

Don't Stop 'till You Get Enough
Rock With You
Billie Jean
Beat It
Thriller

MICHAEL JACKSON'S LAST DANCE

I Just Can't Loving You

Speechless
2000 Watts
You Are My Life
Privacy
Don't Walk Away
Cry
Whatever Happens
Threatened

Unbreakable
Heartbreaker
Invincible
Break Of Dawn
Heaven Can Wait
You Rock My World
Butterflies

Michael Jackson's Last Dance Photo 42. Another look at the bustle under the Marquee as people jockey to get to see the "Altar of Remembrance."

FREDERICK MONDERSON

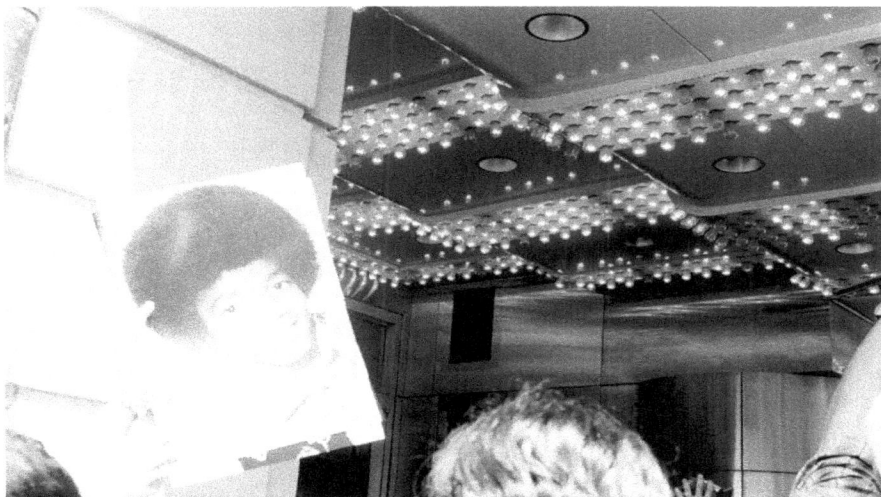

Michael Jackson's Last Dance Photo 43. Michael's photo under the lights of the Marquee before entering.

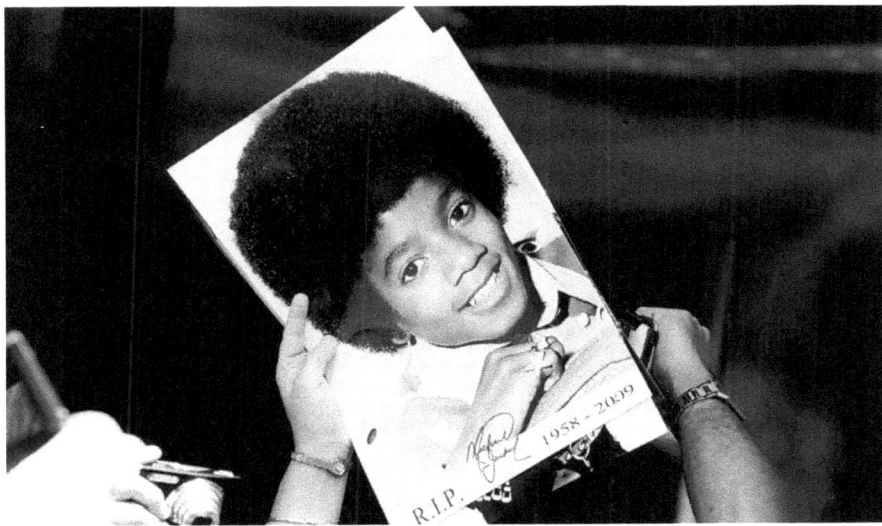

Michael Jackson's Last Dance Photo 44. A clear and true picture of Michael Jackson.

MICHAEL JACKSON'S LAST DANCE

Michael Jackson's Last Dance Photo 45. An MJ button adorns a beautiful shoulder strap of an equally beautiful young woman.

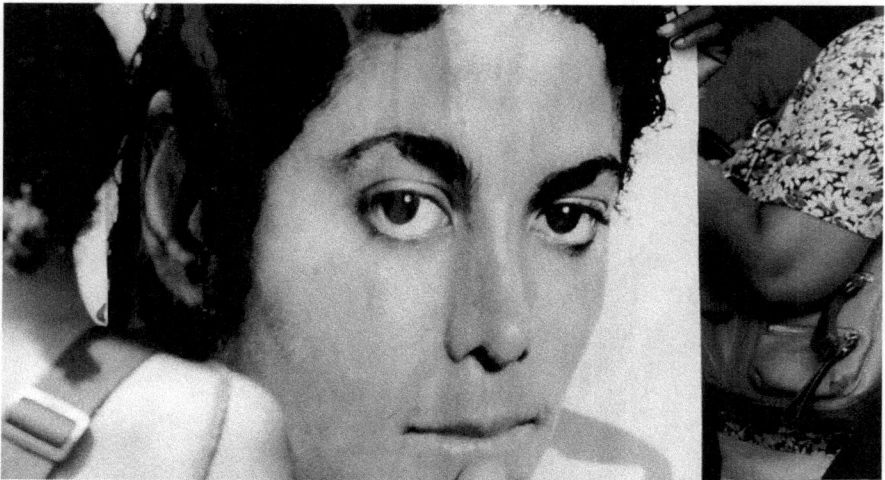

Michael Jackson's Last Dance Photo 46. How Michael seems to be looking back at us.

FREDERICK MONDERSON

Michael Jackson's Last Dance Photo 47. Green T-shirt sports MJ on the back.

MICHAEL JACKSON'S LAST DANCE

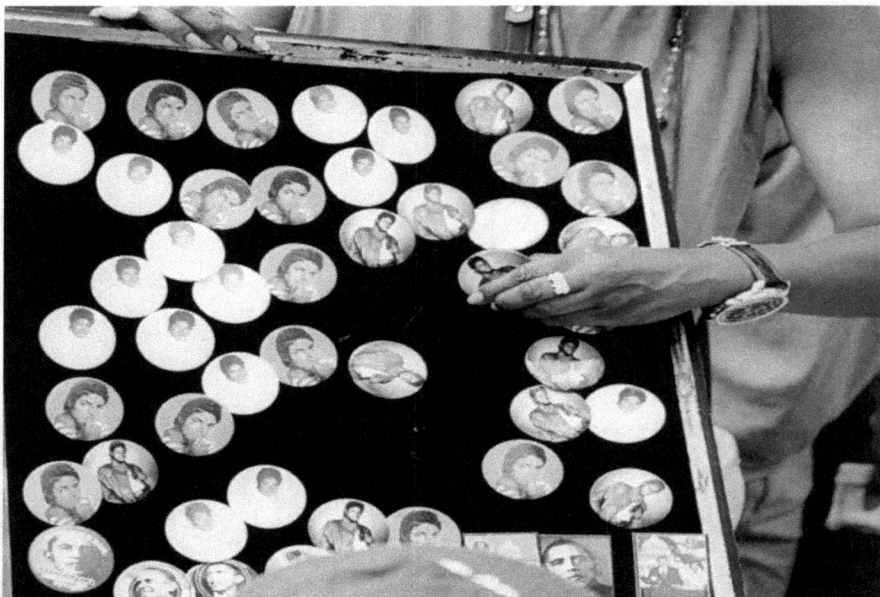

Michael Jackson's Last Dance Photo 48. Vendor hawks Michael and Obama buttons.

Michael Jackson's Last Dance Photos 49. Seems everybody and his brother was selling Michael Jackson memorabilia.

FREDERICK MONDERSON

6. THE MICHAEL JACKSON TIMELINE
By

Dr. Fred Monderson

It is difficult to sketch a timeline about the fascinating experiences Michael Jackson was part of from the time of his first singing outing with a band formed by his brothers and supervised by his father Joseph, a former musician turned steelworker. Information provided for this timeline is provided by *USA Today* Special Edition; The New York *Daily News* "Jackson: A life in the spotlight" by Patrick Huguenin and Gina Salamone, Friday, June 26, 2009, pp. 41-43. In addition, Brooks Barnes's "Jackson's Estate: Piles of Assets, Loads of Debt" *New York Times*, Saturday, June 27, 2009, p. A 11, also provided information for this timeline. In addition, allmichaeljackson.com also provided information.

August 29, 1958 – Michael Jackson is born to Joseph and Katherine Jackson, in Gary, Indiana.

1962 – Joe forms the band with his brothers, Jackie, Tito and Jermaine.

1965 – 7-year old Michael joins a band formed by his brothers Jermaine, Tito and Jackie Jackson. Marlon also becomes a member of the band.

1966 – 8-year old Michael and his brothers wins a talent show at Roosevelt High school in Gary, Indiana. Then they begin to play across the state and in Chicago before touring across the country.

1967- Along with his brothers, Michael performed at Harlem's Apollo Theater's Amateur Night and stole the show. They won the contest. Gladys Knight and the Pips recognized their talent and recommend them to Berry Gordy, founder of Motown Records.

1968–1969 - Michael, as part of the Jackson 5 signed with Motown Records. Their debut album, "Diana Ross Presents the Jackson 5" released December 18, 1969

MICHAEL JACKSON'S LAST DANCE

had No. 1 singles "I Want You Back" released October 7, 1969 and "Who's Loving You?" That same year Michael and the group appeared on The Ed Sullivan Show, December 4th, and from then on his fortunes were on the rise.

Michael Jackson's Last Dance Photo 50. A vendor's collection of MJ's Record Albums.

1970 – The Jackson 5 released their second album "ABC" in May with "The Love You Save" and "ABC" that rose to the No. 1 spot on the charts. The Jackson 5 cartoon was premiered on Television. In September their third album, entitled "Third Album" was released. Later in the year they released a Christmas Album.

1971 – The Jackson 5 released "Maybe Tomorrow," April 12, their first album to not reach the Top 10 of the Billboard Charts. That year Michael began recording under his own name, releasing "Got To Be There." Two hits were "Never can say Goodbye" and "Maybe Tomorrow."

1972 – Michael released the album "Ben" in 1972. The single "Ben" was the title to the movie in which Michael expressed his love for a pet, homicidal rat.

1974 – "Dancing Machine" by the Jackson 5 was released in September and sold over 2 million copies.

FREDERICK MONDERSON

Michael Jackson's Last Dance Photo 51. The sign says it all for Michael Jackson.

Allmichaeljackson.com informs: "During their six years at Motown, The Jackson 5 had worked hard; recording over 450 songs of which only 174 were released. They made a total of ten studio albums and generated ten top 10 US and UK hits. They had made numerous television appearances and toured America several times. Young Michael Jackson had released four albums of his own and generated a major number 1 hit. Under Motown's direction The Jackson 5 had made a massive impact in the music world and Michael Jackson had become the youngest vocalist ever to top the US charts."

1975 – Michael and his brother (minus Jermaine) left Motown Records to sing with CBS Epic Records. January his 4th album, Forever Michael was released.

1976 – "The Jackson 5 Show" began airing June 16, 1976, and ran until March 9, 1977. This was the first time an African American family starred on a TV show. That year they released an album, The Jacksons that reached number 6 on US charts.

MICHAEL JACKSON'S LAST DANCE

1977 – Michael made his musical film debut in the "Wiz" as the Scarecrow, alongside Diana Ross playing Dorothy and Nipsy Russell, the Lion. This was one of the most expensive films made at that time, totaling $24 million. Michael sang 6 songs on the track including "Ease on Down the Road." The Jacksons released their second CBS record, "Going Places" in October, 1977.

1978 – The Jacksons released "Destiny" containing "Blame it on the Boogie," the only song not written by the brothers but by an Englishman, incidentally named Michael Jackson.

1979 – The Jacksons launched "Destiny World Tour" taking them to the United Kingdom and Africa as well as doing several Television appearances. After this, Michael branched off as a solo artist. Teaming up with legendary producer Quincy Jones, Michael produced "Off The Wall," released in August with his award winning "Don't Stop 'Til You Get Enough." This album sold more than 7 million copies in America and 19 million total albums worldwide. This album catapulted him to superstardom. It was his fifth solo album and second with CBS Epic. He won four Billboard Awards for the album. By 1981 "Off the Wall" had sold 5 million copies, but by the time of his death it had sold more than 20 million albums.

1980 – Michael and the Jacksons released "Triumph" with several songs reaching significant numbers on the charts.

1982 – Michael's biggest selling album, "Thriller" sold 48 million plus albums in the United States and ultimately 109 million albums total, making it the highest grossing record in history. It has been certified 28 times Platinum by the Recording Industry Association of America.

1983 – In celebration of Berry Gordy and Motown 25 years' anniversary, Michael performed the legendary "Moonwalk" while singing Billy Jean. This performance rocketed him into megastar orbit. On December 2, 1983, a 14 minute video of "Thriller" premiered on MTV and everything changed in the music video industry. This became the largest selling music home video.

1984 – Michael received 8 Grammy Awards in one night and that year, while making a Pepsi commercial his hair caught fire and Michael suffered 2nd degree burns. The Pepsi Company awarded him $1.5 million. The Victory World Tour united him with his brothers. Michael dated Brooke Shields.

1985 – Michael Jackson purchases the Beatles Catalogue for an estimated $47.5 million. Today it is worth close to one billion dollars. It included the Beatles song

FREDERICK MONDERSON

collection. He would later sell 50 percent of this catalog to Sony Records for $90 million. Some of the songs by the Beatles in the catalog were owned by MIT and Sony/ATV. According to David Lieberman, *USA Today*, Thursday, July 2, 2009, p. B 1, some of the songs include: "Ticket to Ride, Revolution, Yesterday, Hey Jude, Help, All You Need is Love, Sgt. Pepper's Lonely Hearts Club Band, Day Tripper, And I love Her, Please, Please Me, Love Me Do, Lady Madonna, Penny Lane, Blackbeard." Some believe purchasing this Catalogue and marrying Lisa Marie Presley were the sources for much of the enmity directed towards Mr. Jackson. He co-wrote "We Are the World" with Lionel Ritchie.

1986 – Michael was photographed in a hyperbaric chamber, part of his plan to lengthen his life.

1987 – The album "Bad" sells over 8 million copies. The movie director Martin Scorsese produced a video for the album at a cost of approximately $1million.

1988 – Michael was diagnosed with Vertiligio, a disorder in which pigment is lost in the skin and exposure to the sun exacerbates it. Mr. Jackson purchased a 3000 acre ranch in Los Olivosco, 125 miles northwest of Los Angeles and renamed it **Neverland**, the mythical island of Peter Pan, a play place for kids. He spent some $35 million to outfit it with a zoo, amusement park, and 50-seat theater. Elaborately furnished, kids were welcomed there. In 1999, with a staff of some 150 employees, he reported it cost $5 million to operate the play-land annually.

1990 – He was hospitalized with chest pains.

1991 – Michael released "Dangerous." The album sold more than 7 million plus copies.

1992 – Michael was in Africa and received a tremendous welcome, yet the media gave many negative reports regarding his time in Africa. It seems his tours of Europe are never given as negative coverage as was done in Africa.

1993 – A US TV audience of 135 million people watched his 1993 Super Bowl Halftime
Performance, thought to be magnificently exhilarating. He later cancelled a performance
due to dehydration. He did an Oprah Winfrey interview. The *Associated Press* reported

MICHAEL JACKSON'S LAST DANCE

Elizabeth Taylor informed them Michael entered a rehab clinic to overcome addiction to
prescription pain killers. Jordan Chandler, father of Evan Chandler 13, accused Michael of sexual abuse of his son and received a monetary settlement of $14-20 million.

Word is now out that Mr. Jackson was pressured by an insurance company to settle this case. As Mr. Jackson later indicates, it is not inconceivable his success motivated people to encourage the media to hound and help victimize him right up until he died.

1994 – In May, Michael at age 37 married Lisa Marie Presley, in the Dominican Republic. She was 27. The marriage lasted less than two years. Presley filed for divorce in 1996.

1995 – "HIStory: Past, Present and Future Book I" sold more than 7 million copies. He collapsed on stage at the New York Beacon Theater due to exhaustion. Earlier he shot
footage in Hungary, using Hungarian soldiers at a cost of millions of dollars.

1996 – Michael married Debbie Rowe, a British nurse to his dermatologist. The union lasted from 1996-1999. She bore him two children, Prince Michael and Paris. His HIStory concert world tour was seen by 4.5 million fans.

1997 – "Blood on the Dance Floor: History in the Mix" sold more than 1 million copies. Michael was inducted into the Rock and Roll Hall of Fame as a member of the Jackson 5. Michael Joseph Jackson Junior was born in 1997. In the mid-1995 Mr. Jackson spent millions upon millions on videos.

1998 – Paris Katherine Jackson was born in 1998. Before the end of the year Mr. Jackson had borrowed $90, $140 and $30 millions for a total of $260 million from Bank of America against his Beatles Catalogue.

1999 – Debbie Rowe filed for divorce. He parted with Sony. He lists $5 million for maintenance of Neverland and $7.5 million for personal expenses.

2000 – Michael starts sporting a goatee and secures a $60 loan from Bank of America.

FREDERICK MONDERSON

2001 – Michael Jackson releases "Invincible," a commercial success. He is inducted into Rock and Roll Hall of Fame as a solo artist. This induction marks his second such and has never been duplicated by any other artist. Michael pays Marlon Brando $1 million to appear at his 30th anniversary tribute at Madison Square Garden in New York. Michael accused Sony's Chief Tommy Motola of being a racist, just before he released his album "Invincible."

2002 – In jubilation after his birth, Michael dangled his young baby Prince Michael II (Blanket) off a hotel balcony to show off to fans below. He later admitted the baby dangling was a "terrible mistake" claiming he got "caught up in the excitement of the moment." Michael attended Al Sharpton's National Action Network's forum on Racism in the Music Industry.

2003 – Fortress Investment Group buys Michael's Bank of America loan and raises his rates after he defaulted. He released "Number Ones," a compilation of his greatest hits. Charged with child molestation and taken into custody. He splurged, spending millions on furnishings and paintings.

2004 – Plastic surgeon Werner Mang reveals that he rebuilt Jackson's nose with part of Michael's ear cartilage.

2005 – After an expensive trial, a jury finds Jackson "not guilty." He moved to Bahrain as a guest of Sheikh Abdullah. *The Essential Michael Jackson* was issued.

2006 – Sony and Michael Jackson worked out a deal that extended his credit using his share of the Beatles Catalogue as collateral.

2007 – In December, Michael visited James Brown to pay last respects to the deceased idol, laying at C.A. Reid's Funeral Home in Augusta, Georgia.

2008 – Claims of respiratory problems were denied while Michael was involved in arranging a world tour with special appearances. Colonial Capital picked up a default note for $24.5 on Neverland and assumed a joint venture with Mr. Jackson on the property. In November 2008, Michael paid $7 million in Sheikh Abdullah's breach of contract suit. He moved back to California "To be where the action is." He reissued "Thriller."

2009 – Michael Jackson cancels an auction of Neverland artifacts, claiming he did not have time to check the contents. He reportedly appeared wearing heavy makeup, wig and sunglasses at announcement of his "This Is It" series of some 50 concerts in London, starting mid-July and extending over an indefinite period. Seemingly in good health at the Staples Center in Los Angeles, he died hours after rehearsal at 5: 26 pm EST on June 25, 2009.

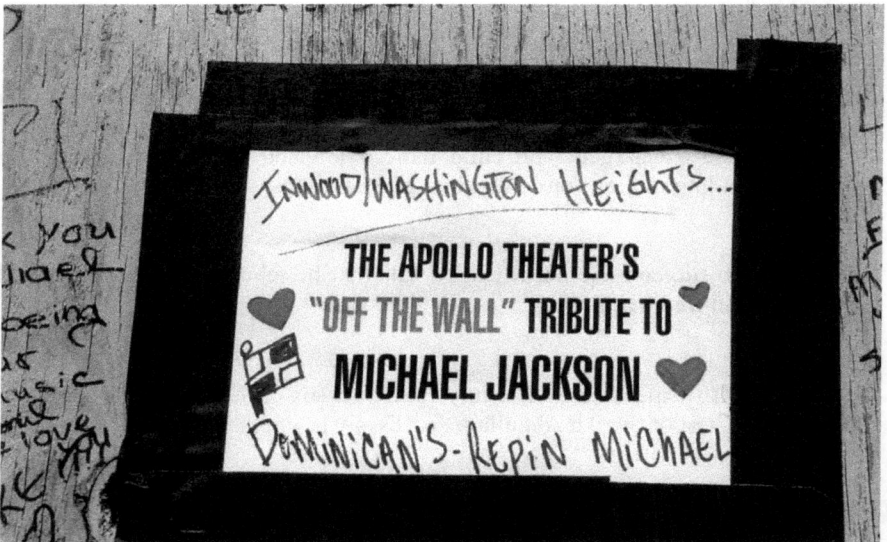

Michael Jackson's Last Dance Photo 52. The sign says it all, posted on the "Great Wall" where thousands will later sign their condolences and thanks to Michael Jackson.

FREDERICK MONDERSON

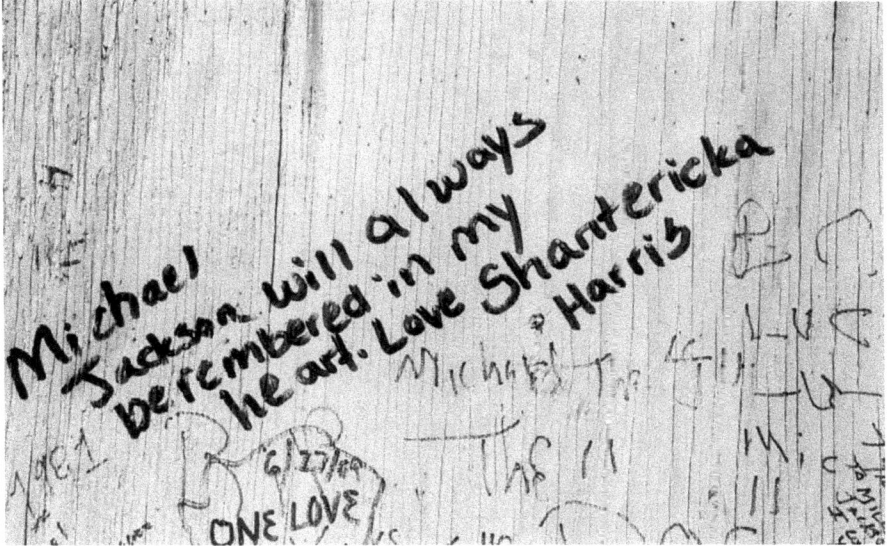

Michael Jackson's Last Dance Photo 53. These writings are self explanatory.

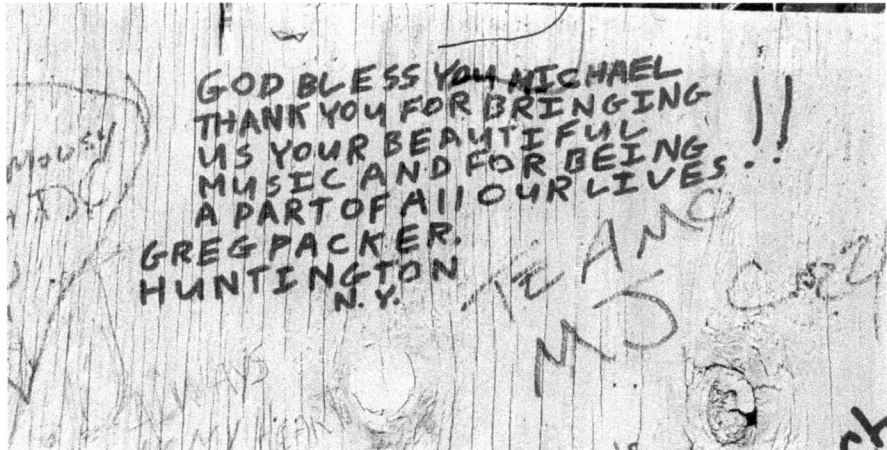

Michael Jackson's Last Dance Photo 54. These writings are self explanatory.

MICHAEL JACKSON'S LAST DANCE

Michael Jackson's Last Dance Photo 55. These writings are self explanatory.

Michael Jackson's Last Dance Photo 56. These writings are self explanatory.

FREDERICK MONDERSON

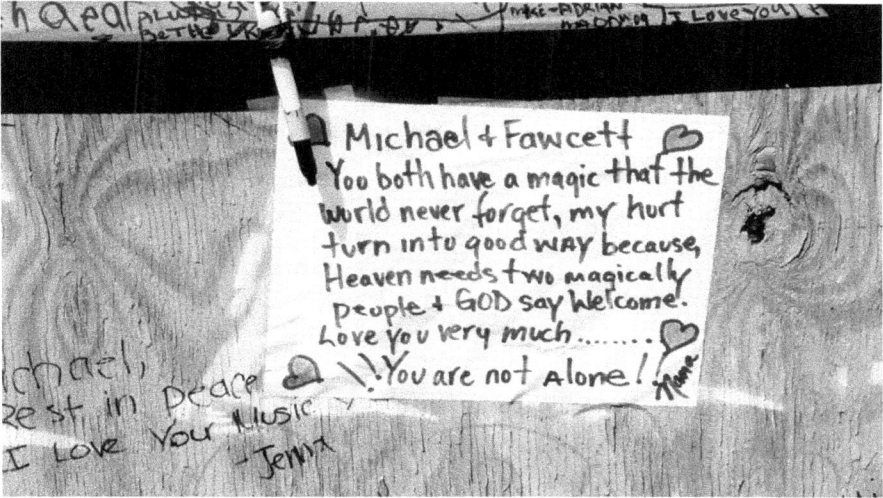

Michael Jackson's Last Dance Photo 57. These writings are self explanatory.

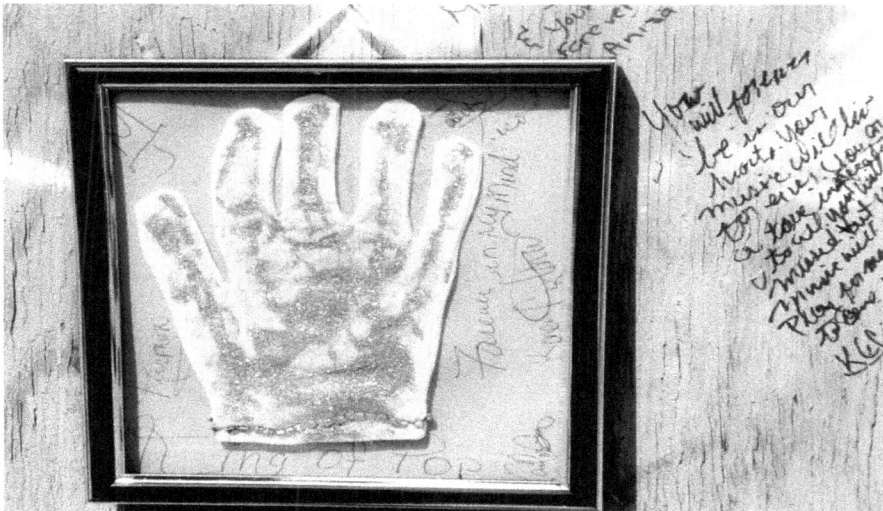

Michael Jackson's Last Dance Photo 58. The Glove and these writings is self explanatory.

72

MICHAEL JACKSON'S LAST DANCE

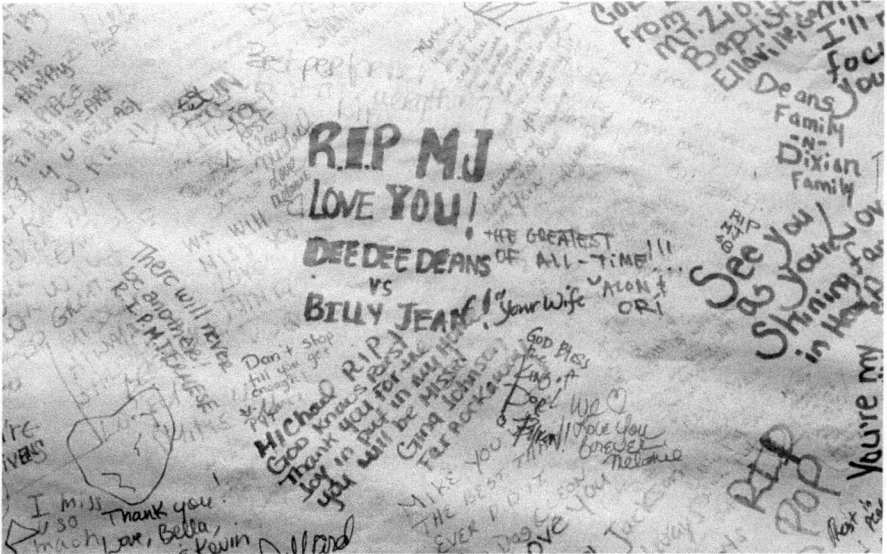

Michael Jackson's Last Dance Photo 59. These writings are self explanatory.

Michael Jackson's Last Dance Photo 60. These writings are self explanatory.

FREDERICK MONDERSON

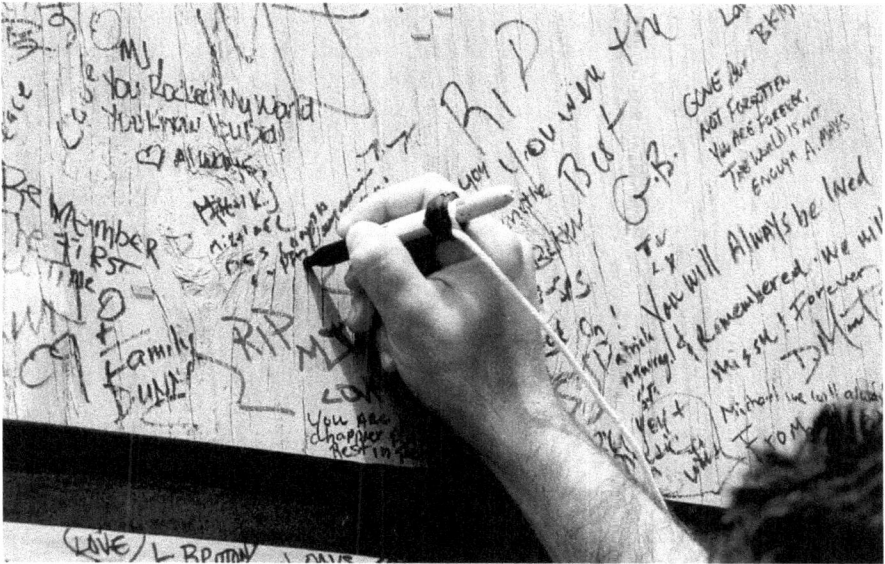

Michael Jackson's Last Dance Photo 61. These writings are self explanatory.

7. PRESIDENTS TO PRISONERS SALUTE MICHAEL JACKSON
By

Dr. Fred Monderson

It's a known fact Presidents Richard Nixon and Ronald Reagan admired and recognized Michael Jackson as a musical and artistic genius. This was particularly so of Ronald Reagan, the actor who easily recognized Michael's talents. The Bushes, certainly young George and especially the "party animal" Bill Clinton would have danced to Michael's soulfully rhythmic and titillating music. While Jimmy Carter may have been somewhat reserved, Andrew Young in the Cabinet may have insisted a Jackson number or two be spin at one of the celebrations.

74

MICHAEL JACKSON'S LAST DANCE

Since young people loved Michael Jackson, President Carter's daughter Amy may certainly have played either the Jackson 5 or Michael's records at her birthday parties in the White House. It is not inconceivable that Barack Obama, while out "sowing his royal oats" whether at Columbia or Harvard would have danced to Michael Jackson, the hottest entertainer of the age, not realizing one day he would end up being the first African American President. Therefore, in his comments upon Michael's passing, the President praised Mr. Jackson as being "the greatest entertainer of our time," though he was not unmindful of the tragedies of this man's life.

During the good times when Michael was topping the charts, America not only loved him but also relished in him as American ambassador of goodwill exporting American culture through his music. During those good times Michael Jackson was the guest wined and dined by the princes and cultural royalty of the great houses on all the continents who chose to be with and be seen with the icon musical "royalty," "King of Popular culture." But, while Michael enjoyed the hospitality of global royalty, he was not unmindful of the plight of paupers and, as such, he devoted large sums of his fortune and made special efforts to aid the less fortunate. His humanitarian nature and efforts to help the less fortunate are renowned. His charity work preceded "Live Aid" and "We are the world" productions and innumerable charitable organizations he supported. The United Negro College Fund was a particular beneficiary of his generosity. As in life, so in death, his will states, portions of his wealth will continue to benefit charities.

Where money was not given, the image and musical genius and influence of the great artist, who performed with passion and electricity, reached into the prisons with a therapeutic effect. More than a year ago, prison authorities in the Philippines launched an innovative dance program to motivate and rehabilitate its inmates. With skepticism the world viewed this new approach to rehabilitate, some even scoffing at it. When U-Tube picked it up and it appeared a sensation on the internet and elsewhere, there was something to this as it became a popular refrain. With Michael Jackson's passing, emotions overwhelmed and the Philippines prisoners were the first to pay homage to their hero whose songs were inspirational and enabled them to emotionally empower themselves through dance therapy as a part of something bigger than themselves in a disciplined and constructive manner. Here is another example of Michael Jackson's influence that did not involve money, yet, has produced a long lasting result that moved these people to a higher plane of emotional and artistic consciousness.

Score another positive and constructive contribution for Michael Jackson whose humanistic path is strewn with many such, even unintentional successes in his effort to share love, help heal humanity and bring out the best in people. Truly,

75

FREDERICK MONDERSON

Michael Jackson was a great soul, imbued with the spark of divinity, all doing the Lord's work!

Michael Jackson's Last Dance Photo 62. Someone left roses for the "King of Pop."

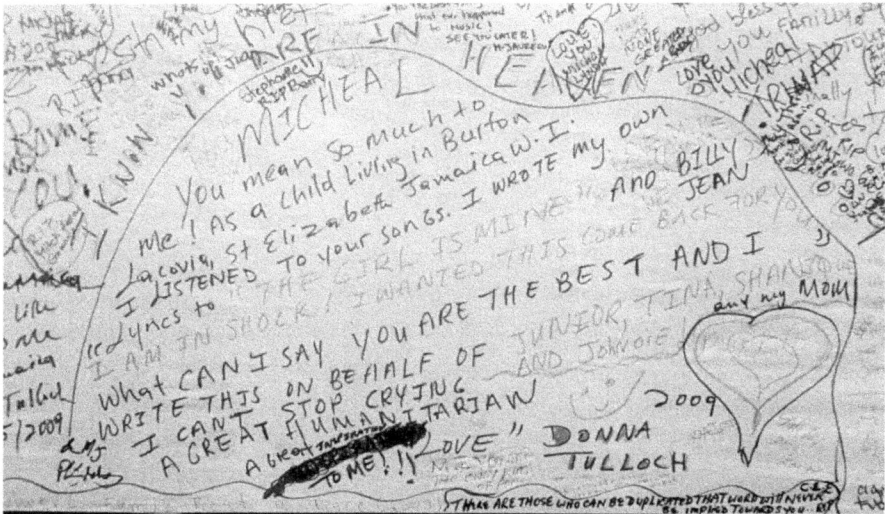

Michael Jackson's Last Dance Photo 63. These writings are self explanatory.

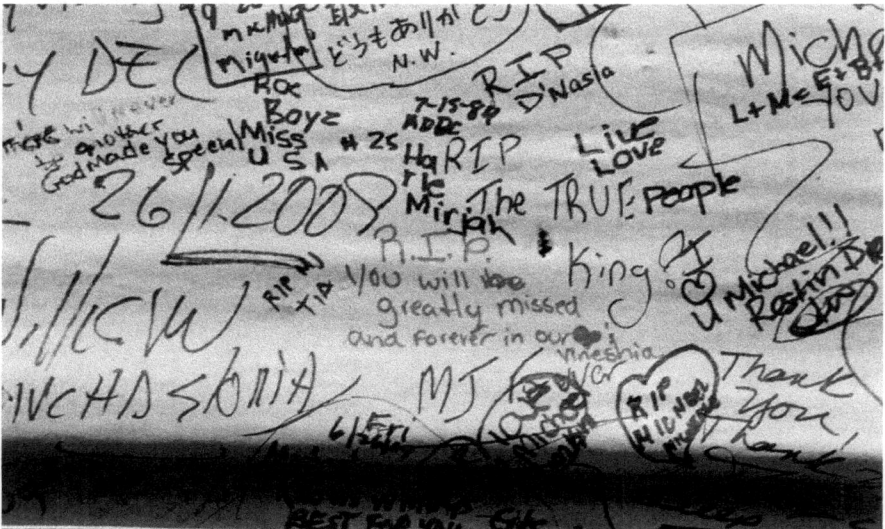

Michael Jackson's Last Dance Photo 64. These writings are self explanatory.

FREDERICK MONDERSON

Michael Jackson's Last Dance Photo 65. These writings are self explanatory.

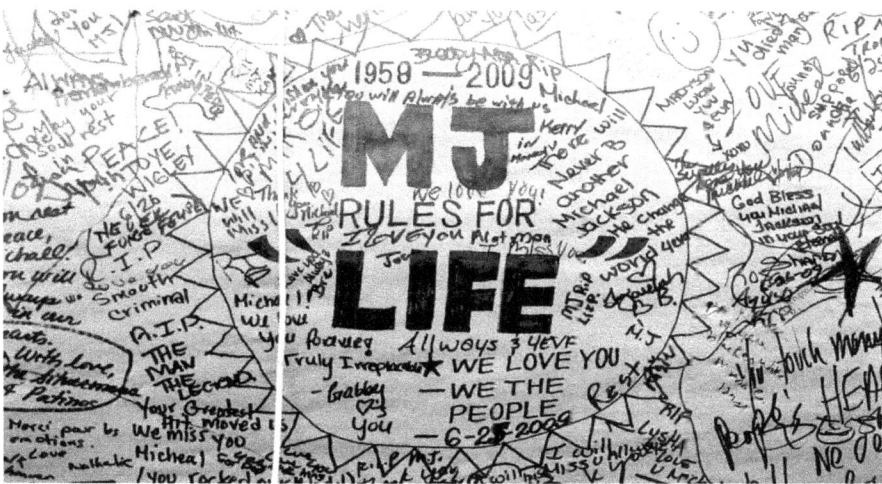

Michael Jackson's Last Dance Photo 66. These writings are self explanatory.

Michael Jackson's Last Dance Photo 67. These writings are self explanatory.

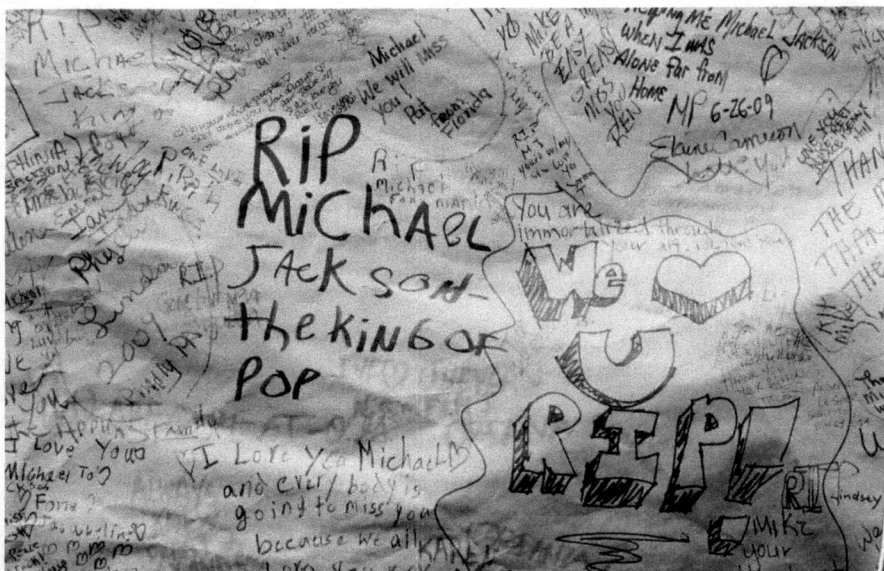

Michael Jackson's Last Dance Photo 68. These writings are self explanatory.

FREDERICK MONDERSON

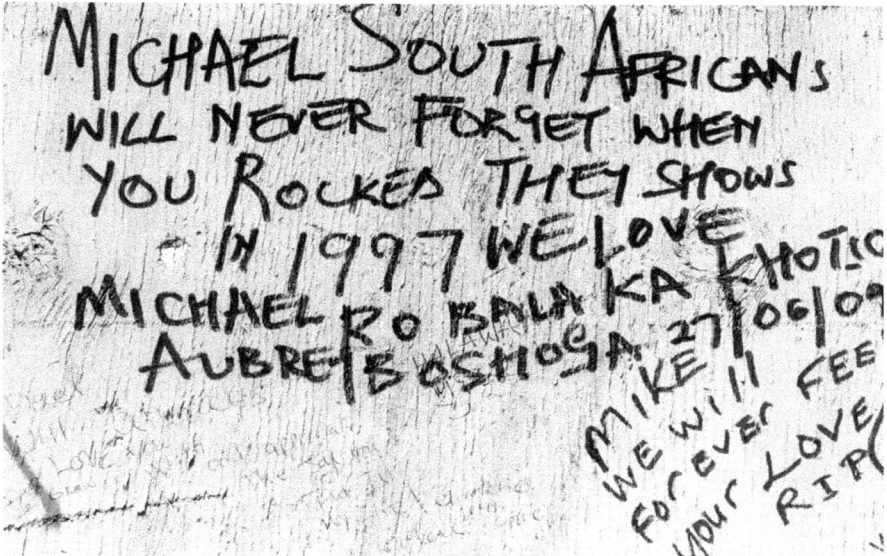

Michael Jackson's Last Dance Photo 69. These writings are self explanatory.

Michael Jackson's Last Dance Photo 70. These writings are self explanatory.

FREDERICK MONDERSON

Michael Jackson's Last Dance Photo 71. These writings are self explanatory.

Michael Jackson's Last Dance Photo 72. These writings are self explanatory.

MICHAEL JACKSON'S LAST DANCE

Michael Jackson's Last Dance Photo 73. These writings are self explanatory.

FREDERICK MONDERSON

8. The Staple Center Memorial to Michael Jackson on July 7, 2009.

The overhead banner read:

IN LOVING MEMORY

MICHAEL JACKSON

KING OF POP

1958-2009

The Michael Jackson memorial ceremony was one of the most watched events in history. It was probably only outdone by the Princess Diana funeral, but people from around the world were not as touched by the Princess as they were touched by Michael. So, while the "counters" say Michael's was viewed by 31 million viewers and the Princess 33 million, they were probably not counting the fact his tribute was carried live across the world. In the United States, Michael's Memorial dominated the airwaves. TV Guide, New York 1, E!, CBS, TV One, NBC, ABC, Fox, Fox News, CNN, HLN, and MSNBC among others aired the proceedings. Let us not forget foreign language stations probably got in the act. Radio stations probably were also involved. Almost all the TV stations did no commentary but simply let the uninterrupted show speak for itself.

By the time most of the guests were seated, the Andre Crouch Choir belted out "Going to see the King."

Smokey Robinson read **Tributes** from **Diana Ross** and **Nelson Mandela**.

MICHAEL JACKSON'S LAST DANCE

Pastor Lucious Smith, family friend, described Michael Jackson as an

"Idol, hero, even a king
Brother, son, father, friend,
Beloved part of Jesus, friend, and family of man

Remember the time
Gone too soon
Never really gone at all

Give love to the world
Moment of remembrance
Moment of healing
Moment of love.

Who is **Diana Ross**? Diana Ross has played an important part in the life of Michael Jackson, a sort of "other mother." She was with him from the beginning of his career, through the ups and downs, and finally stood tall at the end. What a friendship! We first encounter their relationship when he was first introduced to the entertainment world in their first album:

Diana Ross Presents the Jackson 5

We see her again in the movie version of the show "The Wiz."

At the end, overcome with emotion, she chose not to be at the Memorial, but Diana Ross's message was the first Tribute.

Paying the ultimate tribute to a lifelong friend, Michael Jackson chose to name Diana Ross in his Will to take care of his kids, in the event his beloved mother could not! He believed Diana Ross would take care of them as she had taken care of him. What love and confidence!

Michael Jackson was a student of music. He studied Tchaikovsky and Mozart. He also studied the dancing skills of Fred Astaire and all the great dancing masters. He was really impressed with James Brown. Michael was ready and optimistic. He blended pyrotechnics and all forms of costumes and eclectic moves in creating the great dancing he became famous for. To the question, 'Why his global impact?' The answer is simply the music! Music moves people. Michael was free, happy, optimistic, nice, a kind person and very polite. Elizabeth Taylor described him as "wonderful, giving, caring, generous, a great artist."

FREDERICK MONDERSON

The **Artists** who performed were **Mariah Carey** with **Trey Lorenz** who sang "I'll be there."

Lionel Ritchie sang "Jesus is Love."

Stevie Wonder sang "Never dreamed you'd leave in summer." In opening he said, "This is a moment I wished I didn't live to see." He said further, "as much as we may feel we need Michael here with us, God must have needed him more. I'm at peace with my love for Michael."

Jenifer Hudson did an outstanding rendition of "Will you be there?"

John Mayer performed "Human Nature" as an instrumental selection.

Jermaine Jackson performed "Smile."

Usher sang soulfully, Michael you're "Gone Too Soon."

Shaheen Jafargholi of Britain's Got Talent sang "Who's Loving You?"

In closing, the **Jackson Singers** sang "We are the World" and "Heal the World." All sang "We are the World."

Speakers were **Queen Latifah** who read a poem from Maya Angelou entitled "We Had Him!"

Berry Gordy, founder of Motown Records – In his tribute, Gordy said Michael "was like a son to me." He recalled, the "little kid had a quality I couldn't understand, but we all knew he was special." "His performance was well beyond his years. You could feel the happiness in his soul when he performed his songs. With Michael, the Jackson 5 was the only group in history to have their first four hits go to the No. 1 position on the charts. In 1983 they reunited. Michael went into orbit and never came down. Michael Jackson accomplished everything he set out to do. At 10 years old he had passion to become the greatest entertainer in the world. He had 2 personalities. The soft spoken, childlike one and on stage, he was a master, take no prisoners showman. The King of Pop is not big enough. He is simply the greatest entertainer that ever lived. Thank you for the love. Thank you for the joy. You will always live in our hearts."

Kobe Bryant and Earvin "Magic" Johnson –

MICHAEL JACKSON'S LAST DANCE

Kobe Bryant – "In the **Guinness Book of World Records** Michael holds the record for most charities supported by a pop star."

Earvin "Magic" Johnson - "I saw the genius in Michael Jackson. He always had command of himself, the band and the audience. When I was invited to his home and ordered broiled chicken for dinner, Michael ordered Kentucky Fried Chicken. This is a celebration of his life, of his legacy. I want to thank Michael for keeping the doors open."

Rev. Al Sharpton called for "Love vigils to celebrate the life of a man who taught the world to love. Michael never let the world turn him around from his dream. He did not accept limitations. He did not accept limitations. He out sang his cynics. He outdistanced his doubters."

"It was Michael Jackson who brought Blacks, Asians, and Latinos together. He fed the hungry before Live Aid and he created a comfort level. Kids from Japan, Ghana, and France were dancing to his music. There's nothing that can't be don't if you put your mind to it. Michael was not about mess but about his message. He didn't love in vain. I want to say to his three children: There was nothing strange about your daddy. It was strange what he had to deal with! But he dealt with it anyway. Most came here to say good bye, I came here to say Thank you. Thank you, Michael. You never stopped. You never gave up. You broke down barriers. You gave us hope. Thank you. Thank you. Thank you."

Brooke Shields - "Michael was one of a kind. We enjoyed the most natural and easiest of friendships. We both understood what it was to be in the spotlight from a very young age. We laughed. Michael loved to laugh. Michael's laugh was the sweetest and purest of anyone I've known. He was a genius with unchallenged ability. He was honest, pure. He cared deeply for his friends, family and his fans. There was an extraordinary sensitivity about him. He looked with the heart. His favorite song was that written by Charlie Chaplin, 'Smile, though your heart is aching.' Somewhere up there he is perched on a crescent moon."

United States Representative **Sheila Jackson Lee** (D-Texas) also praised Michael Jackson for a life of constructive musical production.

Martin Luther King III and his sister Bernice King.

Martin Luther King III – "They say the sky's the limit, but Michael had no limit. You must discover your calling and be the best you can be. Michael Jackson was truly the best that he was. Martin Luther King did say do your job well, whether you were a doctor or street sweeper. Be the best you could be. Be the best street sweeper. On June 25, here on earth many did pause to say of Michael Joseph Jackson, here was a man who did all that he could to the best of his ability."

Bernice King – "My prayer is that no one fact or fiction can separate you from the love of god. Michael's life and work was inspired by the love of god."

Michael Ortega, Director of Michael Jackson Concert Tour. "We were here practicing. We knew we had to do this memorial here. This was to be his triumphant return to the world. This was his best work. "

Germaine Jackson – "I would like to thank everyone for coming out. We thank you. We thank you. We thank you."

Marlon – "We are trying to understand why the lord has taken our brother. Michael, when you left us a part of me went with you. I will treasure the fun we had singing, dancing, and mother would say boys it's time to go to the recording studio. Despite your disguises, you're my brother, I can spot you anywhere. You wore a crown, you were judged, ridiculed. Maybe now they will leave you alone. Michael was the voice of our angelic trumpet. Whenever we parted and I said I love you, he would say I love you more. Your ultimate reward is in the lord's presence. I thank you. I thank you. When you get to heaven, give my brother Brandon, my twin, a hug."

Paris, Michael's daughter – "From the time I was born, Daddy has been the best father you can ever imagine. I just want to say I love him very much."

Janet – "Thank you for loving our brother. Thank you. Good night."

Pastor Lucious Smith closed with the Benediction. He explained: "All around us are people of different cultures, different religions, and different nationalities. And yet, the music of Michael Jackson brings us together."

While the above performers were clearly visible on stage, it's expected the Staples Center was laden with other celebrities. Various news services gave the names of the following celebrities in attendance: Cicely Tyson, P. Diddy, Rick, Kathy and Nicky Hilton, Lil Kim, Chris Brown, Mickey Rooney, Tatum O'Neal, Larry King.

Emotions probably overcame Quincy Jones who was quoted as saying, "I can't attend any more funerals" and Elizabeth Taylor who wanted to mourn Michael in private.

MICHAEL JACKSON'S LAST DANCE

Michael Jackson's Last Dance Photo 74. All the news stations were in attendance.

Michael Jackson's Last Dance Photo 75. Even more news organizations were represented as a City Cop directs traffic on 125th Street in Harlem, outside the Apollo.

FREDERICK MONDERSON

Michael Jackson's Last Dance Photo 76. Herb Boyd, well known columnist for the New York *Amsterdam News* holds up an original photo of the Jacksons 5 Brothers.

Michael Jackson's Last Dance Photo 77. These folks are at the head of the line to enter the Apollo Theater, Tuesday June 30, 2009. They stood in line for hours to be first.

MICHAEL JACKSON'S LAST DANCE

Michael Jackson's Last Dance Photo 78. From across the street, people get ready to enter the Theater to begin the True Memorial on Tuesday, June 30, five days after Michael's passing, when Rev. Al Sharpton would address the crowd and play MJ music.

Michael Jackson's Last Dance Photo 79. Just before the doors open around 2:00 pm.

FREDERICK MONDERSON

Michael Jackson's Last Dance Photo 80. The sign says it all and so do people's faces in tremendous tribute salute to Michael Jackson, the "King of Pop."

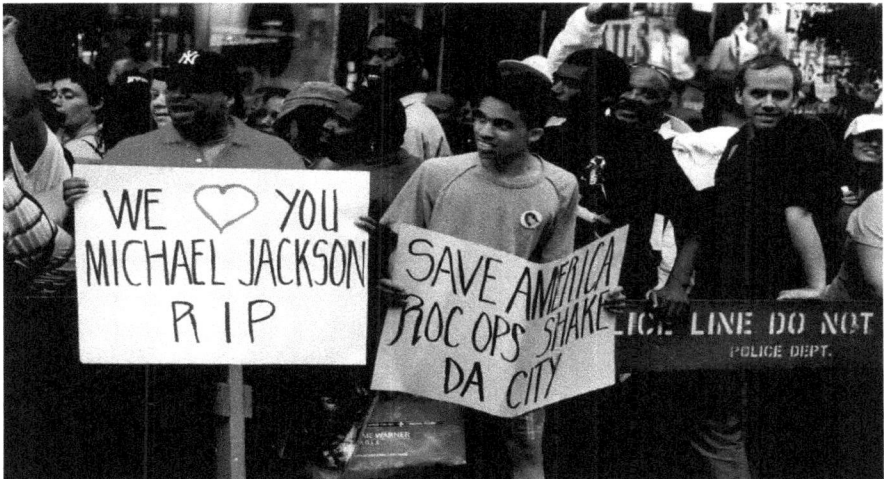

Michael Jackson's Last Dance Photo 81. These folks are all pumped up for Michael.

MICHAEL JACKSON'S LAST DANCE

Michael Jackson's Last Dance Photo 82. People are lined up on both side of 125th St.

Michael Jackson's Last Dance Photo 83. The line stretched towards Lenox Avenue.

FREDERICK MONDERSON

Michael Jackson's Last Dance Photo 84. More of the excitement as fans await the door opening across the street. Notice the line going back farther towards Lenox Avenue.

9. MICHAEL JACKSON, BELOVED
By

Dr. Fred Monderson

The world was shocked at the untimely passing of Michael Jackson, singer, dancer, entertainer, humanitarian; and as spontaneously electric as his music and performances have been, in like manner loyal and adoring fans took to the street at venues worldwide to honor the life's work and passing of an American icon, whom Elizabeth Taylor first dubbed the "King of Pop." From Presidents to Prisoners and Princes to Paupers, the explosive yet gentle artistic giant was mourned for his lifelong contribution to the joyful exuberance of so many, for so long. Equally, in life as in death, media vultures continue to accentuate any human

94

MICHAEL JACKSON'S LAST DANCE

indiscretions Mr. Jackson may have been accused of, though in the eyes of the law, he was found not guilty of criminal charges. Michael Jackson is not unlike so many creative, hardworking and oftentimes intellectually gifted blacks, and people in general, who must creatively perfect their craft, work hard to achieve a well-deserved acclaim, struggle to maintain a socially acceptable squeaky clean persona or brace for the unrelenting onslaught of perennial demonizing of people trying to make a career through the media's sensationalism. This, therefore, was the fate of the songbird Michael Jackson.

Fortunately at this time especially, fans do not wish to see their idol's name and memory further besmirched by critics fueled by envy, greed and opportunism. The outpouring of love and affection for Mr. Jackson and his family at this grievous time, is a tremendous indication of people's long memory of the wonderful moments that Mr. Jackson has provided during their times of celebration of birthdays, weddings, graduations; at parties, concerts, driving to and from work, and any inconceivable number of times and ways he provided sweet music that aided their joyous expressions, lifted their spirits.

Years ago my mother, psychically talented, while observing Michael Jackson performing on TV said, "When this young man dies the world will realize how creatively talented, mystical and spiritual he really was." She has been gone nearly 19 years and now with his passing the vast majority of people will not only miss this musical genius but also come to realize there was something mystical, magical, and indeed spiritual about one who could reach so many, so far, in so many cultures across so many countries and continents, high and low in society. Truly, Michael Jackson's angelic voice seems fueled by divine inspiration which aided his mission as a wonderful American cultural ambassador.

From the time of his passing, the outpouring of love and condolences to his family has shown Michael Jackson was beloved far and wide and the human frailties that marred the later years of his wonderful career seemed inconsequential as fans celebrated his life, refusing to mourn the wonderful spirit they came to admire and love in the person of Michael Joseph Jackson. This creative genius was hard working, disciplined, a tremendous perfectionist who was truly international in outlook and a great musical star, a bright star in the earth's constellation. He was a sensitive artistic genius who became vulnerable to vulturistic chicanery and so, out of fear, became isolated and lonely. After his death and reflecting on that famous interview, Oprah Winfrey explained: "I heard it, I sensed it, but I didn't understand how profoundly lonely he was." Yet he continued to create wonderful music that expressed the deepest sentiments of love, harmony and healing that reflected the true genius of the man.

Michael Jackson's Last Dance Photo 85. More folks, not just across the street on the barriers at 125th, but jamming the sidewalk where vendors were making lively business transactions with Jackson memorabilia.

Michael Jackson's Last Dance Photo 86. Still more folks across the street buying and observing what's going on at the Apollo as fans in line wait to enter the Theater.

MICHAEL JACKSON'S LAST DANCE

Michael Jackson's Last Dance Photo 87. A Michael Jackson impersonator has appeared and the excitement begins to stir as people wait in line to enter the Theater.

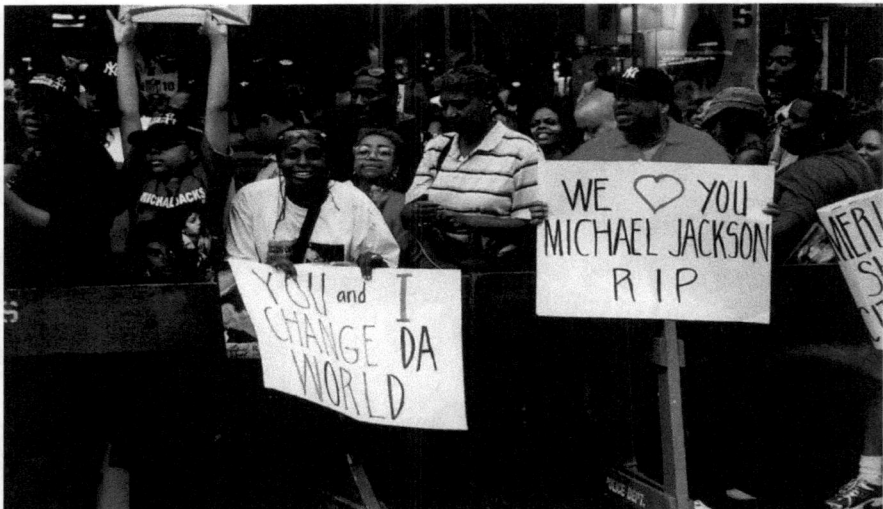

Michael Jackson's Last Dance Photo 88. The excitement is building in the line for those waiting to enter the Apollo Theater to begin the show of Memorial to Michael Jackson at 2: 00 pm. Some have waited for hours just to be among the first to enter the Apollo Theater.

Michael Jackson's Last Dance Photo 89. Author and photographer as part of the fun.

MICHAEL JACKSON'S LAST DANCE

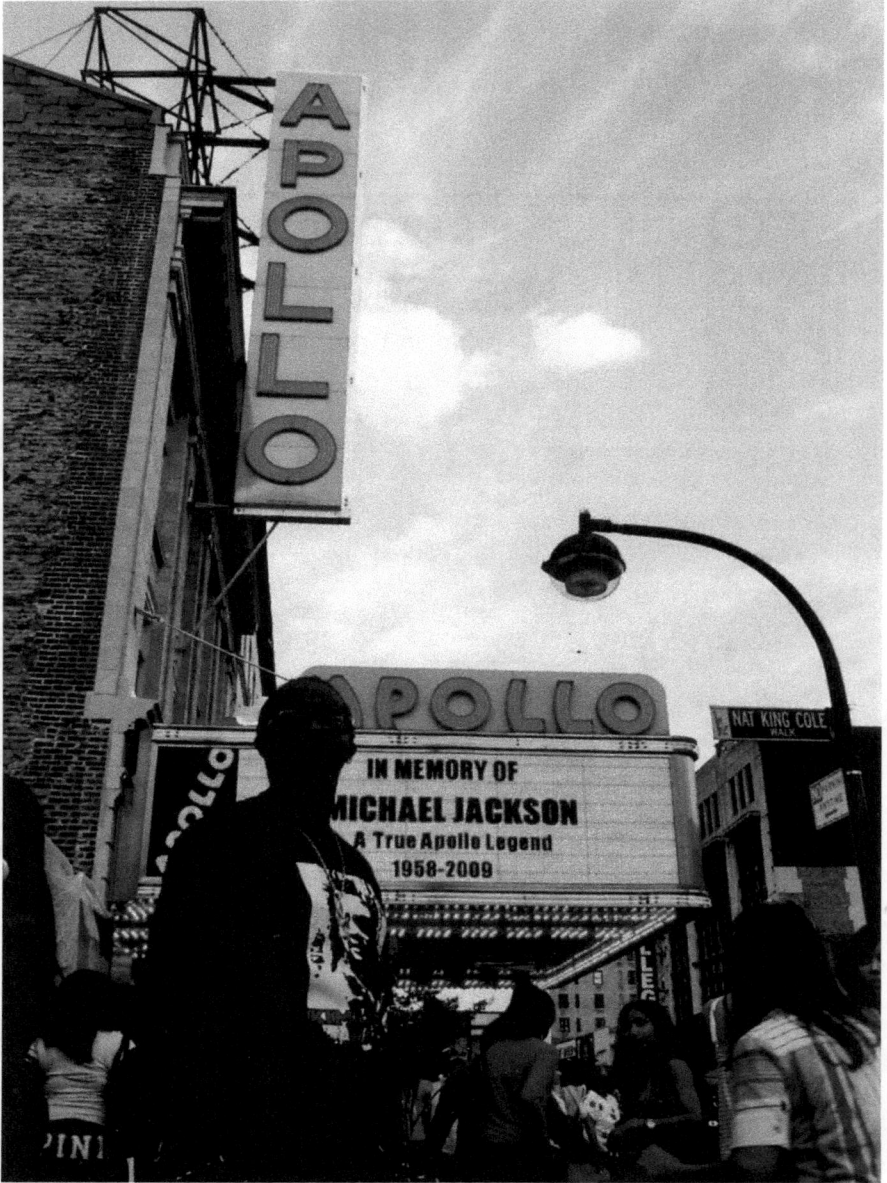

Michael Jackson's Last Dance Photo 90. Nova Felder among the excited fans.

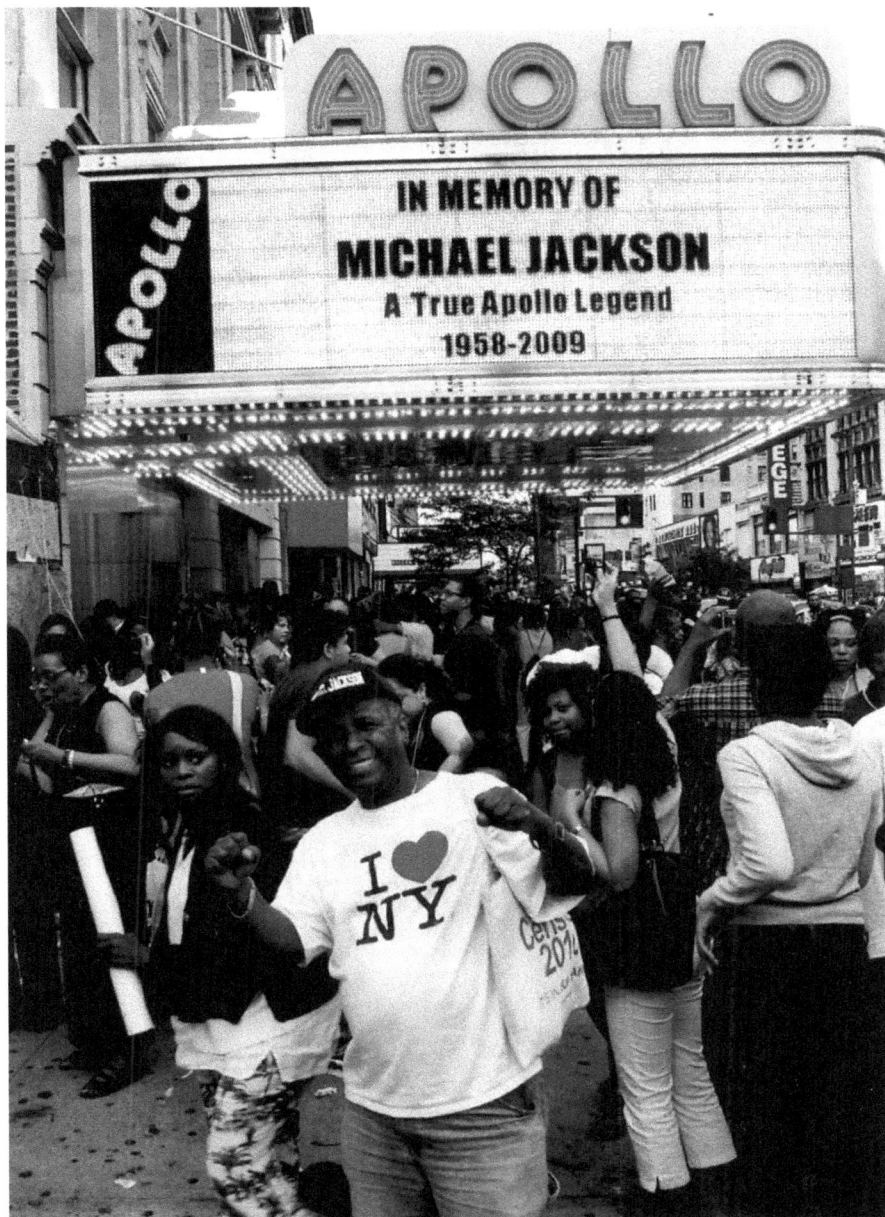

Michael Jackson's Last Dance Photo 91. Part of the excited crowd at this time.

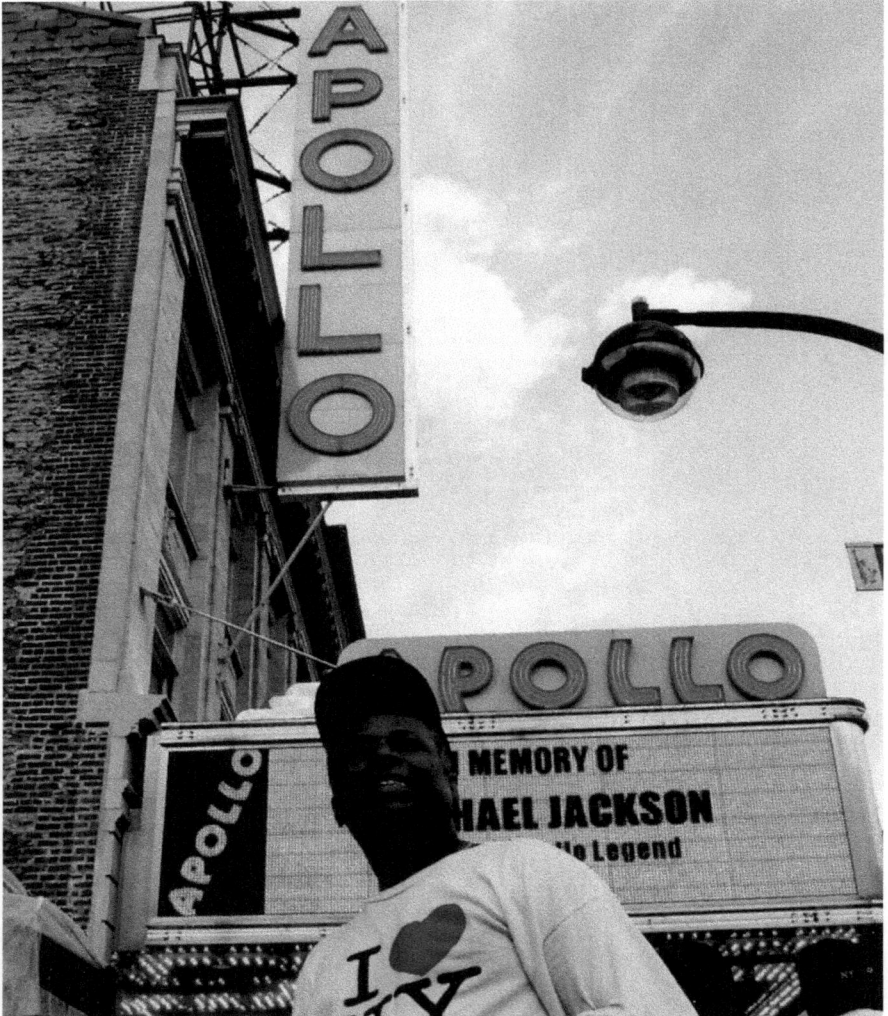

Michael Jackson's Last Dance Photo 92. The author with people viewing "The Wall" and the Apollo Marquee in the rear.

FREDERICK MONDERSON

Michael Jackson's Last Dance Photo 93. The signs say it all for Michael Jackson.

Michael Jackson's Last Dance Photo 94. More of the background scenery with "The Wall" to the left as people sign first "The Wall," then paper, then plastic with other signs.

10. EXPRESSING THE VOICE OF THE PEOPLE
By

Dr. Fred Monderson

Teddy Cubia, June 25, 2009, retired New York City Educator believed: "These are the highest events of our lifetime; the birth of the first Black President and the death of a musical icon, Barack Obama and Michael Jackson."

According to Mr. Cubia, "Michael represented the epitome of artistry, so classic with his style that he transcended the entertainment industry in every ethnic denomination."

Cubia further believed, "Claims of parental misconduct are unfounded. Michael never really grew up. Joe was very strict in his discipline. He wanted to make his diamond in the rough shine. Joe believed and reinforced the notion: the quickest way to Carnegie Hall is rehearse, rehearse, rehearse! Joe disciplined Michael in the elements of artistry to perfection."

Vincent K. Manuel (Teach) – "They feed off us … They benefit from our misfortune and made their fortune. The Rabbi robbed I! It does not matter if you're white or black. Dracula did not come out of Africa … You can't plant peas and get cassava. From 3/5 of a man to King of Pop. We the people like cream, we always rise to the top. Top Contributor Worldwide for Humanity! As it was in the Beginning, We continue to No End."

The Rabbi - Once you become a confessor, whatever is told to you, you are supposed to throw it into the Sea of Forgetfulness. That Rabbi did not do this and sought to profit from his relationship with Michael Jackson. It is like a Catholic priest revealing what is confessed to him. Who knows if Michael Jackson actually knew the Rabbi was taping him and what would have been his response if he could contemplate his deepest thoughts being exposed to the public without his prior knowledge. Others will find it difficult in the future to confess to this individual for fear the religious leader-client privilege would no longer be sacred, secret. That is, no one will trust him anymore for fear he will do a Michael Jackson on them!

Leslie Austin – Michael is the greatest entertainer I have ever seen. My whole family loves him forever. I will always love him and will miss him greatly.

Quincy Jones – June 25, 2009 – "I am absolutely devastated at this tragic and unexpected news. I've lost my little brother today and part of my soul has gone with him."

Tommy Motola, former head of Sony Music – June 25, 2009 – Mr. Jackson was "the cornerstone to the entire music business. He bridged the gap between the rhythm and blues and pop music and made it into a global culture."

Doris Darrington (77) of Gary, Indiana – June 26, 2009 – "He has always been a source of pride for Gary, even though he wasn't around much. The older person, that's not the Michael we knew. We knew the little bitty boy with the big Afro and the brown skin. That's how I'll always remember Michael."

MICHAEL JACKSON'S LAST DANCE

Chloe Rosenberg "On Web, Fond Farewell to Pop Legend" *Daily News* Saturday, June 27, 2009, pp. 8-9, the following are excerpts from comments printed by the news writer.

True Yet Fair wrote: "He changed cultural landscape that only others can dream of. This man is known around the world, in every corner of the earth where no one else is. I am 27 and my name is Billie Jean ... enough said. God bless his talent and his kids who have to live in this world without him. Respect to one of the best musicians to ever live."

Nature's Beauty: "MICHAEL JACKSON!! YOU were one of a kind!! There has never been or will never be another who can come close to your talent. No One will ever compare! You were often imitated – you could NEVER be duplicated."

Tchicky: "They called Michael demeaning names, really hurtful to a man who would never hurt a fly and who contributed his whole existence (really!) from 5 years old to your enjoyment of music. We can never repay you Michael. Your music, your voice will last forever. Thank you, Michael. God Bless. RIP. One Love!"

Hjo4: "Michael Jackson was the GREATEST ENTERTAINER ON THIS EARTH. I doubt if anyone will come remotely close to the late Superstar. He also was a sad and tortured soul. His spirit was broken and he was tired, worn out, his job here on earth was done. His expiration date came and freed him from his pain. Rest in peace Gloved One."

Poetic Justice: You're the best and growing up, you really made my life a much better one listening to your music. Thanks for all you have done. I hope that you are "Moon Walking" your way through heaven's door. RIP."

Rican Princess: "Nobody cares what he did to his face. Nobody cares what he did to his voice. Nobody really cares about the three-ring circus surrounding his life. Michael Jackson was the greatest music artist of our time."

Htotheo: "He was a great artist and he deserves all the acclaim and dignity that he has earned as an icon."

Caring American: "Michael THANK YOU for bringing a lot of happiness and enjoyment to my life. You are part of my growing up to who I am now. I will miss you forever. I wish people would stop looking for negatives about you and think about all of the good you did. We have lost a legend."

Tiffany Howard of Brooklyn, in the New York *Daily News* Saturday, June 27, 2009, p. 24, under **Voice of the People: Mourning Michael** wrote: "Words can't describe "The Way You Make Me Feel," "You made me feel like a "P.Y.T," even though you never said my name the way you did "Billie Jean," You said I was "The Lady in Your Life," and with those words, "You Rock My World." You knew it was "Human Nature" to "Wanna Be Startin' Something" because you were "Bad" – but a "Smooth Criminal." And they would never "Beat It" and "Leave you Alone." Your music helped "Heal the World" in so many ways. That's why we will forever "Jam" and "Rock With You," even until the "Break of Dawn." You'll be remembered as a true "Dancing Machine," a "Thriller," a legend in your own time who has "Gone Too Soon." I hope you know "I just Can't Stop Loving You."

Mike Jaccarino – "Constant pain part of his life" in *Daily News* Sunday, June 28, 2009, p. 6, quoted R. Kelly who expressed his sympathy in the following: "I am truly saddened that my mentor, brother and friend will no longer be with us physically. At the same time I feel so blessed to have been touched by his music, his dance, his lyrics and his pure genius. It is because of Michael's yesterday that I am who I am today."

Jan Ransom and **Bill Hutchinson** with **Tanyanika Samuels** "The Apollo launches tributes" *Daily News*, Sunday, June 28, 2009, p. 5, quoted Rev. Al Sharpton: "He was the king of popular culture and I'm not going to let them reduce Michael to some king of freak show... but Michael was a true genius. To create music that outsold any other artist in his generation, can't no freak do that."

Even further the columnists wrote, "Vendors lining the sidewalk across the street from the Apollo were doing brisk business hawking Jackson CDs, DVDs, posters, photos, and T-shirts. **Nova Felder**, 31, of Queens said he sold five-dozen Jackson videos at $15 apiece on Thursday and had sold out of CDs he was offering for $5 each. 'People are buying it, buying it, buying it,' Felder said."

Tanyanika Samuels' "Rev. Al vows to fight for Michael" in *Daily News* Sunday, June 28, 2009, p. 5, quoted Rev. Al Sharpton: "'If we can look past the shortcomings of Frank Sinatra and Elvis Presley, then we can put into proper perspective any shortcomings Michael may have had,' he said. Sharpton said he knew Jackson was at peace. 'When you get to heaven,' he said, looking skyward, 'turnaround and moonwalk through the gates.'"

Venues for watching the event as shown on the TV screen included: London, Berlin, New Delhi, Harlem, New York, Raleigh, North Carolina, First AME

MICHAEL JACKSON'S LAST DANCE

Church of Los Angeles, Times Square, New York on a Jombotron, the Staples Center, Los Angeles, Neverland ranch, Gary Indiana, Atlanta, Hollywood, Las Vegas. In fact, people around the world watched the historic Home Going ceremony for Michael Jackson.

Errol Lewis columnist of the Daily News in "What Michael meant to me" *Daily News* Sunday, June 29, 2009, p. 27, wrote: "Michael Jackson first entered show business as the youngest product of the Motown record label, a legendary pop-culture juggernaut that had already launched the likes of Marvin Gaye, the Supremes, Stevie Wonder, and the Temptations. Toiling under the watchful eye of Motown founder Berry Gordy, a team of producers and songwriters called The Corporation scripted the look and sound of what they dubbed 'Bubblegum soul.' They took the Motown formula – teen music whose rugged gospel and blues roots were blended with stripes, Doo-wop harmony and bright, catchy hooks – and made it kid-friendly...."

"And by the time we were full grown, Michael was swimming in the deep currents of American musical genius. His groundbreaking solo album, 'Off the Wall,' was produced by Quincy Jones – a dazzling composer/arranger who'd started as a young trumpeter in the Dizzy Gillespie Band...."

"When all is said and done, Michael's trials and tribulations, the snide recitations of court cases and financial woes, will amount to no more than trivia. Michael Jackson and the music he made are baked into too many lives, minds and hearts to be anything but a glorious legend in the end – one that will live well beyond my lifetime and yours."

On **LARRY KING LIVE** July 7, 2009, 9:00-10:00 pm, Dionne Warwick and her son appeared.

On Larry King Twitter, as shown on the TV screen:

EJay – "An excellent home going for Michael."

Rohan – "Michael Jackson was the MAN and the best entertainer."

Angela – "Michael's costumes should be on display at Neverland."

Fran – "Michael Jackson was not just an icon, but a genius with a message."

Brown – "Michael Jackson set the bar for songs, videos and fashion."

FREDERICK MONDERSON

Judy – "Michael Jackson was a great entertainer who did a lot for AIDS and other causes."

Matt – "Michael was an icon of our time, only Elvis was comparable."

Afrida – "Michael was the best entertainer, musician and humanitarian."

Maria – "King of pop and his music and videos will last forever."

Vincent – "Michael Jackson will never die. He will live on in his music."

Lynn – "Michael will live on in his children and Neverland."

Deanna – "I hope Michael gets the peace he never did in life."

Gotham Chopra – Michael's funeral was "very elegant and dignified."

Rose – "Michael's abilities opened the door for African American artists."

Brian – "Michael gave up his life and money, everything for people."

Charmichael – "It takes a lot for me to cry. I haven't stopped."

Patti Austin – "Michael studied the greats who came before him."

L.H. "Michael, the man with a platinum soul."

Rohan Lisa – "Neverland should be owned by one of Michael's charities."

Roxanne – "Michael was a gift to the world."

Al Sharpton on **Anderson Cooper** AC 360, CNN, July 7, 2009, 10: 00-12:00 pm –

"Michael kept going. He did not accept limitations. Michael broke down the color curtain. He brought together Black, White, Asian, Latino. He outperformed the pessimists. Michael never topped. Michael never stopped, Michael never stopped."

"The whole service was almost flawless. He was the one MTV and Rolling Stone put on their cover. He helped create the culture of comfort. He brought changes to your eyes, your biases, your fears. His children were in a web of love."

MICHAEL JACKSON'S LAST DANCE

Vincent Patterson, Choreographer and director – "That's how he developed the moonwalk, working on it for days, if not weeks until it was organic. He took an idea that he had seen some street kid doing and perfected it."

Jamie Fox at 2009 BET music award – "We want to celebrate this black man. He belongs to us and we shared him with everybody else."

Rev. Carolyn Herron of the First African Methodist Episcopal Church in South Los Angeles on June 28, 2009. "He may not be the King of Kings, but he's the King of Pop."

Naya Arinde in "The Phenomenal Michael Jackson – Rest in Perfect Peace," The New York *Amsterdam News* July 2-July 8, 2009, quotes Michael Jackson from a June 2002 Forum at the Rev. Al Sharpton's National Action Network entitled "Music Fairness, Justice and Racism in the Recording Industry" where the talented entertainer stated: "The moment I started breaking the all-time record in sales... I broke Elvis' record, I broke the Beatles' records, the minute ["Thriller"] became the all time [best] selling album in history in the **Guinness Book of World Records** – overnight they called me a freak. They called me a homosexual. They called me a child molester. They said I bleached my skin. They did everything to turn the public against me. It's all a complete conspiracy. You have to know I know my race. I look in the mirror. I know I'm black!"

Rev. Al Sharpton – "Michael made young men and women all over the world imitate us. Before Michael, we were limited and ghettoized. But Michael put on a colorful military outfit, he pulled his pants up, he put on the one glove, and he smashed the barriers of segregated music."

David, now **Governor Patterson** informed the *Amsterdam News* – "His video for Thriller redefined the way music videos are made for ever. He probably succeeded James Brown as the greatest dancer; and he succeeded Elvis Presley as the King of Pop; and he probably succeeded the Beatles in international recognition. I was on 125th Street on Saturday, and I noticed in comparison how all these other artists seemed so distant and far away. People grew up and knew him. Even with his [transformations], they just always treat him as a family member having problems rather that people could relate to."

Charles Barron – Michael Jackson was a black genius who loved his people. The man in the Mirror will be sorely missed, for he has truly gone too soon. Rest in peace my brother Michael, for a job well done."

FREDERICK MONDERSON

Michael Jackson's Last Dance Photo 95. One of the youngest Michael Jackson "impersonators" on the scene prepares for the attention he will get.

Michael Jackson's Last Dance Photo 96. A young MJ "impersonator" stands alone.

FREDERICK MONDERSON

Michael Jackson's Last Dance Photo 97. "Now, what was I thinking?" He must think.

Michael Jackson's Last Dance Photo 98. Another young Michael Jackson "impersonator" just cooling it with the crowd to his rear, behind the barriers.

FREDERICK MONDERSON

Michael Jackson's Last Dance Photo 99. Young Michael Jackson "impersonator" seems ready for the action as he strikes a pose.

MICHAEL JACKSON'S LAST DANCE

Michael Jackson's Last Dance Photo 100. "Impersonator" and beautiful MJ lady fan.

Michael Jackson's Last Date Photo 101. Young "Michael Jackson" seems to have a very vivid fan with an admiring grin as she holds an original photo of Michael Jackson.

MICHAEL JACKSON'S LAST DANCE

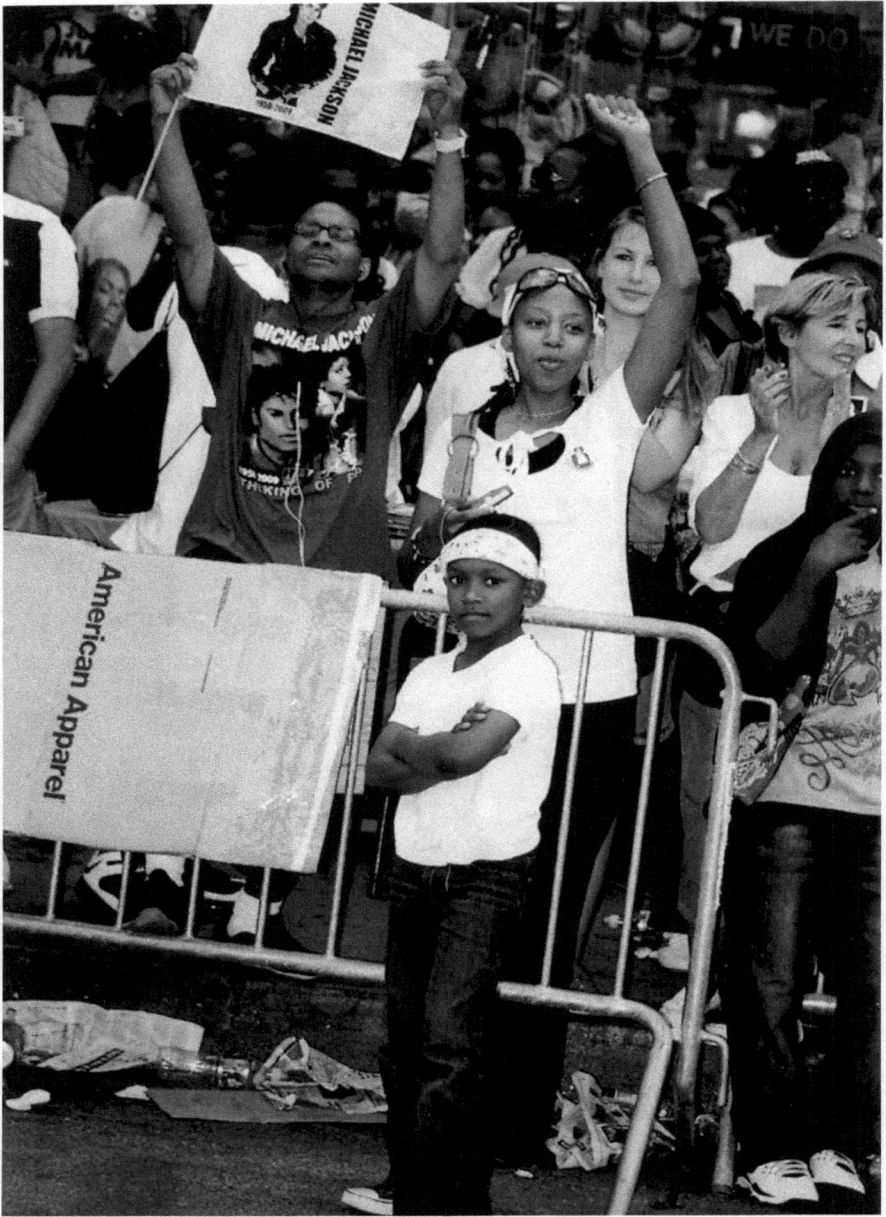

Michael Jackson's Last Dance Photo 102. Young MJ "impersonator" with crowd.

FREDERICK MONDERSON

Michael Jackson's Last Dance Photo 103. A real live Michael Jackson "impersonator" has arrived with news vans in background, especially Brooklyn News 12.

Michael Jackson's Last Dance Photo 104. MJ "impersonator" speaks as the crowd listens, with cops and news vans in the background.

FREDERICK MONDERSON

Michael Jackson's Last Dance Photo 105. "Everybody is a star" as MJ "impersonator."

11. COMMENTATORS ON MICHAEL JACKSON

Donna Brazile, the Democratic strategist and CNN Commentator mentioned Michael's music, movements and his humanitarianism. He stretched "Hands Across America" and was instrumental in 'Live Aid' and 'We are the world' which was done with Lionel Ritchie. "Michael Jackson was dancing and celebrating life itself." Donna thought the Memorial, "an organized event. It was a celebration of his life, work, legacy. Many charities will continue to benefit from his legacy."

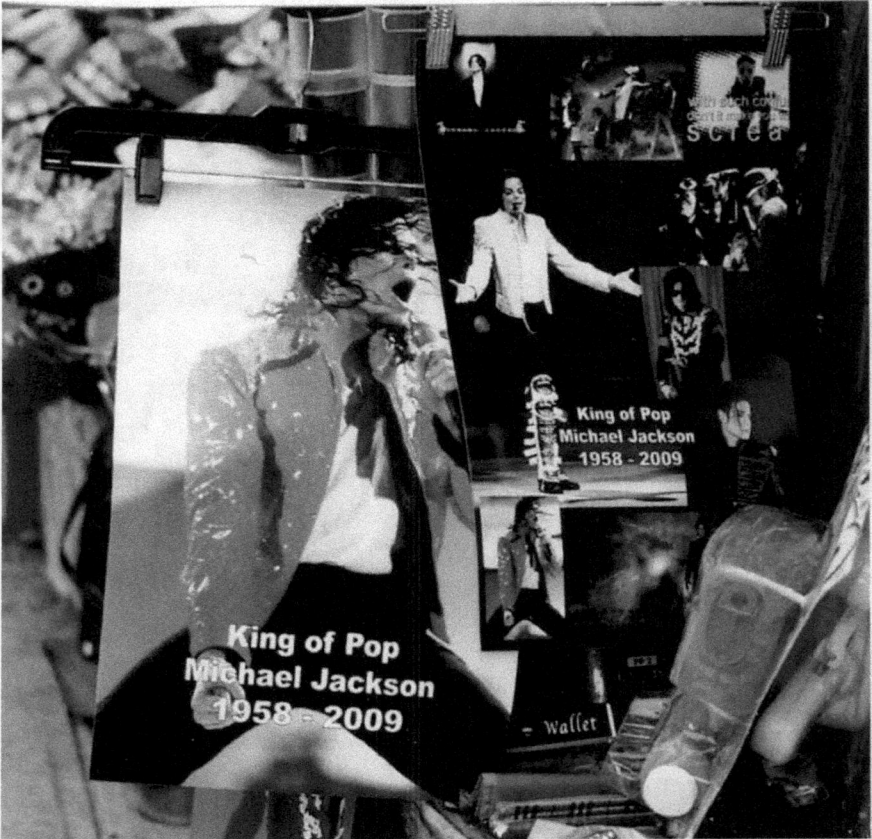

Michael Jackson's Last Dance Photo 106. Memorabilia of Michael Jackson on sidewalk.

"Michael Jackson was huge in the United States but massive abroad. In his spectacular 'We are the world' this is the first time that many entertainers, 25, worked together. Michael gave tremendously to charity. He supported the United Negro College Fund. He is reported as giving anywhere from 300 to 500 million dollars to charity. The children gave his life new meaning. His hat (fedora), glove, jacket, socks, black pants were his singular trademark. There were many Michaels for many souls. There was universal love and respect for his music."

FREDERICK MONDERSON

Roland Martin, a syndicated Radio Host and CNN Host and Commentator reflected on the somber celebration given to Michael Jackson. He stated in the Black Community, the tradition is one of a "Home Going Service." Mr. Martin thought Michael is now "In a better place. He will have no more pain. No more sorrow. No more heartache. There will be no more tortured challenges. Michael loved to perform. There were never any shifting attitudes for Michael in the African American Community. African Americans adored Michael because of his music."

Michael Jackson's Last Dance Photo 107. Michael Jackson's image on back of a T-shirt that reads Michael Jackson – A True Legend - "Rest in Peace."

MICHAEL JACKSON'S LAST DANCE

Michael Jackson's Last Dance Photo 108. More memorabilia of Michael Jackson on display showing the many moods of the great one.

FREDERICK MONDERSON

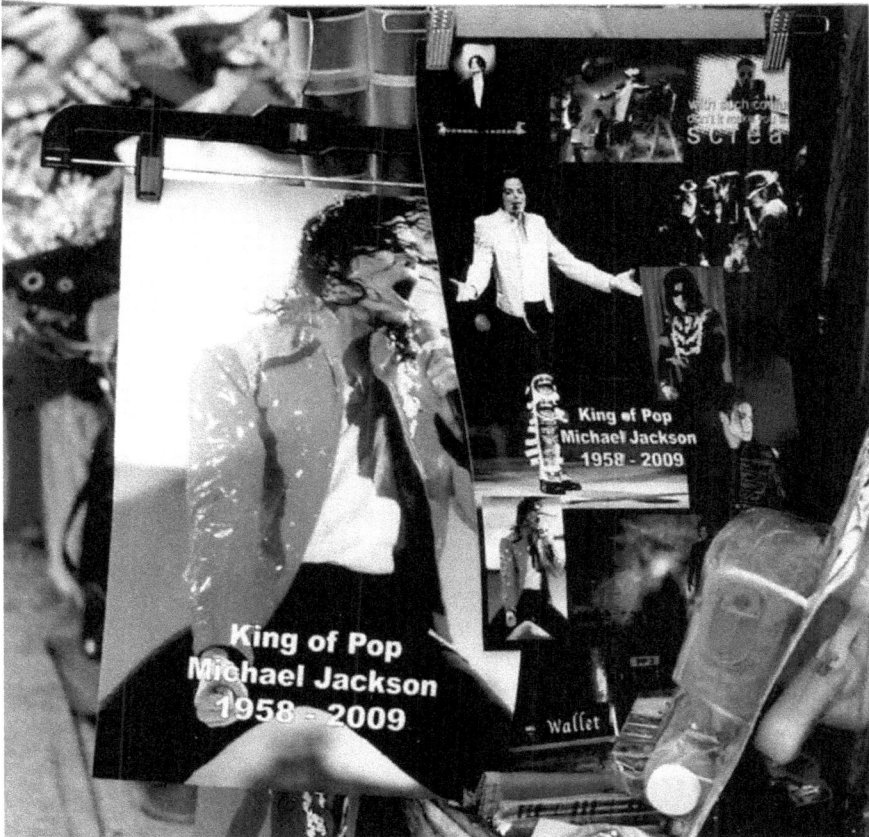

Michael Jackson's Last Dance Photo 109. Photo images of Michael on display.

MICHAEL JACKSON'S LAST DANCE

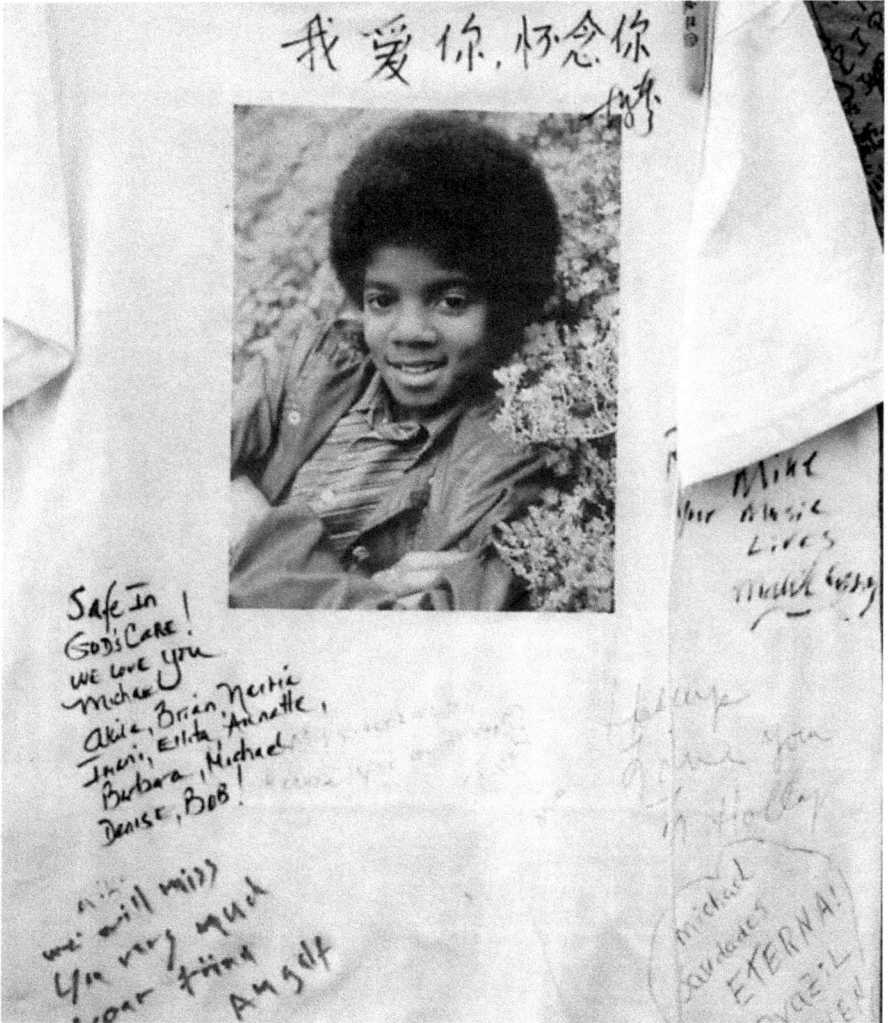

我爱你,怀念你

Michael Jackson's Last Dance Photo 110. T-shirt awaiting autograph by fans.

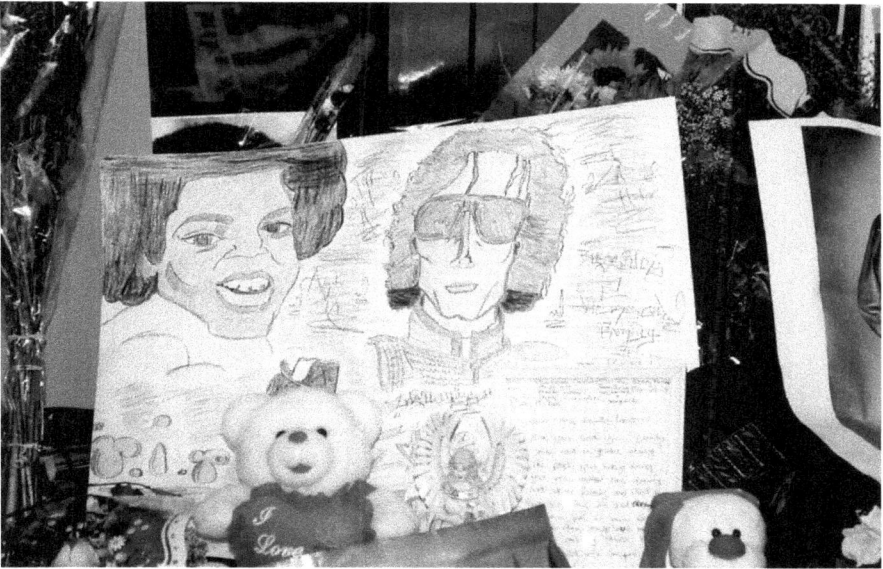

Michael Jackson's Last Dance Photo 111. Someone took the time to draw this image of Michael in their tribute to the "King of Pop."

MICHAEL JACKSON'S LAST DANCE

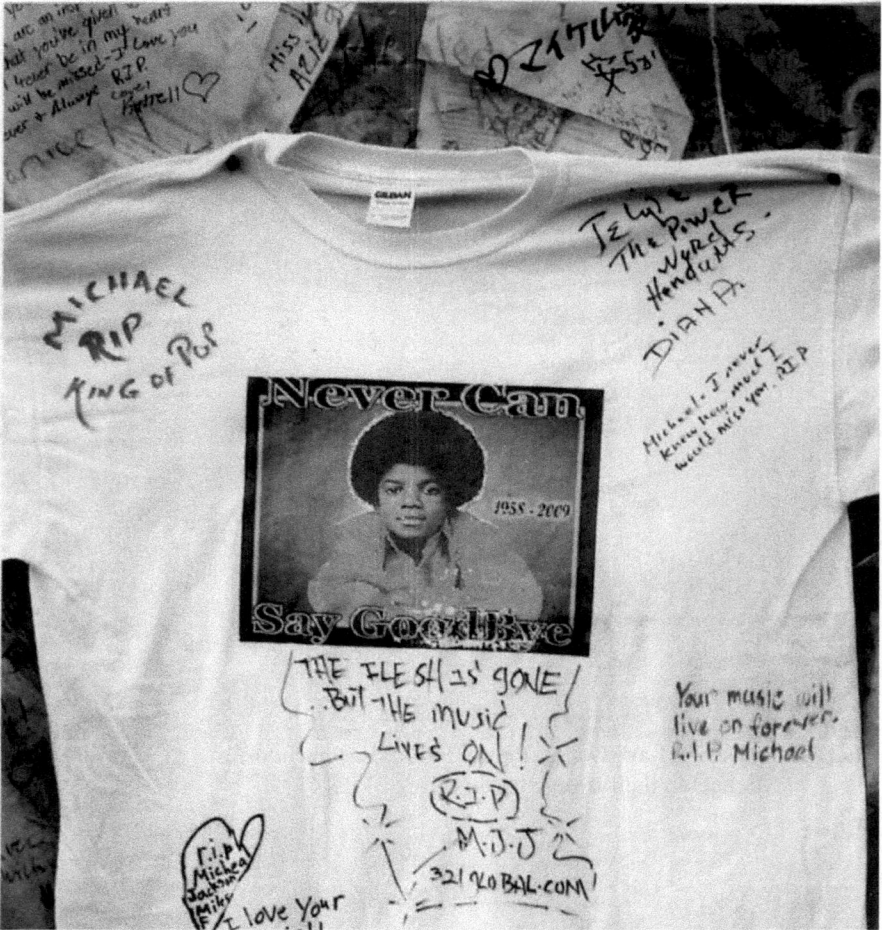

Michael Jackson's Last Dance Photo 112. Another T-shirt with Michael's image awaiting autograph by fans.

FREDERICK MONDERSON

Michael Jackson's Last Dance Photo 113. Another T-shirt awaiting autograph.

MICHAEL JACKSON'S LAST DANCE

12. Michael Jackson in Retrospect

The death of Michael Joseph Jackson shocked the world but more important it shocked some individuals into realizing that life is indeed fragile, tender, even precious and sometimes short. Nevertheless, a philosophical belief holds, "It's not how long you live, but what you do while on earth and what is your legacy." Another somewhat mundane belief is "you come into this world crying, structure your life so that when you depart people will cry because you represent a loss." To both of these admonitions, Michael Jackson is a perfect example of one whose legacy is assured and with tumultuous tears shed at his passing, he will surely be missed!

Michael Jackson was born to Joseph and Katherine Jackson in Gary, Indiana, on August 29, 1958. The second youngest, his male siblings were Jackie, Tito, Jermaine, Marlon and Randy. The twin of Marlon, Brandon, died and in his tribute to his brother asked Michael to give him a hug when he got to heaven. The sisters were Rebbie, LaToya and Janet. Brooks Barnes' "A Star Idolized and Haunted, Michael Jackson Dies at 50" in *The New York Times*, Friday, June 26, 2009, Cover and pages A22-23, writes about the family and that: "They all survive him, as do his parents Joseph and Katherine Jackson, of Las Vegas, and three children: Michael Joseph Jackson, Jr., Paris Michael Katherine Jackson, born to Mr. Jackson's second wife Deborah Jeanne Rowe, and Prince Michael Joseph II, the son of a surrogate mother. Mr. Jackson was briefly married to Lisa Marie Presley, the daughter of Elvis Presley."

Michael began performing with four brothers from the age of five and for more than four decades he remained a fixture on the American entertainment scene. The interesting thing about Michael, unlike many young singers of the present generation, his lyrics were plain, simple, fun-filled and harmless. Whether as a member of the Jackson 5, a band his father Joe organized as a former musician; as a member of the Jacksons; or as a solo act, Mr. Jackson was a prolifically creative song-writer who seemed to own the pop charts. As such, he is the only pop star inducted into music's Hall of Fame twice, as a member of the Jackson 5 and as a solo act.

Michael Jackson first appeared, at the age of 5, with his brothers, in Harlem at the Apollo Theater's Amateur Night and stole the show. Then known as the Jackson Brothers, in 1968, the group was signed by Berry Gordy's Motown Records. Diana Ross probably made the introductions. However, within no time, Michael and the group were a sensation. They changed their name to the Jackson 5. Brooks Barnes (June 26, 2009: 22) notes: "The Jackson 5 was an instant phenomenon. The group's first four singles – 'I want you back,' 'ABC,' 'The

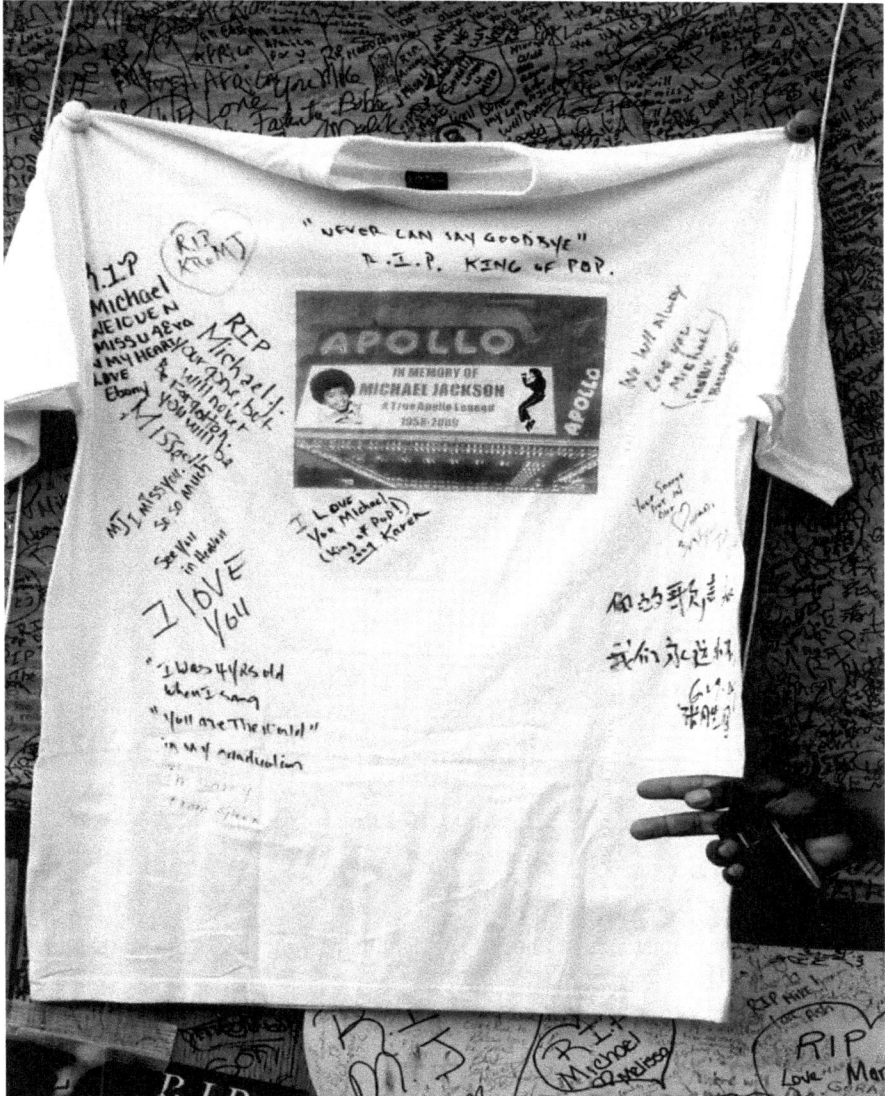

Michael Jackson's Last Dance Photo 114. Before writing saturated the T-shirt.

MICHAEL JACKSON'S LAST DANCE

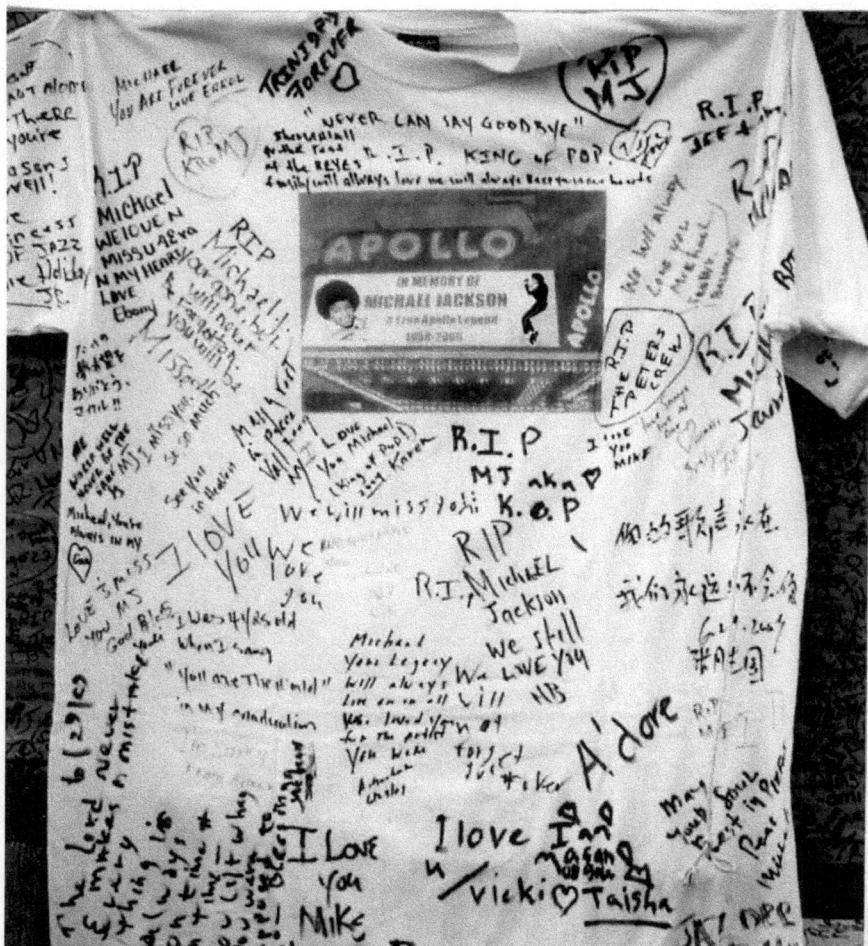

Michael Jackson's Last Dance Photo 115. T-shirt writing shows the shirt saturated with love for MJ.

FREDERICK MONDERSON

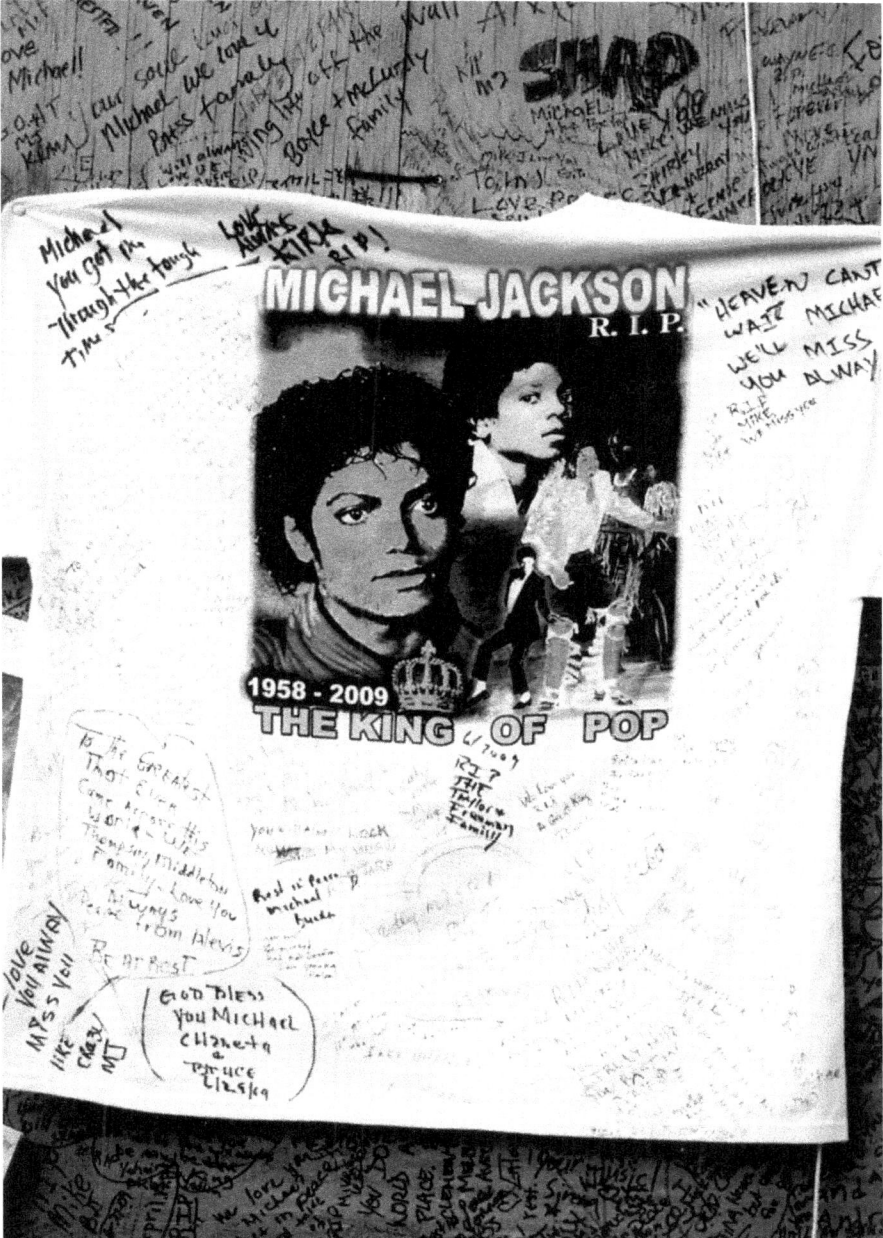

Michael Jackson's Last Dance Photo 116.   T-shirt writing showing love for MJ.

MICHAEL JACKSON'S LAST DANCE

Love You Save,' and 'I'll Be There' – all reached No. 1 on the pop charts in 1970, a feat no other group had accomplished before. And young Michael was the center of attention: he handled virtually all the lead vocals, danced with energy and finesse, and displayed a showmanship rare in a performer of any age."

Michael Jackson's Last Dance Photo 117. A female wears T-shirt with Michael's image as "King of Pop."

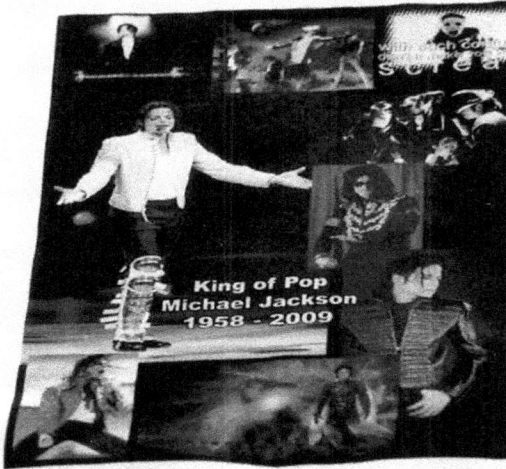

Michael Jackson's Last Dance Photo 118. A collection of images of the "King of Pop."

The next year he began a solo career and a year after that in 1972 he produced "Ben" title song of the movie about a young kid and his pet rat considered a killer animal. While still composing, singing and dancing, Michael Jackson made his movie debut in **The Wiz** in 1978 alongside Diana Ross and Nipsy Russell.

MICHAEL JACKSON'S LAST DANCE

Michael Jackson's Last Dance Photo 119. A beautiful lady holds a classic picture of Michael Jackson that reads "King of Pop" the "Greatest Ever."

Michael Jackson's Last Dance Photo 120. Images of Michael Jackson lining the pavement in front of a vendor's stall.

Michael Jackson's Last Dance Photo 121. A collection of images of Michael Jackson in different stages of his life.

Michael Jackson's Last Dance Photo 122. Classic photo of the King of Pop" all written up with sentiments expressing the love fans feel for their departed hero.

FREDERICK MONDERSON

Michael Jackson's Last Dance Photo 123. More writing surrounding that classic photo of the "King of Pop."

13.   CONCLUSIONS

Michael Jackson lived a rather remarkable life for a black man born in America in the 20th Century. While not concerned with general events surrounding his death, this work sets out to praise and celebrate his life, adding a pictorial focus on Harlem's Apollo Theater Memorial to one of its true heroes. It is designed to present Mr. Michael Joseph Jackson in as much of a positive light as possible so posterity will be able to see beyond the media disfigurement the man was subjected to and his true genius can be remembered.

In many aspects, this is a compilation of the positive things about Michael Jackson so persons interested in his creative genius can have a point of departure into the life of a man divinely inspired with a gift of creativity, humility, and humanitarianism fueled by mystical spiritualism and a magical nature bent on

138

making a difference in the lives of people in as disparate a region of the world, as possible. This is why the world mourned the passing of Michael Jackson because there would be no more creations and hands on concerns about the poor, diseased, and those-in-need of charitable contributions. Thank God, however, Michael Jackson was full of foresight back in 2002 to Will so no matter what, help would always be available for charity.

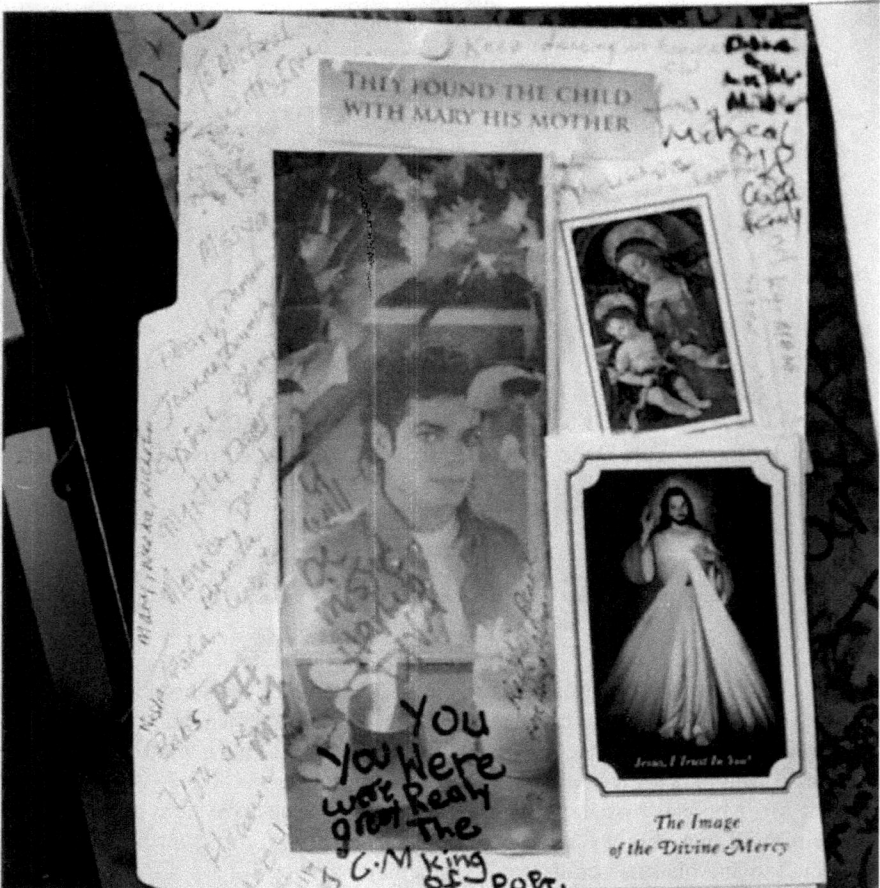

Michael Jackson's Last Dance Photo 124. This one ties Michael to Heavenly Grace.

FREDERICK MONDERSON

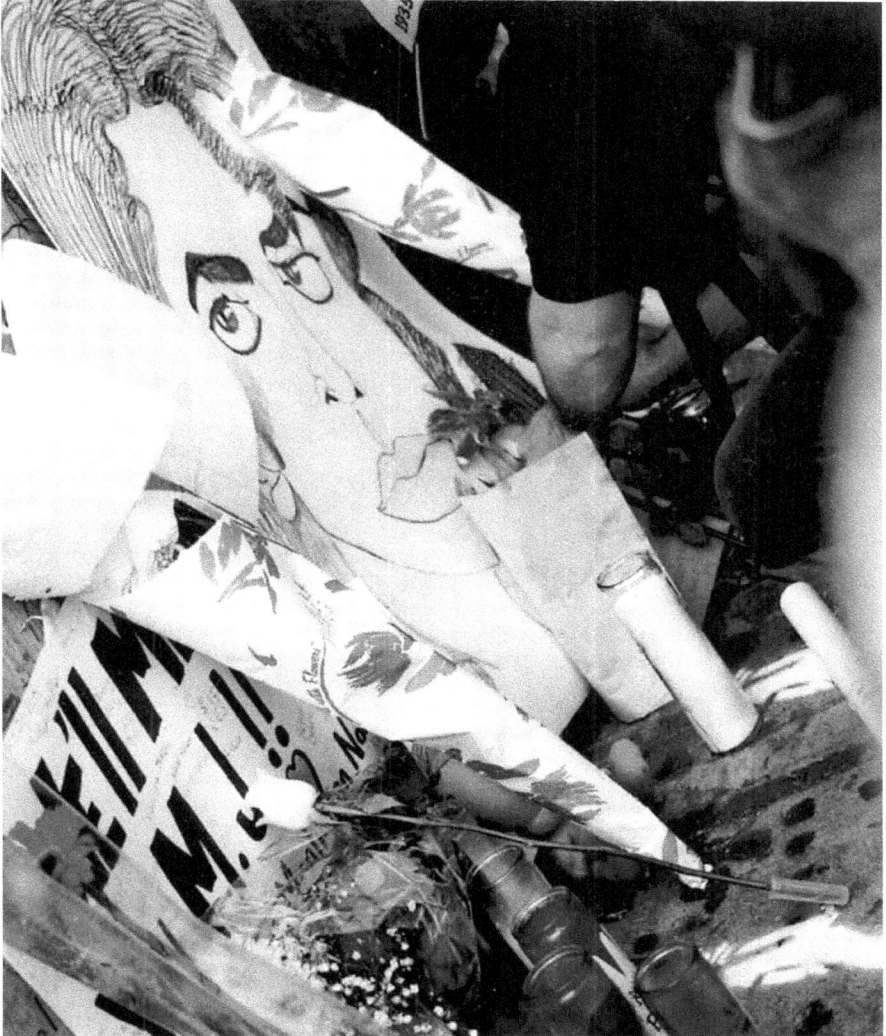

Michael Jackson's Last Dance Photo 125. Illustrated image among the candles and flowers as fans celebrate the "King of Pop" who brought such great joy to their hearts.

All this, notwithstanding, despite the media negative amplification of some sad moments in his history, Michael Jackson has imprinted the world as a creative musical artist, dancer, writer, and humanitarian whose music seems appropriate today as it was two or three decades ago; and may very well be around for two or three more decades.

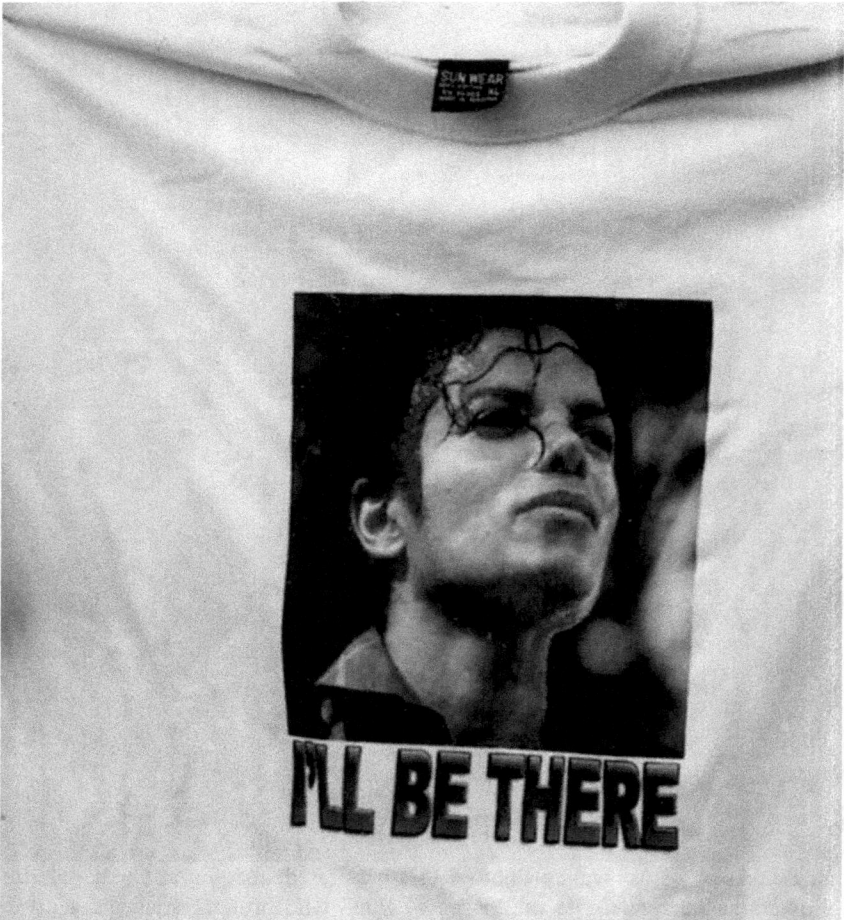

Michael Jackson's Last Dance Photo 126. A new T-shirt before the tributes.

FREDERICK MONDERSON

Michael Jackson's Last Dance Photo 127. That same T-shirt with new tributes.

MICHAEL JACKSON'S LAST DANCE

Therefore, the contents are presented in a manner that readers can make their own deductions about the man who fascinated the world with his music, dancing, entertainment, charitable contributions, concerns about humanity and tremendous efforts to heal the sick and make the world a better place, all accentuating the notion of love as a powerful social exhilir that can bring soothing joy to even the most distressed.

Michael Jackson's Last Dance Photo 128. Another new T-shirt before the tributes.

Michael Jackson's Last Dance Photo 129. That same T-shirt with new tributes.

MICHAEL JACKSON'S LAST DANCE

Michael Jackson's Last Dance Photo 130. This T-shirt hopes for the best!

Michael Jackson's Last Dance Photo 131. Classic photo - Jacksons on *Ebony* Cover.

Michael Jackson's Last Dance Photo 132. Back to the "Altar of Remembrance."

14.   VISCERAL CONCERN
By

Dr. Fred Monderson

Visceral Concern: Since the death of Michael Jackson, establishment Media has used power and influence to continue to defame this great artist and to diminish his legacy and his value to the Black Community and to the world.

PURPOSE: The purpose of this brief inquiry is to:

147

FREDERICK MONDERSON

Establish or deny the authenticity of the negative innuendos and rumors pertaining to Michael Jackson.

To assert the inescapable contribution this brother has made not only to the performing arts but to the positive imagery of American culture worldwide.

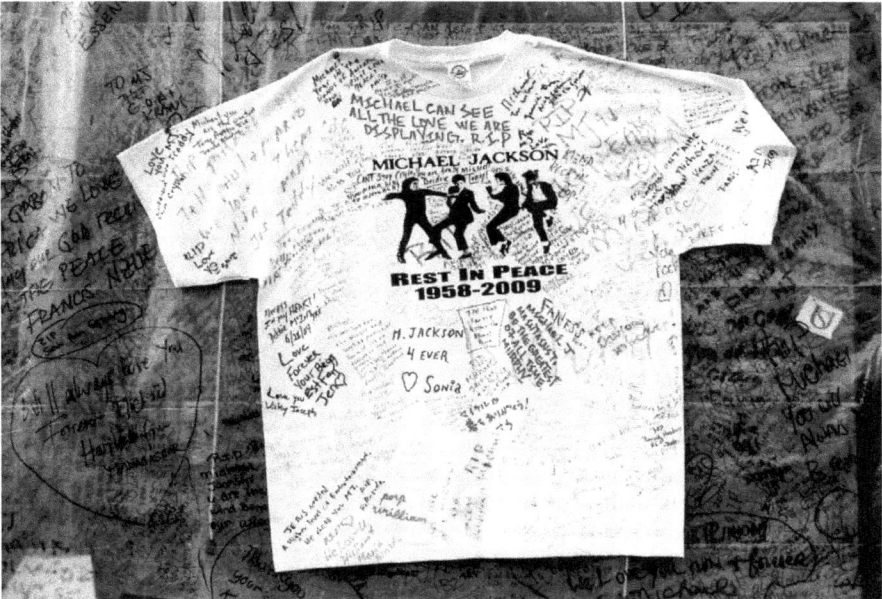

Michael Jackson's Last Dance Photo 133. Amidst the other signings, the T-shirt says much about Michael Jackson and his influence.

My hypothesis is therefore interrogative, which states:

Is there substantive evidence in the record to support the proposition that Michael Jackson was subjected to parental abuse which primarily led to patterns of behavior that were non-traditional and whether this has led to his dependence on narcotics. The Methodological Tools to be utilized will include:

Historical Outline
Cause and Effect

MICHAEL JACKSON'S LAST DANCE

Comparison and Contrast
Systematic Conceptual Scheme of Analysis and this requires:
Purpose
Concepts selected must have relevance
        They must be Precise
        They must contain bases for problem solving theory

Concepts:

        Parental Responsibilities
        Talent
        Internal Interactions
        Father
        Mother
        Family

External Interactions and influences

        Berry Gordy
        Diana Ross
        James Brown
        Media
        Jessie Jackson
        Al Sharpton

Critical Summary:

Parental Responsibility is to maximize the potential of a child. Did Jackson's parents do this?
Siblings' influences and interactions
Matrimonial Relations and his children
People whose financial lifeblood depended on Michael Jackson

The Music Industry with its:

        Producers
        Directors
        Distributors
        Musicians
        Audience
        Intra/Inter group relations (race)

FREDERICK MONDERSON

Michael Jackson's Last Dance Photo 134. More of the "Altar of Remembrance."

Charitable Contributions

National
International

Interpretative Summary

The Body of Work

150

MICHAEL JACKSON'S LAST DANCE

The Michael Jackson Legacy

What people are saying

VISCERAL CONCERN
HISTORICAL OUTLINE

Michael Jackson was born into a very close-knit family on August 29, 1958, in Gary, Indiana. Headed by Joseph and Katherine Jackson, his male siblings were Jackie, Tito, Jermaine, Marlon and Randy. He was the seventh child that included sisters Rebbie, Latoya and Janet. Very early, their father, himself a musician and steel worker, realized his offsprings had musical and entertainment talent. And so, he tried to develop this in hopes one day, they would hit the big time and elevate their social standing in a post-civil rights America where blacks lagged in all fields of endeavor.

Mr. Jackson was by no means a "modern father," because as a child of the Depression he had experienced all the vicissitudes of being black in pre and post World War II America. It is easy to understand his desire to see his children succeed. He would later be accused of using harsh methods to encourage his children to perform. He probably encountered the old adage, "How do you get to Carnegie Hall? You practice, you practice, you practice!" This is the only way the Jackson 5 and Michael "Got to Carnegie Hall!" Wembley stadium and entertained in the great houses of Europe, Asia, Africa, and America. Notwithstanding, the hype by the media and Michael, Joe Jackson like any father loved his family, worked at making them successful and probably exclaimed, "Damn the torpedoes, full steam ahead." Joe Jackson was determined his children would not end up as so many hapless blacks have, who were consigned to the perils of society's ills.

By late 1960s, success came to the Jacksons and by early 1970 they were on top. By the 1980s Michael's rocket had catapulted him into the stratosphere. He had become a household word in America, a global entertainment phenomenon and everyone was dancing to his music, watching his videos and his family was earning cash big time.

Michael Jackson became a victim of his success because, though a powerhouse entertainer, he was a gentle soul who surrounded himself, in his inner circle, with the proverbial "parasites," people who did not have his best interest at heart. The end result, he became eccentric, cultivated the finest tastes, spent money like it was going out of style and did not pay attention to the creeping vultures that began to circle before they swooped down on him.

It's been argued, his lifestyle, the regimen of constant entertainment at the high level of his performance, exertion, unfortunate physical accidents, plastic surgery, all drove him to ultimately become addicted to prescription drugs. Because Michael opened his heart and home to young people, he was accused of being a child molester. The first time he was forced to settle out of court by an insurance company and his attorneys who thought such accusations would not only damage his image, his career, but also detract from his time spent in active production of his craft. Gerry Hopkins, JD, "Michael Jackson: Black or white?" in *Care* (Concerned American for Racial Equality) No. 15 (July 15-24, 2009) makes an interesting statement in response to Long Island, New York Republican Congressman Peter King's disparagement of Michael at his death about being a child molester. He quotes Rev. Al Sharpton at the Michael Jackson memorial Ceremony at the Staples Center, in that "people are gathering well aware of the fact that MJ was found 'not guilty' of every count in the child molestation trial that was brought against him in criminal court by the State of California. King conveniently minimized and disregarded this fact in his monologue about why MJ does not deserve anyone's respect."

Hopkins goes on to write, "Regarding the civil claims which were brought against MJ by Jordan Chandler on behalf of Evan Chandler, MJ did what every other respectable, hard working celebrity (Black or White) would have done – he settled. He settled, not because he could not win a civil trial or because he was culpable, but because he had more productive things to do with his time than to deal with a money-crazed parent who was bent on getting rich the easy way - using fabrications against a celebrity in a sensational trial." Even further he states. "Congressman King also chose to disregard a very important fact, as have the mainstream media in the U.S., that on or about June 29, 2009, MJ's accuser Evan Chandler, whose father, Jordan Chandler had settled the civil matter for a reported $22 million, confessed that MJ did not molest him. This news is available from various unverifiable internet reports. According to these reports, Chandler has since indicated that his father told him to falsely tell the police that MJ had engaged in acts of kissing, masturbation and oral sex. [Attempts by the author to reach Evan Chandler for a first-hand comment were unsuccessful.]

Equally, "no major news media source has been able to substantiate this claim." What I could add, however, this unconfirmed, un-corroborated story is mainly fed by lots of blog commentary at various Internet sites. Importantly, when this researcher tried to Google the subjects by name, lots of entries surfaced. For instance, "Evan Chandler" revealed some 303,000 entries. The names "Jordan

MICHAEL JACKSON'S LAST DANCE

Chandler" + "Michael Jackson" + "Evan Chandler" revealed 17,100 postings. "Evan Chandler" + "Michael Jackson" + "Jordan Chandler" returned 9,120 entries. "Evan Chandler" + "Michael Jackson" revealed 149,000 and "Jordan Chandler" + "Michael Jackson" netted 1,160,000 entries. When I coupled "Jordan Chandler" + "Michael Jackson" + "Evan Chandler" + "I lied" I came up with 1,240. Somewhere in there a poll asking whether the confession that Jordan Chandler supposedly made was correct provided the following: "87 percent said Yes; 6 percent said No; and 7 percent said Maybe." Of course, only if the young man comes forward and confirms publicly that he in fact made the confession would the world know for sure. Until then, if the events described never happened and if he did make the statement, and would not confirm then the world would still wonder about what happened, and all things being equal, he would perhaps still suffer a guilty conscience. On the other hand, perhaps the law may be able charge him with fraud. Then again, the Statue of Limitations may have expired. So much is uncertain as to whether all this is true.

Nevertheless, those who do not learn from history are bound to make those same mistakes. In the second scheme concocted to shake him down, he probably refused yet the DA decided, "I want to nail this guy."

Michael Jackson's Last Dance Photo 135. These sisters proudly display their Michael collectibles against "The Wall" showing three levels of writing tributes.

FREDERICK MONDERSON

Fortunately he was acquitted of 14 charges of child molestation but the damage to his reputation had been incalculable, fueled by powerful media and people of influence. Not just his reputation, the cost to defend himself and the physical, emotional and psychological strain took its toll on the man and his family. These pains probably contributed further to his use of prescription drugs.

Two marriages, challenges to his financial empire, conflict with the music industry, all challenged his fortitude. All the while, the assault continued, against his integrity, branding him with scurrilous names in an attempt to strip him of his fan base. When God is on your side, in every dark storm there is sometimes a window of hope, joy, goodness and mercy. From his marriage to Debbie Rowe he received two children, a boy and a girl, and from a surrogate he received a son. These children brightened Michael's life. They were his all. he devoted patience, love, caring and concern in raising them, mindful as a youthful entertainer he was denied a proper childhood. He had missed being able to play like normal kids, falling down, bruising his knee, having Daddy there to embrace and say sweet and gentle things to the young soul.

Michael was determined the children would have a normal childhood, but he resolved to not spoil them in the process, even as he sheltered them from the public and media wolves.

Rumor mills churned about his finances that he was broke, bankrupt, about to lose all. Michael arranged to do one series of concerts in London, some say a grueling 50 such events, called "This is it." Within hours of the announcement, millions of tickets were sold and Michael began to prepare. Rumor has it; he was in top shape as he rehearsed; an active, energetic, superstar.

CAUSE AND EFFECT

A longstanding friend of mine, Walter Brown has always said, "Don't get on the road." By this he meant, don't start something unless you can see it through; and nothing good comes easy, to get paid, you must work hard and well in all such applications.

If we seek cause and effect in Michael Jackson's experience, we have to accept the realization that success is, as they say, "99 percent perspiration and 1 percent inspiration." In Michael's case, however, it was "99 percent perspiration and 101 percent inspiration."

MICHAEL JACKSON'S LAST DANCE

The fundamental principles of life instilled from a young age by his loving family were able to sustain Michael in times of extreme challenge. Nonetheless, he was able to creatively produce the works he became famous for. Down to the end, he remained a simple, gentle loving soul whose past and future was shaped by the love he received from his family, particularly his mother, Katherine.

Michael Jackson's Last Dance Photo 136. Michael among the candles to "light his way" on the "Altar of Remembrance."

COMPARISON AND CONTRAST

Comparison and contrast is a wonderful tool to examine any phenomenon, but when we apply this calculus to someone of Michael Jackson's stature, it is difficult to find comparisons. His work ethic, his creativity, his blessedness, his caring and concern for the less fortunate, his charity, his explosive performance on stage as he plied his craft, his business acumen, and in so many other ways, Michael Jackson stands unparalleled. In his line of work, the two greatest entertainers Frank Sinatra and Elvis Presley have been compared with Michael and he seems to have best them. The more audacious claims pit both Sinatra and Presley against Michael Jackson and he was declared greater than both combined.

155

Michael Jackson's Last Dance Photo 137. These ladies proudly display their affection for young Michael.

MICHAEL JACKSON'S LAST DANCE

It is difficult to find comparisons to a man who loved and feared god as he did, notwithstanding all his accomplishments. The feelings he entertained and acted on in favor of the poor and sick, those deserving assistance from his successes and those he reached in his charitable endeavors, all this sets Michael Jackson on a plane difficult to compare with others. Let us not forget, **Guinness Book of World Records** thought Michael the most generous of all entertainers and this rightly sets him apart from the others. Quincy Jones, the producer who spent much time and was involved in creating his most successful pieces of work, remarked: "Michael was the most professional person I have ever worked with." Leonard Rowe, the concert promoter, recounts how in later times he told Michael he needed to slow down with the serious dancing, his signature performance workout on stage. In response Michael told him: "I can't do that to the people. I must give my all at all times." Steve Manning, his brother Tito's manager, reminded us Michael was a perfectionist. He was beyond his years. He was very deep, kind, trusting of people. How many, in today's world can boast of such attributes with such sincerity as Michael displayed time and time again. This comment therefore sets him apart from so many in his field.

An even more compelling characteristic of Michael was his faith in people, his belief in loyalty. Michael befriended Dave Dave who had suffered some burn accident and who confessed, Michael "Was like the father I didn't have. He offered me emotional support when I needed it most. He loved me from the time we met." Dave also believed, "Powerful people in Hollywood betrayed Michael. They failed him."

While Celine Dion, on the one hand exclaimed Michael "was not only an extremely talented person. He was also a genius." On the other, Deepak Chopra believed Michael Jackson "Was a mythical person and he died a mythical death." There are not very many people he could, therefore, be compared with.

Michael Jackson's Last Dance Photo 138. This is one excited fan who displays Michael's classic image.

MICHAEL JACKSON'S LAST DANCE

SYSTEMATIC CONCEPTUAL SCHEME OF ANALYSIS and this requires:

CONCEPTS

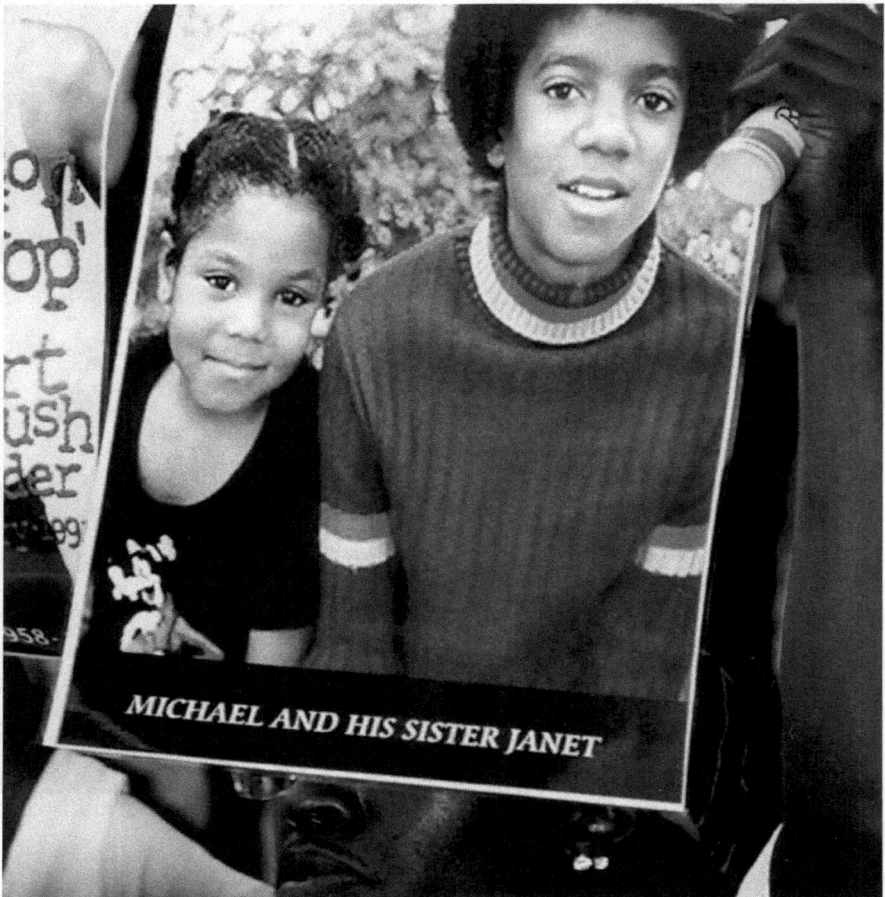

Michael Jackson's Last Dance Photo 139. A fan holds aloft a not often seen depiction of Michael and Janet Jackson.

Michael Jackson's Last Dance Photo 140. Michael works out in this image.

MICHAEL JACKSON'S LAST DANCE

a.   Parental Responsibilities

The role of a parent is to raise a child or children within the constructs of teaching them the right and moral things acceptable in society, and the principles to empower them to become useful constructive citizens in that or any other society.

Michael and his siblings were raised as Jehovah Witnesses, but as he grew older, he became more universal in his religious beliefs. Jermaine his brother, for his part, chose to become a Muslim.

Both Joe and Katherine were involved in raising the children. However, while Joe was brow beat by Michael on the Oprah Winfrey Show Katherine was as much involved in raising him. Evidenced, he loved and supported his mother beyond question.

a.   Talent

Talent is an interesting phenomenon that one has to develop over a period of time. One may be born with the rudiments of talent but it only becomes apparent and practicable through development which can only be manifested through practice. Like all athletes, entertainers, etc., men of talent have to continuously strive to improve this ability.

While Michael Jackson was a talented individual, it was, however, something he worked diligently and consistently to develop and perfect over the ages. We know he claimed his father "beat" him to practice or perform. At the funeral, Marlon referred to his mother insisting they stop playing and go to the studio to practice. But like everything else, Michael's talent dictated he do more than average. He was a perfectionist and therefore he put more energy, vigor, time and effort into perfecting his craft.

At Motown's 25th Anniversary while singing "Billie Jean" Michael unfolded his now famous "Moonwalk." On Oprah he explained it was something he saw kids in the street doing and worked to perfect it. Others told us he practiced for hours, days, weeks to perfect the "Moonwalk" so that when he broke into it, it was perfect. Even further, we are told Michael rehearsed hundreds of songs that never made it into his album collections. At his death we were told he had some 100 recorded songs he never released. These therefore represent glimpses of the efforts he exerted to perfect his talent and this is what brought him to the pinnacle of his career and the megastar status he enjoyed worldwide.

161

FREDERICK MONDERSON

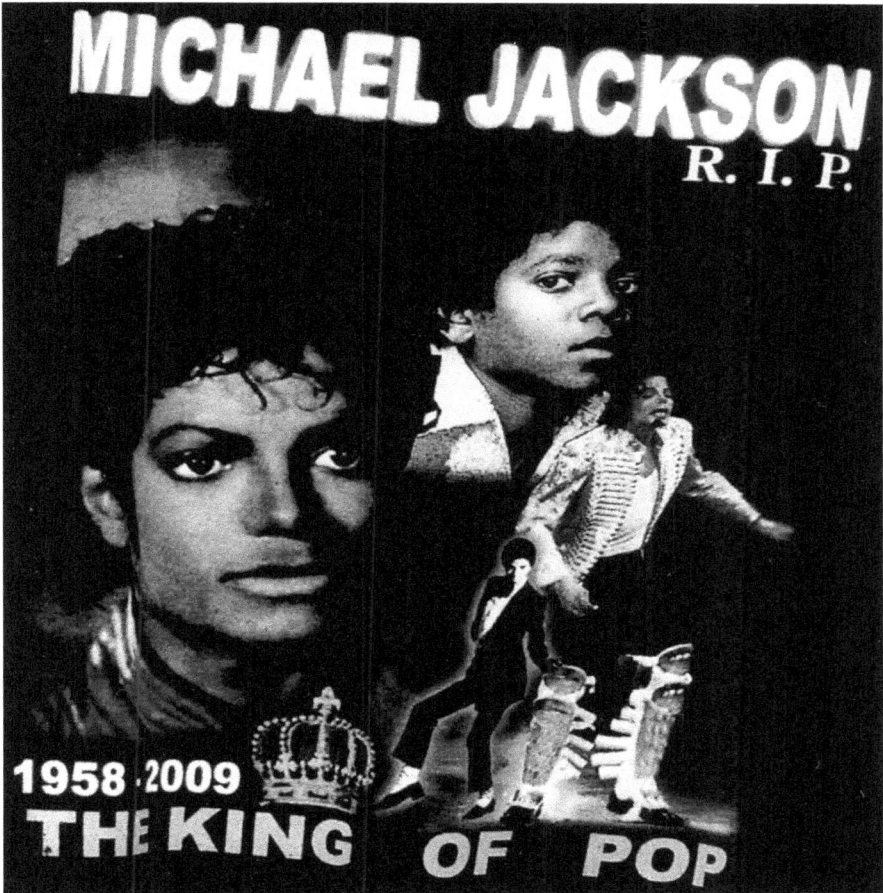

Michael Jackson's Last Dance Photo 141. Truly, "The King of Pop."

b.   Internal Interactions

Family influences on Michael Jackson were tremendous, for, there is nothing like having a house full of siblings to make your time miserable and enjoyable at the same time. For sure, Joe Jackson has been singled out as a stern-disciplinarian, but he must have realized such was the requirements to climb the ladder of success.

At the staples Center Memorial Ceremony, when Marlon, Michael's younger brother spoke, he mentioned how they would play until "mother said it was time to go to the studio." That picture is one of a happy family with the boys and girls supporting each other, and mother right in the middle.

Coming back to Joe Jackson, boys sometimes feel more affection for their mother than their father; and Joe's stern insistence may have bugged Michael. However, as success became apparent, the Jackson 5, Jacksons and finally Michael must have begun to relish in the adulation of the fans, the lights, publicity, rewards, excitement, glare, etc., and the need to practice to perfection would become self-evident. That is why I must conclude, the "rap" Joe received may have been overblown and we would probably have to look to outside or external interactions and influences for some of the problems Michael encountered.

c. External Interactions and Influences

i. Berry Gordy

At the Staples Memorial Berry Gordy praised Michael as the kid with talent and energy. Mr. Gordy, founder of Motown Records, is a business man, out to be successful. Quick to spot talent, Mr. Gordy and his "Corporation" of songwriters very likely began the process of enabling Michael Jackson and equally the other members of the Jackson 5. Caught up in the glare of the spotlight, it is not inconceivable Michael and his brothers would want to practice more to be more successful; reducing the need for Joe to use the rod!

When young men are in the joys of spotlight, girls, women are the most sought after form of entertainment. One has to believe a religious father such as Joe would not approve but Gordy's enablers would pick up the slack. Here would probably begin the enjoyment of perks that accrues from the success Michael and the Jacksons came to expect and enjoy.

Speculation could argue, Joe Jackson, with his religious background and conviction would have objected to the potential path his boys were heading, if at all. In a heated discussion, between an older head and young and restless heads, the argument may have taken this form.

Joe: I don't like the way I see you boys are conducting your lives.
Boys: We're not doing anything wrong.
Joe: Women, booze, cigarettes, who knows what!
Boys: We're stars and should enjoy ourselves. We work hard.

Tempers flare, Joe feels disrespected; he hits out and therein lays the bone of contention. We cannot discount the entertainer's motivation to practice in order to be successful and enjoy the benefits of that success.

This, therefore, would absolve Joe of being too harsh. It would probably spotlight the emergence or birth of enablers who would appear "experts," since they help write lyrics, choreography and could deliver on "intangibles."

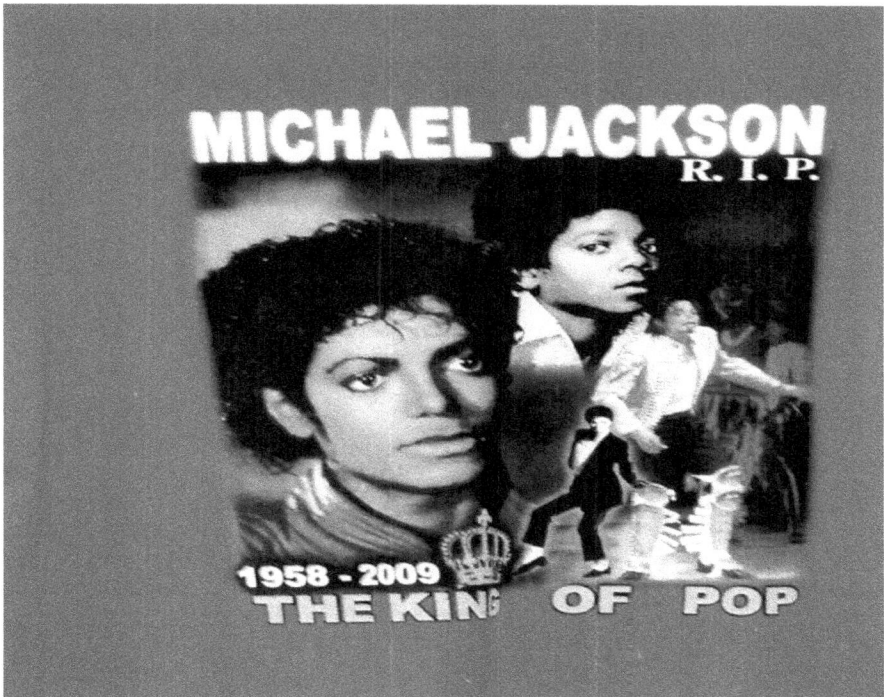

Michael Jackson's Last Dance Photo 142. Images of Michael Jackson "King of Pop."

MICHAEL JACKSON'S LAST DANCE

ii.   DIANA ROSS

Diana Ross has held a very special place in the life, mind and heart of Michael Jackson. She came early and stayed late.

Miss Ross, while herself a star with the Supremes under the Motown Label, took Michael under her wings very early. One of the first albums of the group was "Diana Ross Introduces the Jackson 5." Inasmuch as he loomed large at the end of his life one has to believe through his ups and downs, she remained his dearest friend.   Clearly this is evidenced from the fact Michael loved his Mother Katherine. Michael also thought Diana Ross would be an excellent surrogate mother in the event Katherine could or did not want to be responsible for his children Prince Michael Jr., 12; Paris Michael Katherine, 11; and Prince Michael Jackson II, 7, also known as "Blanket."

All this goes to show Diana Ross was a treasured friend of Michael Jackson. Perhaps through the ups and downs of his two marriages, his accidents, the accusations, trial, name calling, his media victimization, Diana was there to comfort, encourage and advise as a loving sister, mother, friend. Clearly she could not have had any kind of negative impact on him. On the contrary, Miss Ross was probably one of his strongest pillars of support.

Diana Ross, Michael's mentor, hurt so much by his death, declared, "I can't stop crying. This is too sudden and shocking. I am unable to imagine this. My heart is hurting. I am in prayer for his kids and the family."

The relationship Michael enjoyed with Diana Ross is not difficult to comprehend because he was a loving person and herself a successful person, had no reason to feel envious or greedy towards him. Perhaps she was the first to see that profoundly sensitive, loving and extraordinary nature of a man who loved and was loved by so many. This close vantage point cemented their relationship and she would do nothing but enhance the feelings of mutual love and respect they both shared.

FREDERICK MONDERSON

Michael Jackson's Last Dance Photo 143. Mom and son as Michael's fans.

iii. JAMES BROWN

For anyone in the entertainment business, James Brown would have been a tremendous inspiration. The "Godfather of Soul," the "hardest working man in show business," set the high bar for energetic, creative dancing expression.

Michael Jackson's fascination with James Brown began very early in his life. Michael Daly's "His Grim Fascination" in *Daily News* Sunday, June 28, 2009, p. 4, recounts: "Jackson had been a child of no more than 6 when his mother would wake him up to see Brown perform on TV. Jackson had sat mesmerized as he watched Brown move like nobody else did. He decided that was what he himself would do and not long afterward he was doing it." In fact, Jackson confessed, "Right then and there, I knew that's what I wanted to do for the rest of my life."

MICHAEL JACKSON'S LAST DANCE

I should also point out there was a contradiction in Michael, perhaps more than one! Presently there is a recording being presented of Michael's interview with a Rabbi dating back to the early 2000s or thereabouts. In one clip, Michael is heard to say in the "conflict with his father" that he felt "trapped" as a young entertainer who would have to perform for the rest of his life. Yet, he confessed elsewhere as a youngster seeing James Brown dancing, he decided this is what he wanted to do for the rest of his life.

Naya Arinde's "The Phenomenal Michael Jackson – rest in perfect peace," in the New York *Amsterdam News* July 2-July 8, 2009, p. s 6, sports a photograph of Janet Jackson, James Brown, Michael Jackson, Rev. Al Sharpton wearing his priestly collar and two others. The juxtapositioning of James Brown between Janet and Michael is clearly an indication of the love, closeness and friendship they shared.

For sure, Mr. Brown had realized his influences on Michael and as the young phenomenon ascended the charts, commanded the stage and evolved into the global megastar, Brown would have felt proud his work had reached higher heights. In his day, as an energetic busy-body himself, Mr. Brown had had his scrapes with the authorities. For sure he identified with some of the challenges Michael faced. Like all people of goodwill, he probably felt terribly hurt by the ill-will and media trouncing Michael Jackson was subjected to. That's probably when the older Brown would have reached out to Mr. Jackson to comfort and offer friendly support in those troubling times. Such a magnanimous gesture is to be expected from the "Godfather" to one of his young protégés where the love and respect was mutual.

Nearly a year and a half before Michael's demise, the "Godfather of Soul" passed away. His body was memorialized in state at the Apollo Theater in Harlem then returned to C.A. Reid's Funeral Home in Augusta, Georgia. Michael Daly, in New York *Daily News* (June 28, 2009: 4) tells how Mr. Jackson came to pay respects to James Brown. "Jackson arrived around 12:30 a.m. on this December day in 2007, and stayed for nearly five hours. He began by walking into the chapel. He strode directly up to the gold-plated coffin newly back from lying in state at the Apollo Theater. The lid was raised and Brown lay in a bed of cream-colored satin. 'He leaned over and kissed him on the forehead,' Reid said."

"The skin would have been cold under his lips, but Jackson did not recoil. He reached down to adjust Brown's hair so a lock, hung down, as in so many photos."

Such actions are only indicative of pure love for an idol who would have had a tremendous influence on one's conquest of fame. From the time of his mother's

167

insistence on watching James Brown on TV until his death more than five decades later, Mr. Brown's impact on Michael was immeasurable. Every step he took in concert he was probably guided mentally by images of and encouragement from James Brown. Clearly, James Brown was a positive influence on Michael Jackson.

Michael Jackson's Last Dance Photo 144. Classic Michael against "The Wall."

iv. MEDIA

The Media's obsession with Michael Jackson continued in death as in life; and if we could use as a gauge within two weeks of his passing, it's hardly imaginable what it has been for nearly two decades. In assessing the New York papers, *The New York Times*, the *New York Post, Daily News, USA Today, AM New York,*

MICHAEL JACKSON'S LAST DANCE

Newsday, *Metro*, the New York *Amsterdam News* and *Daily Challenge*; excepting the latter two, in keeping with their positions as the paper of record, the *Times* has had the best coverage and the *Post* the worst. The others fall in between, closer to the first than the last.

Powerful media interests and their surrogates and allies in the entertainment industry have waged an unrelenting scorched earth campaign designed to destroy Michael's name and ability to generate funds for his livelihood and undercut his fan base. At Al Sharpton's "Music, Fairness, Justice and Racism in the Industry Summit" in June 2002, Naya Arinde's "The Phenomenal Michael Jackson ..." Michael said it best without naming entities involved in the "conspiracy" against him, nor the strategies they employed. He explained it thus: "The minute I started breaking the all time record in sales... I broke Elvis' record, I broke the Beatles' records, the minute ["Thriller"] became the all time [best] selling album in history in the **Guinness Book of World Records** – overnight they called me a freak. They called me a homosexual. They called me a child molester. They said I bleached my skin. They did everything to turn the public against me." He continued, "It's all a complete conspiracy. You have to know I know my race. I look in the mirror. I know I'm black!"

If we go back a decade before this summit, we begin to glimpse realities of this statement. "Michael Jackson: Crowned in Africa" in *Ebony* (May, 1992: 34, 38, 43) provide glimpses of the media's negative treatment of coverage of the superstar. For example, the media reported: "The trip was a public relations disaster for Michael Jackson" when in fact this was not so. Another misstatement reported: "The singer cut short an African tour after a stopover generated the wrong kind of excitement." Quite the contrary, in Gabon he was greeted with "Welcome Home Michael." One youngster is quoted as saying: "Michael is love, love, love. I want to be like Michael!" Again the paper falsely misrepresented the popular star by reporting; "He held his hands to his nose because the African nations smelled." What a hurtful thing to say! Even further: "He collapsed from the heat and he went to London for a medical appointment." This was clearly a false statement! Even more disgusting was the claim: "He refused to shake hands with Africans." The *Ebony* article pointed out, however, Michael, in fact, never wore gloves or a mask as he has done in the United States. The crowning insult is that: "He is neither black nor white and is not a good role model for children." The *Ebony* article decried all these contentions as being grossly false and, given the facts, Michael never agreed to perform his songs that were played throughout; he sat on a golden throne; and had principally expressed the "desire to visit orphanages, children's hospitals, churches, schools and playgrounds." These false reports are not misstatements and would crescendo over the next decade as more and more false charges or claims and reports were made designed to poison the public's views of Michael Jackson, superstar. It should be pointed out also, the *Ebony* article quotes these happenings before the later claim of child molestation which came some two years later. Therefore, there must have been a predetermined motive for the negative press. Perhaps, Michael was right when he later admitted it was his success that turned the media against him.

In an accompanying piece, Michael Jackson is quoted as saying: "I really believe that god chooses people to do certain things, the way Michelangelo or Leonardo Da Vinci or Mozart or Mohammed Ali or Martin Luther King is chosen. And that is their mission to do that thing. And my goal in life is to give to the world what I was lucky to receive: The ecstasy of divine union through my music and my dance."

Michael Jackson is what is called a cross-over artist and the bulk of his fans; men, women, and children, sometimes two or three generations were white either in America, Europe or elsewhere. They bought his records, more than 750 million albums, and untold numbers of singles and generated more than 4 billion dollars in sales. He had risen to global superstar status, and this creative, energetic, dynamic cultural entertainment express is what the media and its cohorts sought to derail. Hence, they hounded him in life and again in death into dimensions unimaginable.

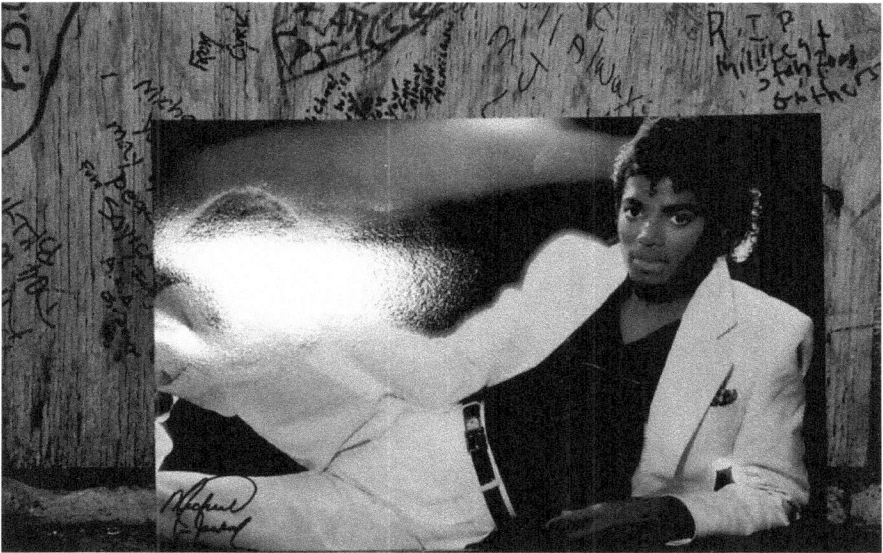

Michael Jackson's Last Dance Photo 145. More classic Michael against "The Wall."

MICHAEL JACKSON'S LAST DANCE

After years of being a recluse, taking time to properly parent his 3 young offsprings, Michael felt strong enough to challenge the "hounds of hell" and make his London comeback. Unfortunately, it was not to be!

v.   JESSE JACKSON

Jesse Jackson has been a civil right icon for half a century and he has come in for his share of negative press. For much to that time as he struggled to improve American socio-body politic, much of this has been in tandem with Michael Jackson's rise to fame and the many calamities, challenges he faced along the way. Jesse Jackson has been a friend and adviser to the Jackson family. In their moments of calamity he stood with them to insure in their enquiries the media did not go overboard on the family. This notwithstanding, the media as they often have, continued their questioning that were not sympathetic at this time of grief and sadness.

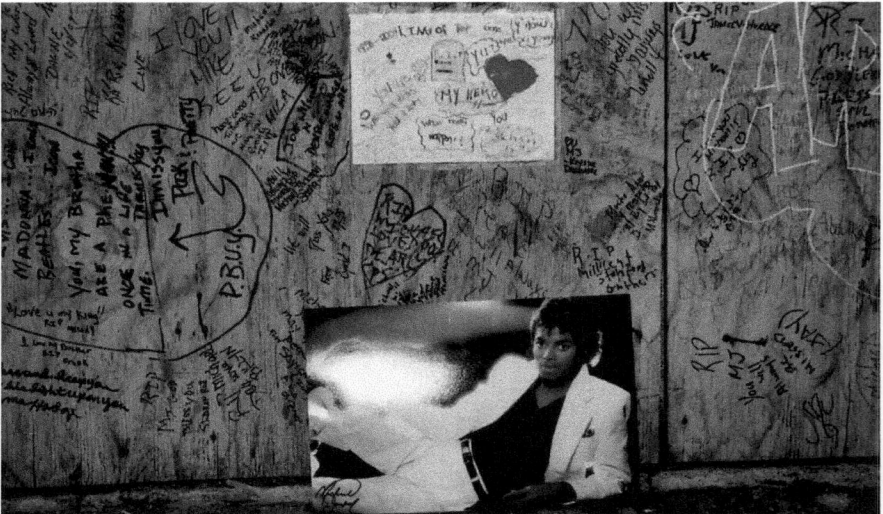

Michael Jackson's Last Dance Photo 146. More classic Michael against "The Wall."

Nevertheless, where people stand at the end is sometimes an indication of where they have stood along the joyful and sometimes saddened path. Jesse Jackson's role with Michael Jackson has not been highlighted in the media and absence any negative publicity in this regard we have to assume his input has been constructively low key. As such then, he cannot be associated with enablers who relished in the negative side of Michael Jackson.

iv. Reverend Al Sharpton

Of all people victimized by negative publicity, none surpass Rev. Al Sharpton, a man who has dedicated his life to the betterment of causes for black and white, inside and outside America. Despite what may be said of Rev. Sharpton, where he stood with the Jackson family at the end is also an indication of where he too stood along the way. Himself a child performer, this time, however, as a man or boy, of the cloth, he too traveled the rocky road of the African American experience of some victories, many defeats, but still, demonstrating an unquenchable fiery determination to persevere until all is right one day.

Rev. Sharpton boasted of being a friend of Michael Jackson for thirty-five years, which takes them back to 1974, or thereabouts, when Michael was in the throes of leading the Jackson 5 band-wagon after churning out such hits as "I Want You Back," "ABC," "Stop, The Love You Save May Be Your Own," and "I'll Be There!" That means when Michael left Motown Records in 1976 and signed with CBS Epic Records, they were buddies.

Along the remarkable hit parade they grew into manhood one rehearsing to sing and dance and perform the sweet Ballard of soulful music; the other, rehearsing and preaching the word of god and ultimately becoming a credible civil rights activist who dared to be a candidate for the Presidency of the United States.

When asked what friends are for, the answer is, to be there when you're needed to lend thoughtful and compassionate words of support in trying times, no matter how often; friends do not turn their backs on friends! Instead, they defend the integrity of their friends when they are unable to do so, and even when they are.

Much has been published in quotes about the comments Al Sharpton has made in wake of Michael Jackson's untimely death.

To begin, inside the Apollo Memorial he told the audience: "He isn't Jacko, as some have called him in their attempts to denigrate him. We are here to salute a

MICHAEL JACKSON'S LAST DANCE

legacy, to praise an icon. He's ours and we don't care what other people say. Without him there would be No Oprah, No Tiger, No Obama."

He asked the audience to be the ones "to tell our stories and to talk about Michael's legacy. He wasn't a freak, he was an innovator... he was our extraordinary entertainer and we love him with extraordinary love."

To further show that brotherly love, born of a long lasting friendship, Sharpton even further informed those in attendance: "Michael Jackson represents to us something that we understand, and when the whole world turned on Michael, we never turned on Michael."

"Michael made young men and women all over the world imitate us. Before Michael we were limited and ghettoized. But Michael put on a colorful military outfit, he pulled his pants up, he put on one glove, and he smashed the barriers of segregated music."

With this said, and after emphasizing their 35-year friendship, Sharpton exhorted: "I call on people around the world to pray for him and his family in this hour. I have known Michael, since we were both teens, worked with him, marched for him, hosted him at our House of Justice, headquarters in New York, and we joined together to eulogize our mutual idol James Brown. I have known him at his high moments and his low moments."

Michael Jackson's Last Dance Photo 147. Young Michael against "The Wall" blinded by the glare that may be his guiding light.

FREDERICK MONDERSON

CRITICAL SUMMARY

Parental responsibility to maximize the potential of a child. Did Jackson's parents do this?

It is a given, it's a parent's responsibility to maximize the potential of a child and Joseph and Katherine Jackson can certainly lay claim to that contention. The truth of the pudding is in the tasting or eating. All of the Jackson children, perhaps with the exception of Rebbie, were successful musically with Michael exceptionally, more so.

When we examine the records of the Jackson 5 achievements, those of LaToya and Janet and finally the astonishing successes of Michael, Michael's foundation and preparation were firm.

A valid question here would be how did Michael's parents help achieve his successes?

Joe Jackson and Leonard Rowe, Music Director and Concert Promoter friend of Michael Jackson appeared on Larry King Live Monday, July 20, 9:00-10:00 pm in what Iris Finsilver, Debbie Rowe's (Michael's second wife) longtime friend later described as: "Joe's interview is a bombshell."

When asked essentially about how he raised Michael, wearing an exposed gold chain with Africa pendant around his neck, Joe responded: "I didn't harm my son. I loved him. I still love him." "Michael was raised properly." "I didn't beat my son. Beat dates back to slavery days, slave masters' actions against their slaves. Many people in America spank their kids. If they tell you different they're lying." "I raised him as you would raise your kids."

In a poll conducted during the Larry King Show, the majority of respondents indicated: "The father was responsible for the kid's success."

Larry King asked Joe Jackson "If you could do it all over again, what would you do better?"

Joe responded: "Working two jobs, promoting my boys, I would have been more wary of the media." Therefore, while Joe may have been a stern disciplinarian, Katherine was more the motherly, loving type. She would coax, cajole, and use love, kind words to get her way, as any mother would. Like all loving mothers, she was with him in his successes, and in his trials and tribulations. We see her performance at his trial for child molestation. Quite frankly, before all of that, Michael's 2002 Will sums up his relationship with his mother. To Will that Katherine Jackson be responsible for raising his 3 children, Michael felt she would offer them the same kind of love and tender support she gave him.

Still, it is always difficult and heart wrenching when a parent has to mourn and bury a child, and according to Joe, Katherine was taking it hard. He, on the other hand, was feeling the pain inside.

Michael Jackson's Last Dance Photo 148. Young Michael with the salutes.

Siblings' influence and Interactions

The outpouring of love and sympathy shown Michael Jackson publicly at the Staples Memorial by his siblings is indicative of the relationship they enjoyed throughout their lives. Brothers and sisters growing up in a loving household, provided with a meaningful central focus will always strive to perfect that focus. In the interacting process, they would offer supportive influence to each other, in a sort of "We must all come along together" philosophy. This is what the Jackson siblings experienced and lived.

Perhaps the best thing Joe Jackson did for his family was to form the musical band which seems to have bonded them in a lifelong mutual relationship of love and

FREDERICK MONDERSON

support. That bonding lasted for the duration. This would certainly be a factor in their overall successes. While private images are difficult to come by, public images of musical performances, photographs, etc., of the family together, they always seem to be bubbling over with joy and happiness. There must have been something special Joe injected in their relationship that enabled the Jacksons to be ebullient and constructively positive in their outlook and public expressions whether in good times, in trials or tragedy. Clearly therefore, Michael seems to have loved his many sisters and brothers because they too seems to have loved him greatly.

Another point gotten from Joe Jackson's Larry King Live interview is his attempt to debunk claims Michael did not go out to play with other kids. He said: "Michael never had a dull life. He had his sisters and brothers to play with."

Recognizing what became an urban phenomenon of "young people killing young people" Joe was ahead of that curve. By forming the band, getting them involved in music and entertainment, he saved his children. Imagine that many siblings and none ended up dead or in conflict with the law. Putting it best, he said, "All the kinds Michael's age," presumably from Gary, Indiana, "are now dead."

On a more positive note, reflecting further on sibling's influence and interactions, we could see a number of important developments that attest to Michael's life, as explained in the Larry King interview with Jermaine Jackson at Neverland Ranch. Jermaine told Larry King Neverland represented "a special connection with Michael." It was "a place of ultimate joy, ultimate happiness, ultimate peace, and ultimate wonderment."

Neverland, comprising 3000 acres, was bought from William Bowen in 1988 for $16 million. "Michael was incredible. This was happiness. He brought different parts of the world here. This was his creation, his idea. It is a place where childhood is relived. We celebrated birthdays, held parties. The children visited. The nieces and nephews loved Uncle Michael."

Larry King remarked "Neverland is a place of beauty, serenity, calmness."
Jermaine told Larry: "The media turned this into a negative place." Larry responded: "I never expected it. It's nothing I ever dreamed of." He added further, "This is some place. I could live here."

Jermaine took Larry to a tree Michael would climb and compose and write songs, lyrics, melodies, his ideas. Then he would get to his drawing board and put these ideas into song. Jermaine told Larry that Michael was "gifted. He does everything at a higher level." Larry King responded again, telling how he was "flabbergasted in a positive way." He further commented on the "Fairy tale nature, fun, carnival atmosphere" found at Neverland.

Then Jermaine took Larry King to a high point on the land and showed him over there "Mount Katherine." Imagine! A mountain named for a black woman in America, it's no wonder the media "tore the place apart." Michael had become too powerful, too early, for a black man!

All this notwithstanding, Neverland was the culmination of positive siblings interaction that supported Michael throughout the ups and downs, the happy and sad times and will continue with the love in assisting his children and his legacy. Too bad, the child molestation charge of which he was acquitted turned Neverland into a monster chamber. So much so, Michael died detesting the piece of earth he loved dearly. Imagine, again, for this he was found not guilty. And we may add, the earlier child molestation charges were reportedly falsified by a young man who confessed his father made him lie to get rich.

Michael Jackson's Last Dance Photo 149. More classic Michael from *Ebony* Cover.

FREDERICK MONDERSON

Matrimonial Relations and his Children

Michael Jackson was married twice, once to Lisa Marie Presley and once to Debbie Rowe. His marriage to Lisa lasted some 20 months. Regarding his marriage in the Dominican Republic, Tracy Connor's "King of Pop Saw his End – Lisa Marie" in *Daily News*, Saturday, June 27, 2009, pp. 6-7, explained "Presley, then 27, and Jackson then 37, were secretly married in May 1994 in the Dominican Republic."

For some time this was under wraps as Conner recounts: "They initially denied tying the knot and when they finally admitted it, many dismissed the union as a publicity stunt to distract from child molestation charges against Jackson. The celebrity couple steadfastly denied it. They kissed at the MTV awards and awkwardly insisted they were indeed having sex on 'Primetime Live.'" The marriage lasted some two years.

Upon his passing she penned in her On Line Page, the marriage was not a sham. She admitted: "It was an unusual relationship yes, where two unusual people who did not live or know a 'normal life' found a connection, with some suspect timing on his part. Nonetheless, I do believe he loved me as much as he could love anyone and I loved him very much." The article continued: "When they married, she wanted to 'save him from certain self-destructive behaviors and from the awful vampires and leeches he would always manage to magnetize around him.'"

Within two years after his divorce from Lisa Presley, Michael Jackson married Debbie Rowe, an attendant in his dermatologist office. Michael and the British born secretary were married in Australia and she bore him two children, Michael Jr., and Paris. Within another two years, they were divorced. Speculation was rife about events surrounding their separation but it appears, for a settlement, Debbie agreed to let Michael have the children to raise, because he could be a better provider.

Even more speculation surrounded whether Michael was the real father of the two kids. On Larry King Live, July 20, 2009, 9:00-10:00 p.m., Iris Finsilver, Debbie Rowe's long time friend told Larry, "Michael is the father of those kids." She reiterated, "I know 100 percent Michael was the father of Faris and Prince." She added even further, "Debbie loved Michael more than anyone in the world."

R.I.P. 1958 - 2009

Michael Jackson's Last Dance Photo 150. A lovely Sister proudly holds an original Michael Jackson photo.

FREDERICK MONDERSON

Michael had a third child, called "Blanket" by a surrogate mother with his "donated sperm." One thing is certain, Michael loved those children; they meant the world to him. That is why he tried any number of strategies designed to shield them from the public scrutiny he was exposed to as a growing child.

All this notwithstanding, Michael seems to have come under undue media scrutiny in those challenging times. He was accused and hounded over claims of child molestation but while Michael claimed it was his astounding successes in the entertainment industry that contributed to his troubles; others commented the audacity of marrying Elvis' daughter added to the assaults on his character.

In the Larry King interview with Joe Jackson and Leonard Rowe, Rowe said when he first met Michael he would not drink a soda and was against drugs and alcohol. One has to wonder whether pain of injuries, pressures of his marriages, the role of the press, the parasites who surrounded him and challenges to create artistically all drove Michael to prescription drugs.

PEOPLE WHOSE FINANCIAL LIFEBLOOD DEPENDED ON MICHAEL JACKSON

When a musical album or single is released, the lyrics, beat, tone, singer or even the band gets some form of credit when the song is considered a hit. Sometimes people write songs the singer sings. However, the people behind the scene, the producers, directors, distributors, arrangers, other musicians and fan audience all have a bearing on the final output of the song and the pushback on the musician. Michael was caught in the middle of this phenomenon and while his longevity in the entertainment industry may have taught him much, he probably fell victim to the "Gulliver Syndrome" because they were too many "enablers" in a symbiotic relationship that "wore down Gulliver."

In an interesting follow up to the Joe Jackson interview on Larry King the previous night, Larry brought out "clean cut" Jim Moret and Roger Friedman to investigate and refute much of what Joe and Leonard had said the night before. Both seemed to paint Joe as an uncaring monster rather than a father, whom the poll the night before gave credit for his son's success. Friedman painted Rowe as a pariah, referring to legal problems with R. Kelly, etc. Larry also quoted a statement from

MICHAEL JACKSON'S LAST DANCE

AEG detailing Michael's involvement in every aspect of the negotiations for his comeback, "This Is It," concert.

First of all, the duo used Michael's own words from the Oprah interview to contradict his father's claims of not beating or abusing his son. Larry accepted AEG's statement that could not be verified since Michael could not speak for himself and no close adviser privy to the inner workings was produced. Yet, Joe and Rowe were discounted. Again, in that Oprah interview, the host queried Michael about whether he was "a virgin." She had referred previously to his dating Brooke Shields. While not specifically asking if he and Brooke had sex, she wanted to know if he had ever have sex. As if responding to the question as to whether he and Brooke had had sex, Michael simply replied, in the most coy, simple, flattering, soft spoken manner "I am a gentleman." Others, without referring to anyone specifically would have said, "Sure I have had sex" etc, in the most bravado manner. But this response in a simple angelic manner could have absolved this man from any and all wrongdoing. Yet so many have victimized this wonderful soul, this is indeed a tremendous travesty.

Joe never appeared a man of much learning and was not very articulate in his responses yet this was no way to ridicule and discredit him. However, some of what he said was not really addressed.

"Rowe is the kind of person Joe would hook up with" said Jim Moret. So we paint these two people, Michael's father and Rowe as a couple of shysters. Such is a matter of opinion from people who were never sympathetic to Michael Jackson in the first place. They certainly, and most certain Jim Moret never sought to absolve Michael of any improper behavior.

Roland Martin CNN commentator on Campbell Brown hosted that night by John King was asked to comment referring to Joe's actions. He agreed with Joe that the children of Michael's age "whom he never played with" "were all dead, on drugs or in jail." Roland, representing Joe said: "I will discipline my child. Beating was discipline. He is the father. It is a question of perspective."

Randi Kaye, CNN correspondent, pointed out Joe lives in Las Vegas. She referred to the Oprah and Bashir interviews Michael gave in his own words. The behaviors in the Oprah interview refer to Michael as an adolescent.

A serious question can be posed here with ramifications on all this. We know Michael was in the music limelight from an early age with his brothers. The image projected is that he loved what he did. He certainly sounded and looked happy when he entertained and sang. A valid question here is, at what point did this highly intelligent young man and his brothers realize if they are to continue to enjoy the adulation of being on top they must practice intently? That is, at what point does success self-motivate them rather than being whipped, beaten, driven to practice to do something they loved, enjoyed, were building a tremendous fan base and were being rewarded financially.

In the Oprah interview, it seems Michael in addressing the question seemed to say, "I don't know if he felt I was his golden child...." Did Michael feel golden? Seems like they cut off the other portions of his statement and focused on this one line only. Did he realize gold has to be polished otherwise it becomes tarnished? Do these considerations absolve Joe?

If we lay great store in Michael's words what about his claims of racism in the entertainment industry? He accused Tommy Motola of Sony of being a racist. At Sharpton 2002 Summit he is quoted as giving reasons for all his troubles. How valid is that claim? He claimed he never abused any children. How valid is that claim?

Lisa Marie Presley talked about the "vampires and leeches" surrounding Michael. Did they go away 12 years after or got fatter blood sucking?

Other statements made by Joe and Rowe to Larry King that Moret and Friedman never addressed were:

1. Whether other people had agendas about Michael's money and further if they really cared about Michael's well-being.
2. Some people wanted to appear as "caring as Mother Theresa." Can the "two experts" Moret and Friedman fit this mold?
3. Can it be disproved Joe, Rowe and Michael were in a recent meeting with Michael and AEG (Randy Philips). Joe says "I was shouting with Philips because Michael wanted to get paid in English pounds not US dollars because the pound was worth more." He said they told him "by the time things will work itself out the dollar will be worth more." The dollar has never been worth more than the pound sterling.

4. If the meeting, and Joe and Rowe were there, Rowe may very well be credible. He said: "Michael told me, Rowe, I want you to look out for my money. I have kids. I don't want to come back from London broke." Is this a likely possibility?

Michael cannot testify on his behalf today. Who knows what he was thinking in those last days. While he was singing and dancing people could have been stealing him blind.

MICHAEL JACKSON'S LAST DANCE

Let's add some more to this. The changing sands of time allow everything to change in time.

The 2002 Will did not have to be written in stone and change not considered in 2009. After all, the Will's Executors were apparently fired by Michael at a later date, yet, they appear as "lily white clean cut guys" determined to execute Michael's wishes at his death.

No one can point to any good intentioned person who was watching Michael's back. No one can truly say how Michael felt about his dad at the end. In the "final battle" of negotiations, who best to go into it with than your dad as someone you can trust who will truly watch your back. After all, can we prove Joe was not in the meeting, shouting at AEG's Phillips? Can it be proven Rowe was not in the meeting? If the meeting did occur and they were both there, does it mean they were rehabilitated in Michael's sights and mind. Is this a basis for later questionable behavior on part of anyone?

Rowe told Larry "AEG's actions were unethical." We get lost in how many concerts Michael was involved in, 10, 31, or 50. But, did the unethical behavior extend beyond mere questions of the number of concerts?

Again, we're not dealing with acolytes and choirboys here. It's understandable the entertainment business is very challenging, excruciating, the term "cut throat" is not out of the question in a highly competitive industry involving lots of money.

Joe Jackson did not come across as a man of great schooling but he:

Remained married to Katherine for nearly 60 years.

Starting as a steelworker, he sired a very large family, raised them all to be successful, no jail, no deaths, no illegal drug use, except Michael's addiction to prescription drugs designed to alleviate his pain and suffering, which came after he was an adult.

Who could question his love for his son?

Joe's call for a Congressional investigation into events surrounding Michael's death is something that will get serious consideration.

Larry King said Joe Jackson was from the age of "Spare the rod and spoil the Child." We give credence to some of what Michael said such as his father using corporal punishment. Friedman on Larry King told us someone told him Joe would lock Michael in a cupboard.

FREDERICK MONDERSON

Michael Jackson's Last Dance Photo 151. Original Michael in the big Afro.

MICHAEL JACKSON'S LAST DANCE

How strange it is we discount what Joe Jackson and Leonard Rowe say but accept what Roger Friedman says.

Let us not forget, Brooke Barnes' "A Star Idolized and Haunted, Michael Jackson Dies at 50" *The New York Times* June 26, 2009, Cover, quotes Berry Gordy, the Motown founder who helped develop the Jackson 5, told CNN that "Mr. Jackson, as a boy, 'Always wanted to be the best and he was willing to work as hard as it took to be that. And we could all see that he was a winner at that age.'"

CHARITABLE CONTRIBUTIONS

Michael Jackson was very charitable, more so than most in his line of business. The **Guinness Book of World Records** named Michael Jackson as the Number 1 charitable contributor, or "the most charities supported by a pop star." They give a total of some 38 charities Michael supported. His generosity has been both national and international and it is interesting how the news media has played up troubling parts of Michael's life but have ignored this important humanitarian side of his life.

In "The Phenomenal Michael Jackson – Rest in Perfect Peace" Naya Arinde in the New York *Amsterdam News* July 2-July 8, 2009, p. 3 gives a partial listing of his contributions. His website Allmichaeljackson.com gives a more complete listing as follows:

Aids Project LA
American Cancer Society
Angel Food
Big Brothers of Greater Los Angeles
BMI Foundation, Inc.
Brotherhood Crusade
Brothman Burn Center
Camp Ronald McDonald
Childhelp U.S.A.
Children Institute International
Cities and Schools Scholarship Fund
Community Youth Sports and Arts Foundation
Congressional Black Caucus (CBC)
Dakar Foundation
Dreamstreet Kids
Dreams Come True Charity

FREDERICK MONDERSON

Elizabeth Taylor Aids Foundation
Juvenile Diabetes Foundation
Love Match
Make-A-Wish-Foundation
Minority Aids Project
Motown Museum
NAACP
National Rainbow Coalition
Rotary Club of Australia
Society of Singers
Starlight Foundation
The Cancer Center's Atlanta Project
The Sickle Cell Foundation
TransAfrica
United Negro College Fund (UNCF)
United Negro College Fund Ladders' of Hope
Volunteers of America
Watts Summer Festival
Wish Granting
YMCA – 28th Street/Crenshaw

Michael supported many international charitable foundations and in his many travels he commiserated with the poor and under-privileged wherever he went. Beside the list of 36 above, he also supported UNESCO and Charles Prince of Wales Prince's Trust. After the allegations of child molestation his contributions to Charles Prince of Wales Trust was refused and he was vehemently told don't call again. However, with the acquittal and the Internet revelation that Evan Chandler and his dad lied, one has to wonder how those at Charles Prince of Wales Trust now feel about their cutting Michael off at the knee! Yet still, his "This Is It" Tour in London was a sold out phenomenon so where does this leave the Trust and its administrators!

In 1992 he was in Gabon, West Africa and signs greeted him thus. "Welcome Home Michael." This says much and such a welcome was probably duplicated wherever he went in Africa. It is amazing, however, that this particular trip generated such negative publicity in the media. It is inconceivable that anyone coming off a plane in a country and seeing such a welcome at the airport and everything that goes with it; could act or think in a manner that is in anyway inappropriate. That *Ebony* 1992 article highlighting the negative publicity the Media gushed on Michael was certainly before he was accused of child molestation and perhaps we see here the roots of the media's negativity towards a successful black performer.

186

MICHAEL JACKSON'S LAST DANCE

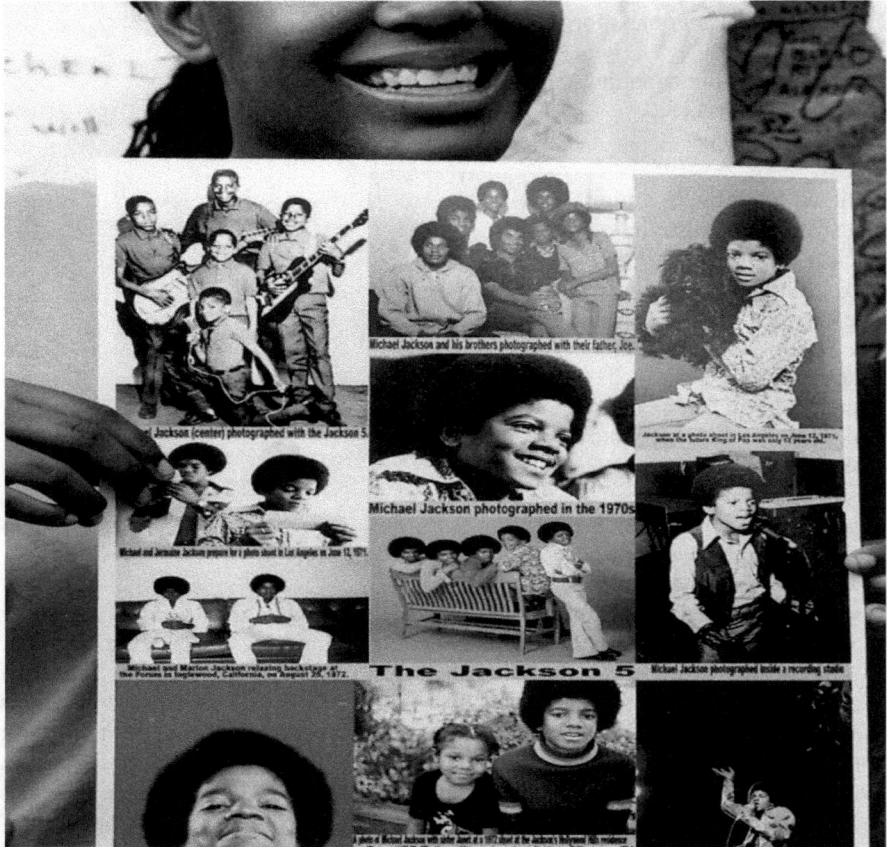

Michael Jackson's Last Dance Photo 152. A varied collection of young Michael.

INTERPRETATIVE SUMMARY

In death Michael Jackson remains as enigmatic as in life. While his genius and musical dynamism is unparalleled, his creative abilities has impacted the globe, his humanitarianism was backed by untold millions of dollars bequeathed to charity. He was born into a close knit family but in many attempts to develop same in a nuclear relationship was unsuccessful. Physical mishaps and the challenges of being a world class entertainer forced Michael into prescription drugs to alleviate

187

FREDERICK MONDERSON

the pain and to keep on going in a world that demanded the best in an unending manner. Despite it all, Michael Jackson persevered, created musical lyrics that were oftentimes simple but conveyed a powerful message that resonated across states, nations, religions and culture with a healing potency etching his memory into the minds and hearts of people for all times.

All this notwithstanding, success is its own enemy in that ill-intentioned persons look for the speck in your life rather than the beam in theirs and end up waging campaigns that become insensitive and hurtful, as they harm or hound their target unending. Much of this characterizes the life, experiences and ultimately death of Michael Jackson. One thing is unmistaken in his experiences; Michael Jackson made a lot of money for himself, those in association with him, those who promoted him and those who hounded him. He also made careers for the latter and those covered him.

Michael Jackson's family, his father, mother, siblings have had a tremendous impact on his life. For many years his father Joe has been villainized for similar to what radio host Bev Smith's sister Cookie told CNN's Soledad O'Brien, "My mother was a Drill Sergeant." Sure, Joe ran a tight ship as an old school disciplinarian but looking at the ultimate outcome of his brood, as successful practitioners of their craft, the methods produced the desired results.

Of course, as an adult, Michael Jackson publicly accused his father of parental abuse through corporal punishment, depriving him of a normal childhood. This non-traditional pattern of child-rearing in this special circumstance, we are led to believe, caused Michael to develop a dependence on narcotics. Such an accusation does not hold true. There was more to this since Michaels's mother was also involved in the process of maximizing his potential as a child. Perhaps she used more gentle persuasive methods that were subtler that those of his father. However, Michael did make mistakes. As he matured he moved from the safety and security of family promotional protection to gradually exposing himself to the viciousness of entertainment management as he indulged in self-management.

As his star got brighter and the constellation of his entourage got bigger, he failed to realize the entertainment industry also expanded and got stronger. Through his trials and tribulations and as he got less prolific and began to rely on past performance, even when he made the decision to re-enter the ring, the opposition had grown beyond his control and the one true friend he could truly rely on, Joe, had been alienated, brow-beaten, ridiculed, yet, in the end like old faithful, he would still be there to "shout at Randy Philips" on Michael's behalf. Where was Oprah, where was Bashir, where were all the others whose name was associated with him negatively?

MICHAEL JACKSON'S LAST DANCE

To get a better look at the process of that alienation, we can step back and look at some aspects of the evolution of Michael Jackson from child star to global entertainer. In the conflict between Michael and Joe Jackson, the son claims the father was harsh in his treatment to encourage him to maximize his potential. From available images of expressions of joy during performances or posturing, Michael certainly conveyed the image of a happy child. He never "went outside to play" because the streets were rough and because he had a "ton of siblings" who sufficed. As far as Joe Jackson was concerned, better if my kid is inside practicing his craft than being outside and exposed to the hopelessness the streets promised in a small town at the tail end of the civil rights movement. But then again, if we focus on Michael and the Jacksons, we ask at what point fame, the glamour, glitz and finances motivated and self perpetuated them to want to practice their craft and optimize in their chosen profession?

In the constant challenge to be successful, one's entourage from cook to chauffeur including lawyers, doctors, accountants, agents, all somewhat dependent on the star and existing under the radar, somewhere in that group is the making of trouble. There is the question of jockeying for favorable proximity to the star and the turncoat who doesn't get his way, silently or outspoken. A very good "Maitre D" or manager, a sort of "lawyer to watch the lawyers" is needed here and he or she too must be kept in check.

In the interview with Larry King, Joe Jackson was asked, "If you had to do it all over again, what would you do different?" Two things he said makes a lot of sense. The first is, "I wish I was more wary of the media." Even more important, however, particularly relating to the end, Joe confessed, "I wish I had done more to help Michael." As he explained, in his view, he was "not able to get to Michael" because, as Leonard Rowe said, people were "controlling Michael's life." Michael Jackson was "not allowed to make decisions." Even further, "People were brought in to run Michael's life."

Larry continued, "How could you the father not get to your son?" To which Joe responded, "I was being blocked. I wish I had gone in there and kick the door down." Again, we must consider no matter what relationship transpired between this father and son, Joe was in the AEG meeting relating to the final tour!

Once this house is squared away, then the people in the music industry must be dealt with. That is, songwriters, producers, directors, distributors, other musicians, concert audiences and global fan base, and let's not forget the question of race in intra, inter-group relationships.

It's admitted, Michael was addicted to prescription drugs to relieve bodily pains and also to calm his body down to get the badly needed rest, sleep.

189

FREDERICK MONDERSON

A couple of important notes are evident. In AEG's rebuttal to Joe Jackson's claim, they produced a note of explanation to Larry King indicating Michael was in full control, participating in negotiations, planning rehearsals, etc. No reference was made to Joe's claim that he was "shouting with [AEG's Randy] Phillips" regarding the manner in which Michael wished to be paid in "pound sterling rather than dollars" for the concerts. Therefore, failure to deny Joe's claims put him in the meeting together with his son, Randy and Leonard Rowe. No matter what anyone would contend. Despite Jim Moret and Roger Friedman who tried to discredit both, Michael Jackson, his father Joe Jackson and Leonard Rowe were all at that meeting with AEG's Randy Phillips arguing on Michael's behalf.

"Holier than thou" Friedman tried to paint Leonard Rowe and even Joe Jackson as shady characters. Forget about Joe, since he is number one, but Leonard Rowe was invited to a private funeral for Michael. Why were Jim Moret, Friedman, and so many others "holier than thou" not invited? Since we do not have the official list of all invited guests, they could have come out and described what happened at the funeral which would have authenticated their presence and given credibility to much of what they said about Michael.

Again, the most anyone could say, "Joe beat Michael for his own good." This was an old school father who lived through the Depression, civil rights movement, all forms of discrimination against black people; he was entitled to be strict with his children to make sure they do not end up as losers. Mothers and fathers were often heard to say to children, "I brought you into this world and I will take you out!" Of course this is just an expression but it's a palliative for betterment of the child.

Friedman maintained Leonard Rowe was sued by R. Kelly and another and had to repay millions. Sure he was a shady character but he was handling millions. He is "The devil I know!" Remember in the presidential elections and the newsman told Colin Powell, "Obama is a Muslim!" He said, "So what!" We know "Thieves respect thieves!" Both sides can say "I know what you did last summer." Now, if Larry King had asked Roger Friedman whether they were other shady characters in the entertainment industry, he could have probably and truthfully responded, "Yes, millions."

Michael knew the "Devil he was dealing with" in the person of Leonard Rowe and he certainly knew Joe Jackson. He certainly must have thought "These two old shotguns will certainly cover my back." The "Devil you know is certainly better than the devil you don't know!"

MICHAEL JACKSON'S LAST DANCE

Hypothetically speaking, if you're going into hell to negotiate with and challenge the devil, you don't take angels and saints with you. You arm yourself with devils, tricksters, conmen, who think like the opponents in any high stakes deal.

Jim Moret said Michael was not eating and kept saying, "They're trying to kill me." He was delusional and the question is did he really say this. If Jim Moret could hear this, so too could Joe Jackson and Leonard Rowe. Did Friedman also hear this? Was it first hand or did he hear it as hearsay. Michael's manager confessed he was not in the meeting with Michael and AEG. However, he did say after, Michael told him "we must get rid of Leonard Rowe." Who can authenticate this? Another question here is, why would Rowe be in the meeting to "watch Michael's back" and come out being told he was no longer wanted? This statement seems questionable on part of the manager.

The digressions aside, let us return to Joe and Rowe. Having established their presence at the meeting, we must give some credence to what was told Larry King.

Michael was not in control of his own finances.

Michael was controlled by the promoters of the London concert.

The two sides did not see eye to eye.

Michael wanted to get paid in British pounds rather than US dollars because the pound was worth more.

"Michael told me" Rowe said, "I want you to look out for my money. I have kids. I don't what to come back from London broke." This is not an unreasonable statement.

AEG's actions were unethical.

Michael is quoted as saying, "Rowe I only agreed to do 10 shows for AEG. I can't do 50 shows." Fifty was against Michael's physical condition. In an interview with a close associate of Michael who worked on his sounds and was familiar with the demands of the industry, he was quoted as saying; "A 50 year old man doing 50 shows was inconceivable" given the physical exertion Michael was famous for.

These concerts were not like those given by such singers as Julio Iglesias or Frank Sinatra, whose chords were so fantastic, the entertainers hardly moved. Michael not only moved, he had the audience moving and 50 concerts, rightly speaking may not have been in his physical or mental well-being.

FREDERICK MONDERSON

Michael Jackson's Last Dance Photo 153. A vendor's powerful collection of educational DVDs across the street from the Apollo Theater on 125th Street.

Claiming that "foul play was involved in Michael's death" Joe Jackson called for a Congressional Investigation because of the "suspicious activities" surrounding his son's last days. The work of law enforcement will shed light on this.

PRIMARY BIBLIOGRAPHY

Moonwalk by Michael Jackson
Michael Jackson: *The Magic and the Madness* by J. Randy Tarraborelli
Michael! By Mark Bego
Michael Jackson *The Golden Touch* by Paul Honeyford
Michael Jackson Thrill by Caroline Latham
Michael Jackson Body and Soul by Gordon Matthews
Michael Jackson The Man In The Mirror by Todd Gold
"*Michael Jackson: The Legend Continues*" presented by Motown
"*The Jacksons: America's First Family of Music*" presented by Marlon Jackson
Footage Viewed:
The Jacksons TV series, Destiny World Tour London, American Bandstand 10th Anniversary.
www.imdb.com
www.wikipedia.com

MICHAEL JACKSON'S LAST DANCE

15. LEGACY OF MICHAEL JACKSON
By

Dr. Fred Monderson

History has always shown "Good triumphs over evil" and the goodness Michael Jackson exhibited over more than four decades as an entertainer, humanitarian, philanthropist and businessman, and father, son, inventor and human being in general manner so pleasing to the almighty, is what posterity will remember of a man, many times victimized in unproven allegations.

At the Apollo Tribute, Tuesday, June 30, 2009, Rev. Al Sharpton commanded the audience to "tell our stories and to talk about Michael's legacy. He was not a freak, he was an innovator ... he was an extraordinary entertainer and we love him with extraordinary love." Herb Boyd in the *Amsterdam News* (July 2 - July 8, 2009) informed how "love for Michael is universal, and there is no better testament to his power and influence as an artist and entertainer than the millions around the globe who were shocked by his sudden death as they were awed by his incomparable talent."

Checked early, the work of the wolves, vultures, vampires and zombies who fed at his lucrative trough will be forgotten in time. Along with their architects, they will either be consigned to footnotes in history or overshadowed by the sheer bulk of the positive contribution of a mega star of towering fame, not unlike a comet, that only passes this way "once in a very long time."

First, Michael Jackson will be remembered for his enormous body of work, particularly the earliest and freshest of his productions that exhibited great magnitude, vision, simplicity and charged fun-filled emotions. His lyrics, style and grace appealed to many people across race, culture and religion where parents, white, black, brown and yellow, felt comfortable with their children listening to and imitating young black boys in their living rooms. The Jackson 5 recorded 14 albums with Motown Records, and Michael also did 4 solo albums with the company. Yet, these early creations simply set the stage for the maturing genius of an emerging solo artist with extraordinary talent, who, in teaming up with music impresario Quincy Jones, produced even more mega hits following his departure from Motown.

193

FREDERICK MONDERSON

One commentator wrote, in "Don't Stop" ('Til you get enough) - the music riveted attention: Jackson' imperial achievement 'Thriller.' The first single 'Billie Jean' began with a uniquely undulating bass line that Jackson topped with a frenzy of curt breaths and huffy exhales. The interplay between Jackson' Jim Farber's "A Wacko yes, but also a genius in many ways," in *Daily News* Friday, June 26, 2009, p. 4, referred to Michael and Quincy's "Off the Wall" production as, "a work that gave their mix of funk, soul, jazz and pop a universal stamp. From the opening track - (Don't Stop) His falsetto had both vulnerability and confidence and the music ruled the dance floor." Then he writes about "Jackson's inventive vocals and the forceful music entranced pop fans in every country around the world."

His creative genius, coupled with energetic performances full of life and exhibiting incomparable dance moves enabled "Off The Wall" and "Thriller" and their videos to break down the segregated walls of MTV and, importantly, aiding the music station's solvency. It also opened the door for African American performers to be aired on MTV's popular cable TV network. Michael won 8 Grammys for "Thriller," the most by a single artist. The album boasted 7 No. 1 hit singles. It sold more than 100 million copies worldwide. After its 1982 release, it stayed 37 weeks on the charts as No. 1. "Off the Wall" had sold more than 20 million albums worldwide after its 1979 release. Michael's efforts revitalized economic aspects of the music industry in devastating musical brilliance.

Year after year, Michael Jackson wrote and produced award winning music that sold millions of records and he continued to fill venues when on tour and in concerts. Excitement and anticipation awaited his every performance and this was no doubt the case with his last scheduled set of appearances. Randy Tarraborelli, who wrote a biography about Michael Jackson informed: "The primary reason for the concerts wasn't so much that he wanted to generate money, as much as it was that he wanted to perform for the kids. They had never seen him perform before."

Naya Arinde (July 2-July 8, 2009) described him as a "man who changed the music game with his singing; dancing; writing and producing." Michael also vocally protested racism in the music industry. Michael Jackson had a down-to-earth quality about him. In June 2002, Michael asked the National Action Network audience "What's more important than giving people a sense of escapism?" "What would life be without a song, joy, laughter and music?"

Selling more than 750 million albums, plus untold numbers of singles, of which 13 were No. 1 as a solo artist, the winning of 13 Grammy Awards, 8 for "Thriller" and awarded 2, a never before and since accomplished, introductions into the Rock and Roll Hall of fame; one as a member of the Jackson 5 and one as a solo artist, Michael has had a very distinguished creative career These distinctions established Michael Jackson as an unparalleled and extraordinary entertainer possessing talent seemingly inspired by divine guidance. Again, Michael's soft

194

MICHAEL JACKSON'S LAST DANCE

spoken nature seemed spiritually and mystically divine and his humanitarian nature underscored that godly connection destined to do good for those in need.

As an interesting article by Edna Gunderson in *USA Today* (July 2, 2009) entitled "The King of Pop reigns over Music Charts," graphically chronicles initial purchasing reactions to the passing of Michael Jackson, because of his melodious sweet harmonic and joyful expression in his songs and videos; their sales are sure to set trends for generations and generations of love and respect for the man and his music.

His message was clear, just like Michael! Even more important, and this should be a reminder to all, while Michael Jackson' legacy is assured it is also not tarnished, thanks to the efforts of Rev. Al Sharpton and others who would not let the media wolves devour the lifeless body and image of "our golden boy." Sharpton's message at the Apollo Memorial was unequivocal: "We love and will defend our heroes." That is, from the destructive machinations of the vultures, vampires and unsavory characters who not only sully people's character and image, but grow rich in the process.

Even more significant, Michael's legacy is also evident in his good works, his humanitarianism, and his charitable work through contributions and physically visiting the "trenches of maladies." Michael has been praised, beyond his creative and artistic genius, as being a "take no prisoners showman and entertainer;" but also as a shrewd businessman and one who shared his bread. He was also a master at give back! This generosity certainly went a long way in "netting" his enemies' "swoop down" in his most vulnerable moments!

Because of the symbolism of Michael Jackson and the Jackson 5 in the early years of their careers; in aftermath of the Civil Rights Movement, Black newspapers particularly Ebony, Esquire, Jet, and many others including Peoples Weekly, Time, TV Guide, Glamour, Ladies Home Journal, Life, Newsweek, Vogue, Publishers Weekly, and other magazines, radio and early TV programs carried the image, spread the word and this helped raise people's consciousness to their goodness, creativity and otherwise. This local exposure helped stamp his enormous imprint on black and white culture. Such groundswell response is what encouraged Michael Jackson to begin his low-key give back that later mushroomed into **Guinness Book of World Records** recognition of his charitable giving. Michael underwrote projects, he visited the sick, and he fed the poor, all this at home and abroad. He "helped cancer stricken children, burn victims, terminally ill children, and those with illnesses as AIDS and juvenile diabetes." He worked for social justice! He visited and assisted the less fortunate in Africa and when he finally realized the gravity of poverty in Africa he formed the Heal the World Foundation. Then he produced, wrote and performed, with Lionel Richie, "We Are the World" and "Heal the World" and played his part in "Live Aid."

195

FREDERICK MONDERSON

In as much as one's legacy is also shaped by what that individual leaves behind and since Michael Jackson left much of his work, the revenues gained there from will continue to support his charitable works. Michael's mother, Katherine, and family members of like mind including his children, will most definitely seek to see his charitable gift-giving continue. Possibly, they will support other ventures in his name; so, decades later, when a poor person wherever, at some auspicious or inauspicious occasion benefits from a meal, a coat, footwear, schools supplies, a clinic, etc., they will always remember to say **GOD BLESS MICHAEL JACKSON** because he deserved it.

Whenever **THE WIZ** is performed, his version will be remembered!

The 1983, 25th anniversary of Motown Records etched Michael's fame in the minds of many. At that event, his poise and pose, grasping his black fedora in sequined glove, black jacket, silver vest, high water pants, showing white socks in black shoes, and explosively breaking into "Billie Jean," then unleashing the fabulous "Moonwalk," electrified the audience and untold millions watching. It was as if the Apollo rockets catapulted Michael into orbit, forever to remain above the stratosphere, physically, spiritually, mystically and in earning power. That enormous earning power allowed him to invest in such ventures as the Beatles' Catalog for which he paid $47.5 million and "Neverland" for which he paid $16 million. In addition, called an energetic eccentric, he invested in artwork and other collectibles that today enhance his holdings, all sound investments.

Even more significant, record sales in his honor after his passing, reportedly will erase all outstanding debts owned by his estate and Michael Jackson's earning power will also benefit from his "100 unreleased tracks," as they are put to album form by the estate for faithful fans. The statement "We have a live album in the can" based on his last concert rehearsal, adds to the enormous body of work of the masterful and consummate entertainer. People will always want to hear for the last time that sweet melodic voice and the unparalleled videos which will drown out any negativity concerning his person by merchants of that hue. This is why, in retrospect, the Apollo Memorial Tribute in Harlem was so timely important to beat back negativity, encourage constructively positive outpouring of praise and prayers, before the wolves could organize from their insidious play book. In many ways, the Apollo organizers gave back to Michael as Michael gave and gave back in those creative and humanitarian efforts to assure his own creative genius legacy.

THANKS for the memories Michael; you will always be in our hearts!

196

MICHAEL JACKSON'S LAST DANCE

Michael Jackson's Last Dance Photo 154. The tributes are self evident.

Michael Jackson's Last Dance Photo 155. More self evident tributes.

Michael Jackson's Last Dance Photo 156. The tributes are self evident.

Michael Jackson's Last Dance Photo 157. The tributes are self evident.

198

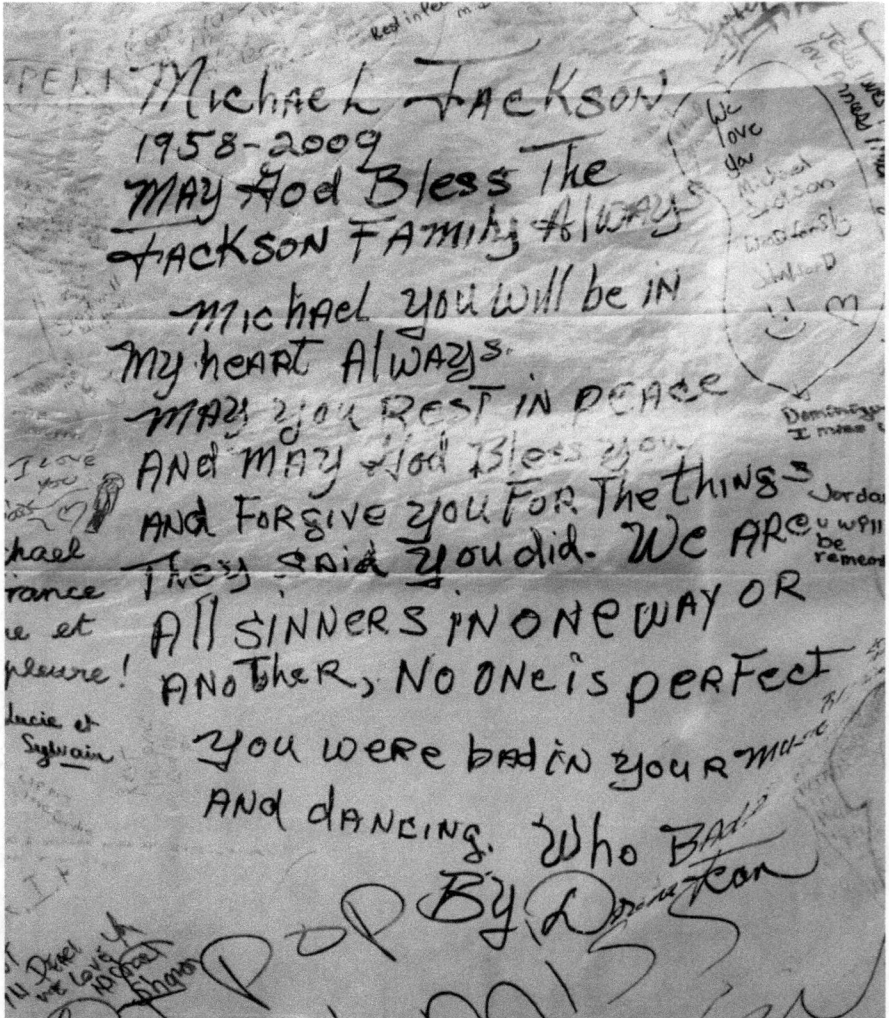

Michael Jackson's Last Dance Photo 158. The tributes are self evident.

FREDERICK MONDERSON

Michael Jackson's Last Dance Photo 159. The tributes are self evident.

Michael Jackson's Last Dance Photo 160. The tributes are self evident.

MICHAEL JACKSON'S LAST DANCE

Michael Jackson's Last Dance Photo 161. Signing "The Wall" for Michael Jackson. The tributes are self evident.

Michael Jackson's Last Dance Photo 162. The tributes are self evident.

16. MICHAEL JACKSON POSTSCRIPT

As the shocking details of Michael Jackson's purported drug use and addiction surfaced after his death, TV stations and other media were having field-days feeding at the trough of the pop star's misfortune. I seem to remember having a conversation with someone about a mutual friend who was inflicted with the AIDS virus and he was quick to point out, the fellow had an illness and we needed to be compassionate about his illness. The same can hold true for Michael Jackson who equally suffered from an illness, which is the malady of addiction to prescription drugs.

As a successful person, challenged by the rigors of his profession and the demands to consistently produce at an optimum level, in this case, producing award winning hit songs, the physical demands on the entertainer, probably accidental misfortunes, his skin condition and plastic surgeries, all started him on the road to using prescription drugs. Perhaps the hurt from the child molestation allegations and the disappointment of "betrayal by important people in Hollywood" have also been instrumental in the pain Michael endured. We should never forget, Leonard Rowe, one time friend and concert promoter, in that interview along with Joe Jackson on Larry King Live, confessed when he first met Michael some thirty years ago, let's say around 1978, Michael was afraid to drink a soda! How then did he transform into the addicted monster the media gorges on in satiation as they sensationalize the latter developments in his life.

Not being sympathetic, showing empathy or commiseration at the pop star's descent into the hellishness of prescription drug addiction and the toll it has taken as he tried to manifest a semblance of normalcy, move in and out of recluse; yet feed the demands of a fan base constantly wanting more from their idol, is a demanding experience few could imagine. The media was very insensitive in this respect.

The tragedy of Michael Jackson's later lifelong road of pain, suffering and ultimately ruin, can essentially be attributable to three sets of circumstances, each playing itself out singularly, yet interacting.

First, we must list the demands associated with entertainment performance excellence such as long hours spent in perfection of his explosive and exerting dance routines; the creative exertion that earned him superstardom, as an entertainer like no other; his mishap in the Pepsi Commercial; and the numerous plastic surgeries he underwent to transform his physical appearance. Whether this

MICHAEL JACKSON'S LAST DANCE

latter self-mutilation is dissatisfaction with his appearance as a black man, as some have perhaps, wrongfully argued; or, the necessary sacrifices to accomplish the universal a-raciality some believe he sought to accomplish, we'll never know. However, the price of success in whatever venture is oftentimes arduous and many times painful, extremely painful. The result is he ended up dead. To this we can add the rigorous financial and other challenges to him and family as well as the embarrassment of the ordeals of accusations of child molestation; accused, charged, but never anything conclusively proven!

As in any major "coup" or accomplishment, seldom can anyone claim "I did it alone." The general consensus is there's more "We" than "I." Sure, Frank Sinatra claimed "I did it my way," but the belief is that he was helped. Equally, Bernie Madoff, wants the public to believe he single-handedly orchestrated a $50 billion Ponzi scheme over a great many years, unknown and unaided by others. Michael Jackson, on the other hand, was surrounded by an enormous entourage of enablers, in addition to producers, writers, directors, agents, lawyers, doctors, friends, managers, the list is endless of people coming and going out of his life. A recent probe indicates he used 19 aliases to obtain prescription drugs as his addiction worsened. There were plastic surgeons, dermatologists, medical nurses, personal servants and employees. Are we to believe no one knew what was going on? No one had the "marbles" to say, "Wait a minute Kid, you're on the precipice of the cliff." Well, he fell over! Meanwhile, the media has not been kind to Michael Jackson. In 2002, he complained at Al Sharpton's National Action Network forum on racism in the music industry that, after he broke music record sales, he was villainized, the media being a useful and willing tool. This has not stopped up until his death and beyond. Let's face it, sensationalism about Michael Jackson sells papers and attracts viewers on TV programs.

After his death, local papers featured headlines among others that truthfully read "The Vultures are Circling" and "Wolves at the Door." Now the vultures have landed and wolves are in the door! As the Coroner stalled in releasing the results of the autopsy and the realization Michael was addicted to prescription pain-killers, viewers were especially glued to their TVs to be apprised of the next piece of juicy scandal. As the "exception proves the rule," Jim Moret and other TV personalities appeared on CNN, to report on Michael or to replace Larry King, certainly other networks and newspapers followed suit. Jim Moret as the "clean cut" reporter type delved into Michael Jackson and the caption showed he covered Michael's child molestation trial. He also covered O.J. Simpson's trial for CNN. He was part of the dynamic fanaticism manifested at "Camp OJ" along with Greta Van Susteren, Dominic Dunn for *Vanity Fair* and Jeffrey Tubin of CNN who were among those who "indulged" with the sensationalism created around this black man on the ropes, incidentally also found not guilty of murder. Such "feeding" probably began with Bryon Styron's Nat Turner's execution, Marcus Garvey's trial and imprisonment, the hounding of Paul Robeson, Mohammed Ali, Mike Tyson, etc. Nevertheless, many modern analysts, commentators, reporters, from unfortunate circumstances jump started lucrative careers that are today respected in their fields.

Two months after his death, before his burial events focus on doctors who administered to Michael, perhaps their actions contributed to his death. Claims of child molestation and sexual abuse have subsided, gone away, which question their originality. The media focused on Michael's words criticizing his father Joe on *Oprah*, but disregarded his own words he was innocent of child molestation, that he was hounded because he broke all records in the music industry and for ultimately possessing the Beatles' song catalogue. Jermaine confessed on Larry King Live that Joe was a good father, he was strict and that such were child raising methods of his generation. He held a positive view of their father pointing to the successes of the Jackson children raised by Joe Jackson.

In the case of Jim Moret, representing Larry King recently, as he focused on Michael's drug addiction and enablers in the process, he seemed to lose sight of the sensational young singer Nisha who told him: "Michael was the nicest human being I met in my life." When asked, "What was the nicest thing he ever said to you," she responded: "If you take an average singer and give them a wonderful song, they will do well. If you take an amazing singer and give them a wonderful song, they will do amazingly well." This truthful and heartfelt assessment rocketed her youthful confidence and career. Such is a fitting epithet for Michael Jackson, whose unfortunate ending, capping an extraordinary career, was entrapped in the frailties of human realities, destructiveness and the powerlessness of excess. If only the media had been less sensational, more kind and compassionate, who knows when Michael got to the fork in the road, he may have turned right rather than left. Notwithstanding, he has left his mark, his legacy, his foundation, his trust, his charities, his earning power, and though now dead, he still makes the news.

Some commentators have argued since science is so highly developed in its focus on the brain, the Coroner's removing a piece of Michael's brain to test for drug substance was really an attempt to seek to understand his outstanding genius. They can do that you know!

What a remarkable individual he was who has indelibly imprinted musically upon his generation and generations to come because he expended great energy crafting his creative abilities to rise to the very top in so many categories of human artistic endeavor.

Further, some have argued, it seems the media is so obsessed with reporting bad news, it could not report a positive story. It could not, even if, as E.F. Hutton used to say, "It would sneak up, slap you on the bottom and say, I'm here." The "clean

MICHAEL JACKSON'S LAST DANCE

cut" types would not give legs to a story saying Michael Jackson entered a Jacuzzi with a friend suffering from AIDS to show brotherly love; or that, two warring factions insisted "Let's suspend fighting, Michael Jackson is passing through," and afterwards returned to their previous belligerence; or his asking the need and then getting up to secure a glass of water for State Senator, now Governor, David Patterson, of New York.

Finally, let's not forget Paris' final and emotionally charged plea at the Memorial and the general consensus "Michael Jackson was a great father." He was also a good friend, an insistently well read and creative artist; a wonderful humanitarian and in his social relations a compassionate and caring individual who should be remembered for the many positive things he did rather than the few frailties he was accused of as a human being.

This brings us back to the intent of the Apollo Memorial and the foresightful-ness of Rev. Al Sharpton. Instantly upon Michael's death Sharpton called for the Apollo Tribute because he had been a friend of Michael Jackson and Michael was a True Apollo Legend. Equally important, as himself a victim of Media vilification, familiar with the wrongs done Michael by orchestrated media, Al Sharpton rightfully got out, ahead of the curve, to steer the perception and help shape and preserve the true legacy of Michael Joseph Jackson. He was a singer, songwriter, dancer, entertainer, humanitarian, child professing love to creatively heal the world to make it a better place for you and me. Now with Jordan Chandler's purported "Internet Confession" that his father, Evan Chandler, made him lie about the child molestation charges, one has to wonder about the nature of people and why the media never, to this day, relentlessly got to and ferreted out the truth that would have aided rehabilitation of Michael's name, image and psychological we-being. Still, in the final analysis, it is the extraordinary creativity expressed in his body of work that will define how Michael Jackson is remembered for decades to come, and not the trumped up charges so many believe were false.

Michael Jackson's Last Dance Photo 163. A fan signs second layer of "The Wall"

Michael Jackson's Last Dance Photo 164. Close up of a fan signing on "The Wall."

Michael Jackson's Last Dance Photo 165. Two fans sign T-shirt on "The Wall."

Michael Jackson's Last Dance Photo 166. The tributes are self evident.

MICHAEL JACKSON'S LAST DANCE

Michael Jackson's Last Dance Photo 167. The tributes are self evident.

Michael Jackson's Last Dance Photo 168. The tributes are self evident.

FREDERICK MONDERSON

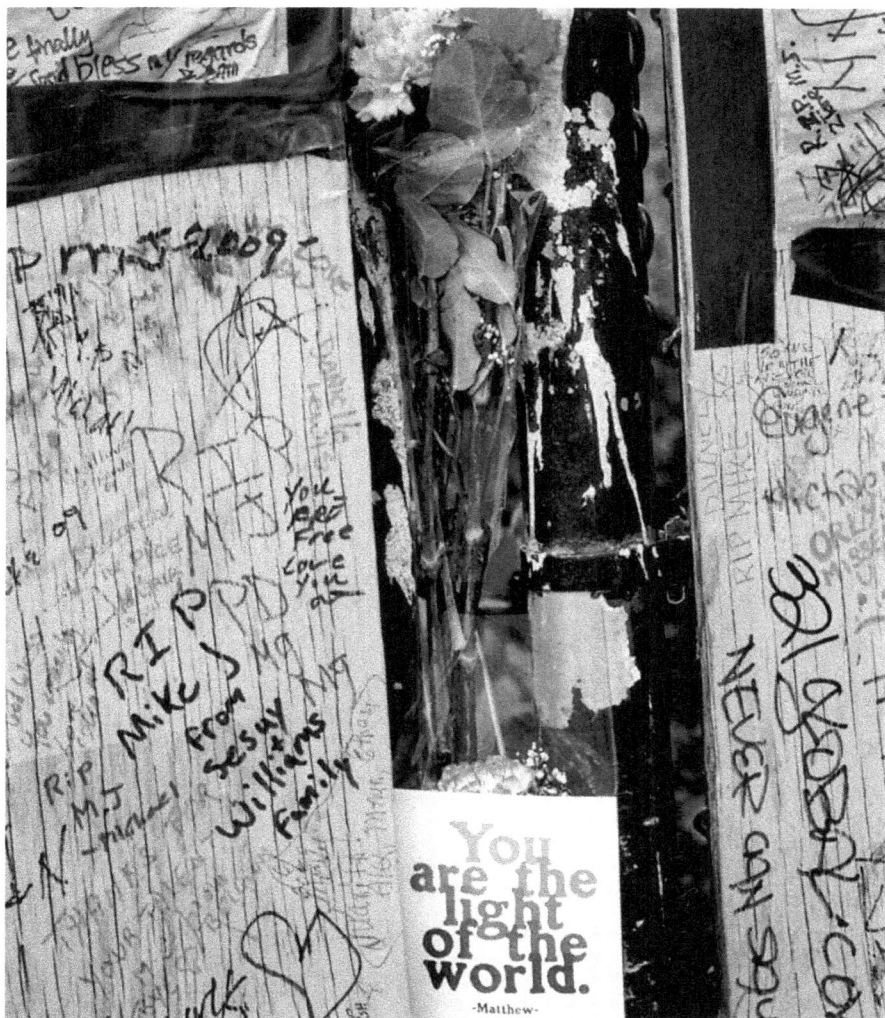

Michael Jackson's Last Dance Photo 169. The tributes are self evident.

MICHAEL JACKSON'S LAST DANCE

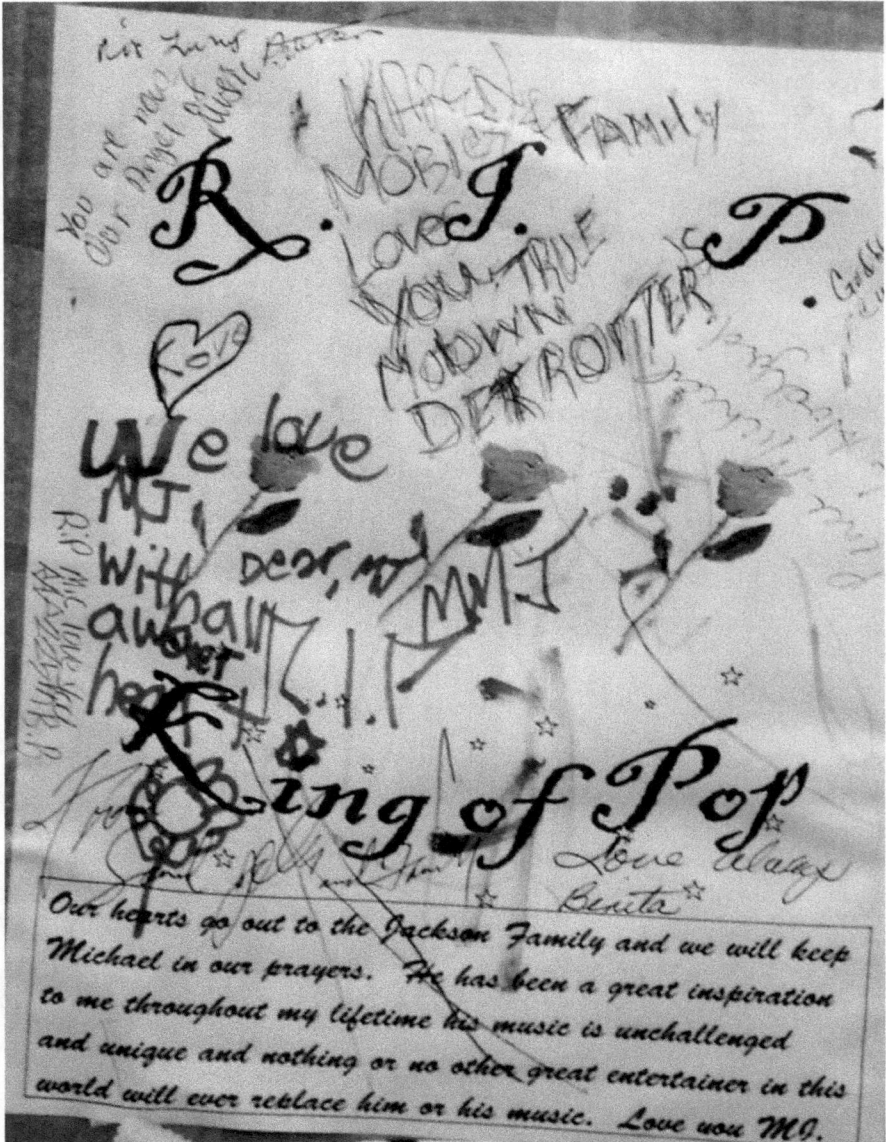

Michael Jackson's Last Dance Photo 170. The tributes are self evident.

Michael Jackson's Last Dance Photo 171. The tributes on T-shirt are self evident.

17.   MICHAEL JACKSON POST, POST SCRIPT

It seems the whole story about Michael Jackson may never be fully known and in light of the media's current emphasis on his addiction and prescription drug use, it's wonderful to have any form of good news.

On Tuesday, August 4, 2009, Larry King interviewed Frank Dileo, former and then re-hired manager of Michael Jackson. Frank, expressing great empathy and sadness at the loss of his friend, indicated he managed Michael from 1984 to 1989, and again was rehired in March, 2009, to be part of his entourage in the upcoming "This Is It" tour sponsored by AEG.

First, Frank said he got a call there was an ambulance at Michael's residence and when he arrived at the hospital, a nurse informed him Michael "would not make it." Then he called "Katherine first" to explain the situation. Then he "called Joe Jackson who was already informed by others. With a doctor and social worker" he "informed the children their father had passed away."

Frank Dileo pointed out Michael Jackson was "a kind soul, who would not harm a child." Larry King mentioned his interview with Joe Jackson and Leonard Rowe and brought up the number of shows, remarking Leonard said Michael only agreed to 10 shows. Frank said no. Both he and Michael read the contract and that Michael wanted to best Prince's 21 concerts. He wanted the **Guinness Book of World Record** officials to witness his record 50 shows, because "Michael is a very competitive person." He talked about a minimum and maximum number of shows and that "there was ticket potential for 85 shows."

Jim Moret then joined the group and said: "Frank, Brooke Shields and Paris revealed a different side of Michael." He did add, however, Michael was odd.

Frank responded, "Sometimes odd can be confused. I learned a few things off Michael Jackson. Michael knew how to sell tickets." Then Larry King asked about child abuse accusations. Frank responded: "Michael was a kind soul, who won't harm a soul. The people are moochers. I told Michael to fight the first accusation. I knew he was innocent." Surprisingly, Larry King offered, "Well that seems to be going away now." This fell flat. No one responded, especially Jim Moret, to an accusation fueled by media sensationalism that persecuted a good man, damaged his image and imagination and threatened to stain his legacy. In retrospect the Al Sharpton's immediate insistence after Michael's death, the need for the Apollo Memorial and the desire to protect his legacy from false accusations, was a stroke of brilliance, "beating back wolves at the door."

213

FREDERICK MONDERSON

Again, Larry brought up Leonard Rowe and the last meeting. Frank admitted he was not there at the Beverly Hills Hotel and Bungalow but that Michael, Joe, Leonard and Randy Phillips were there. He added Leonard did receive "The Letter" from Michael severing their relationship. Michael told him after the meeting, "Frank we have to remove Leonard." No one commented on Joe Jackson's earlier claim he was "Shouting with Randy Phillips." Frank closed by saying "allegations about Michael and children are not true." He said further, "Michael did not like family interfering in his business."

How strange, this was a manager Michael fired or severed in 1989 and again rehired in March of 2009. We are to believe everything he said, including Michael's statement regarding Leonard Rowe. However, we need not believe anything Rowe said, question Joe's intent and disregard or not pay much attention to the manager's claim that Michael was innocent of child molestation! Larry did not ask Frank if Michael explained why Joe was shouting at Randy!

Now, in view of this fellow Jordan Chandler's purported confession that his father, Evan chandler, insisted he frame Michael for money is an issue the media should follow relentlessly to clear the man's name they have so insisted was true and made so much money and ratings. This story has grown tremendously since it was first published on the Internet. It has been mainly carried by blogs. One report claims it was a hoax. Another pointed out: "No major news media source has been able to substantiate this claim."

The Urban Politico, an Internet source, of July 5, 2009, under the heading "All I want to say is they don't really care about us" has written:

"Sometime after Michael's passing last week is when the rumors started to buzz around the Internet that, if true, would confirm what many of us believed to be true 16 years ago: Michael Jackson didn't do it."

"I don't know if Jordan Chandler truly made this admission or whether it's just the internet rumor-mill hard at work, but what I do know is that the facts on the Chandler side of the story have never seemed to add up. If the boy really was molested, then it is difficult to imagine why the family of the "victim" was not at all concerned with pressing charges when it had the chance to do so after the financial settlement. So after the multi-million-dollar settlement was reached, I suppose the family figured justice had been served?"

"In sum, I'll reiterate that I am unable to verify if the alleged admission by Jordan Chandler actually took place. But if it did, that must have been an awful lot of guilt resting on that man's heart for the past 16 years."

Nevertheless, the important thing about this book **Michael! The Apollo Memorial** is that all along the focus has been on showing Michael Jackson in a constructively positive, humanitarian manner, as a tremendously creative artist and never accepting any false claims against "Michael, the Archangel." Whether or not the Chandler supposed confession is true, only God knows since many have tried to substantiate the claim. Notwithstanding, Michael cannot be hurt by this allegation anymore, but maybe, and if the "confession" is true, then the young man will have to face himself and his conscience for many years to come.

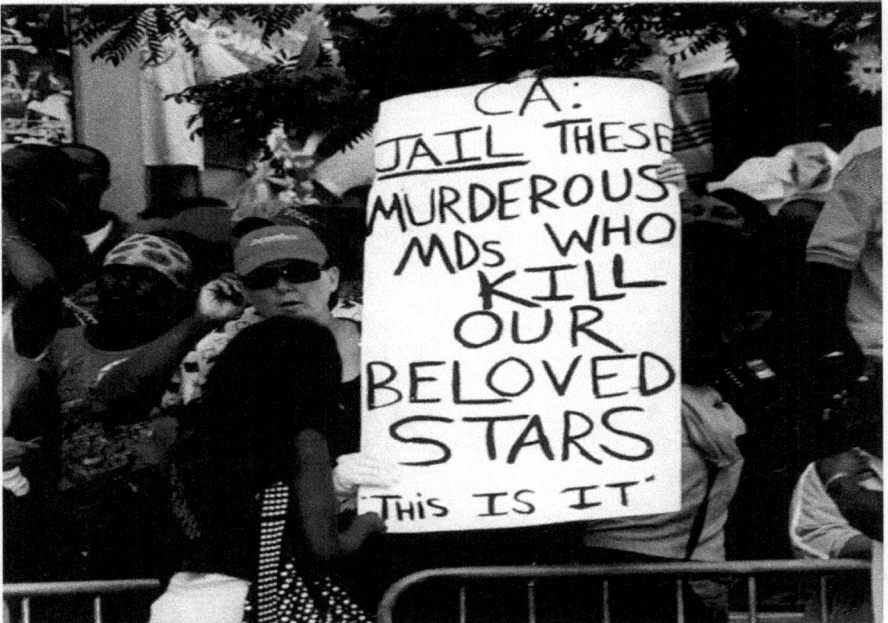

Michael Jackson's Last Dance Photo 172. This sign's message is unmistakable.

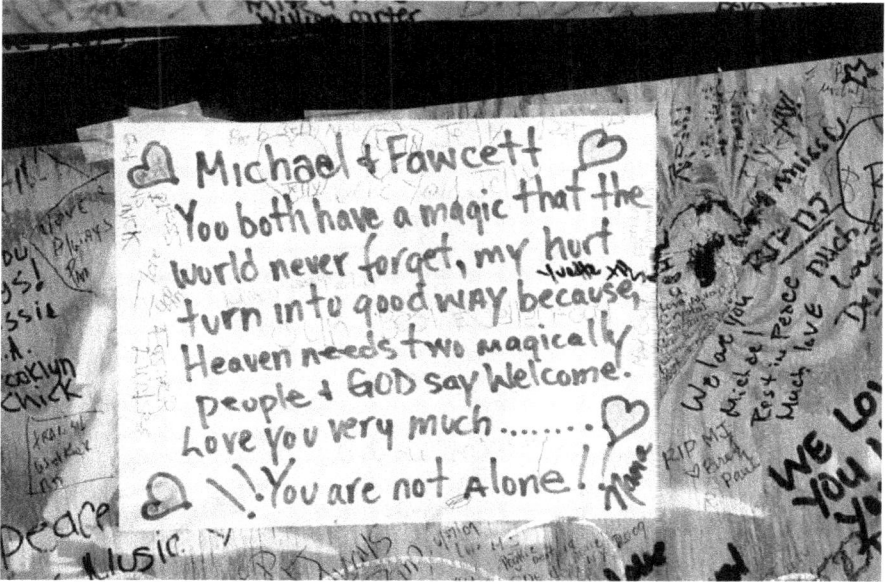

Michael Jackson's Last Dance Photo 173. The tribute is self evident.

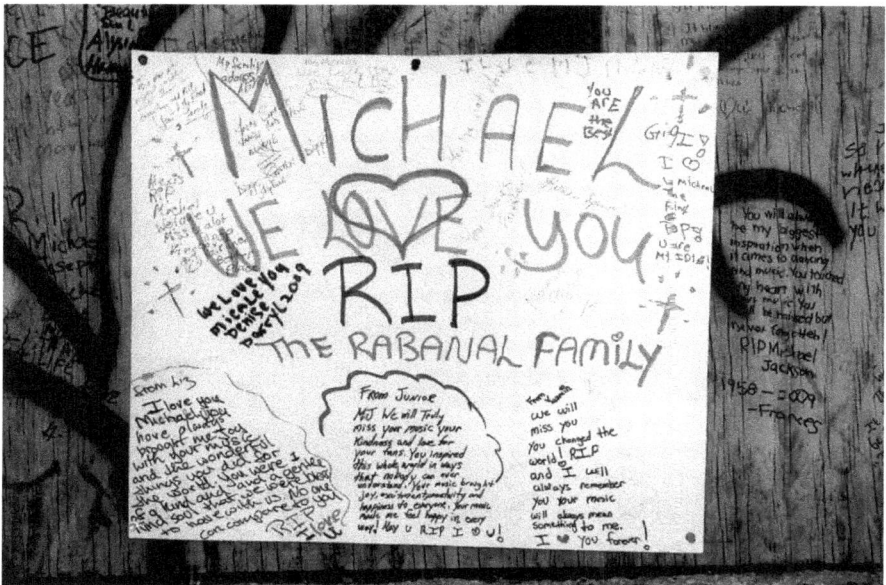

Michael Jackson's Last Dance Photo 174. The tribute is self evident.

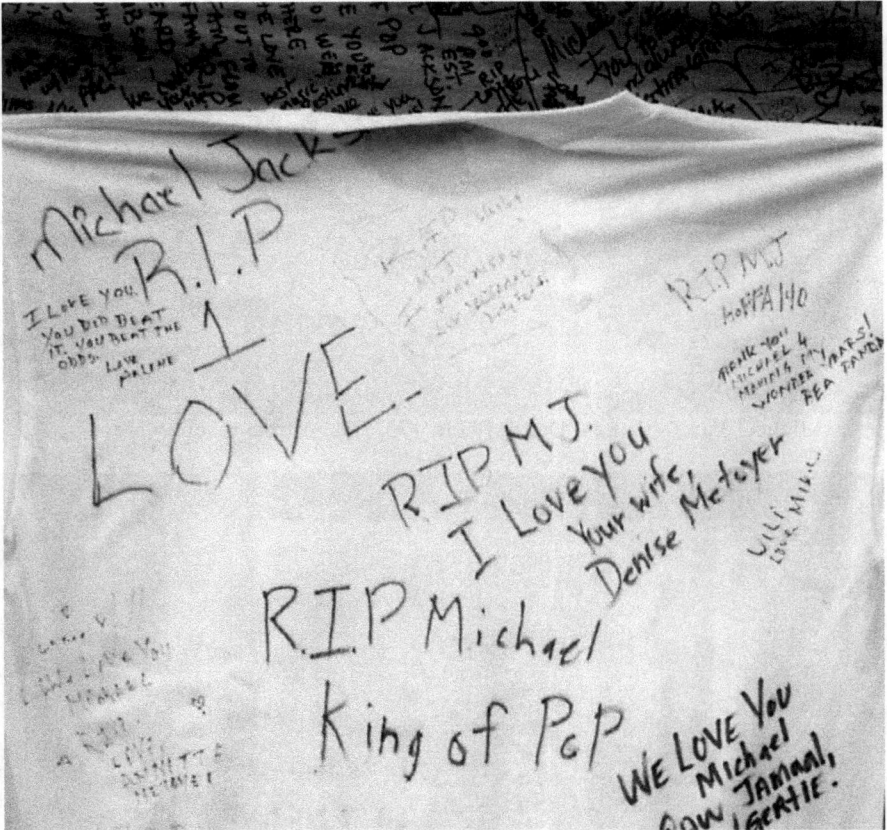

Michael Jackson's Last Dance Photo 175. The T-shirt tribute is self evident.

Michael Jackson's Last Dance Photo 176. The T-shirt tribute is self evident.

MICHAEL JACKSON'S LAST DANCE

Michael Jackson's Last Dance Photo 177. The tribute is self evident.

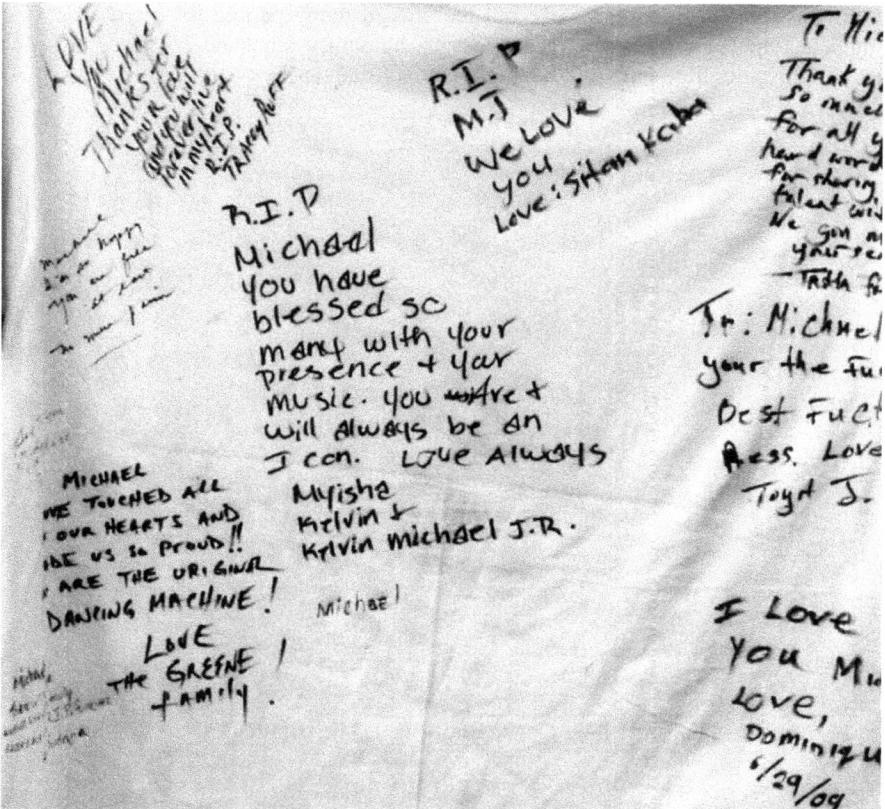

Michael Jackson's Last Dance Photo 178. The tribute is self evident.

18. MICHAEL JACKSON: THE FINAL WORD

Michael Jackson was indeed a very special breed of humanity, one who comes along perhaps once in a century. When you combine the many talents he possessed, his work ethic, care and concern for humanity and charitable mindset, we have the essentials of a really good person. When you combine these attributes, if his efforts to please, pleasure, protect and plead, protest and take significant steps to protect the wonderful nature of humanity and the world we live in, by

MICHAEL JACKSON'S LAST DANCE

some religious standards, he would have approached "sainthood." However, while personally religious, he lived a life that globally brought much joy and pleasurable moments that soothed the hearts and feelings of many people for many years. So much so, his passing was a great loss to humanity since he so gracefully and unselfishly sought to help and heal in whatever manner he could.

Michael Jackson's Last Dance Photo 179. The tribute is self evident.

While many may offer thoughts garnered from their associations with Michael Jackson, whether for personal gain or not, they should really channel their aim to rehabilitate a wonderful soul, painfully exploited in his lifetime. That is, their efforts ought to be directed at "solving the mystery" of accusations that have tarnished the career and persona of an extraordinarily gentle soul. Yet still, and oftentimes, in the hustle and bustle, we seldom get a glimpse of the "inner workings" of such a gifted yet un-pretentious person. One such occasion occurred, and for those who may be fans yet never enjoyed a "close-up" with Michael, the famous Oprah interview provided such a glimpse. This certainly does not emphasize the bashing of his father for Michael rehabilitated Joe at Oxford University

Conducting her interview as any host would, Oprah ventured into a personal side of Michael. Framed in a manner, she first asked whether he was dating Brooke Shields and received an affirmative nod. Next, in a loaded question she insisted people wanted to know whether Michael was a "virgin." After all, she stated

221

essentially, "You sing of wanting to 'Rock with you all night.' "We want to know who you rocking with!"

But, Michael, in that gently soft voice and unpretentious manner responded seemingly as no one else would. He told Oprah, "I am a gentleman and would never discuss that." How gentlemanly of him, for so many others would want to project their macho nature, boasting and if not telling all, certainly coming close to leave the audience on the cusp to draw conclusions that seem pointedly self evident.

 That is the Michael so many imagined but seldom get to know. Importantly, from that simple response one could easily dismiss the allegations the media straddled him with for so many years. Out of respect, as with any historical figure, they should further investigate and clear his name so Michael could be properly rehabilitated and take his proper place among those who preached and practiced the good for all humanity.

Michael Jackson's Last Dance Photo 180. Colorful DJ who rocked those lucky enough to get inside the Apollo to hear Rev. Sharpton at 5:25 EDT June 30, 2009, 5 days to the hour when Michael passed away.

MICHAEL JACKSON'S LAST DANCE

Michael Jackson's Last Dance Photo 181. Jonelle Procope, President and CEO of the Apollo Theater foundation addresses the crowd as to why the Theater is memorializing Michael Jackson as it celebrates its 75th year in 2009.

Michael Jackson Last Dance Photo 182. Film-maker Spike Lee addresses the crown insisting we should shun negativity towards Michael Jackson.

MICHAEL JACKSON'S LAST DANCE

Michael Jackson's Last Dance Photo 183. Spike Lee continues to insist the crowd shun negativity towards Michael Jackson because this is not what the man was about.

Michael Jackson's Last Dance Photo 184. Rev. Al Sharpton at the microphone and calls the crowd to pay attention to what he has to say regarding Michael's tribute.

Michael Jackson's Last Dance Photo 185. Rev. Sharpton and Spike Lee at the podium making a comment about what Michael Jackson represented and stood for.

MICHAEL JACKSON'S LAST DANCE

Michael Jackson's Last Dance Photo 186. Big poster image of Michael Jackson was flashed on the big screen to the rear as people spoke and music played in celebration.

Michael Jackson's Last Dance Photo 187. One of two big bouquets for Michael.

228

MICHAEL JACKSON'S LAST DANCE

Michael Jackson's Last Dance Photo 188. Another big bouquet for Michael Jackson.

FREDERICK MONDERSON

Michael Jackson's Last Dance Photo 189. With a DJ on stage, the crowd is
entertained with Michael Jackson's songs as the place heats up.

MICHAEL JACKSON'S LAST DANCE

Michael Jackson's Last Dance Photo 190. A close up of part of the crowd in the Apollo Theater paying homage to the deceased idol entertainer.

Michael Jackson's Last Dance Photo 191. Another look at the crowded audience.

FREDERICK MONDERSON

Michael Jackson's Last Dance Photo 192. With DJ on stage the crowd rises to its feet to dance to the music of Michael Jackson played by the DJ-team.

Michael Jackson's Last Dance Photo 193. Rev. Al Sharpton addresses the crowd.

Michael Jackson's Last Dance Photo 194. Al Sharpton raises his hands to the crowd.

Michael Jackson's Last Dance Photo 195. Another close up of the crowd in the Apollo Theater.

Michael Jackson's Last Dance Photo 196. Another close up of the crowd.

Michael Jackson's Last Dance Photo 197. Beautiful basket of flowers adds to the ambience of the occasion.

19. Michael Jackson: Thoughts on the Funeral

Michael Jackson was finally buried September 3, 2009, 70 days after his passing on June 25. Himself a legend, he will lay alongside great musical and movie legends at the historic 290-acre Forest Lawn Cemetery in Glendale, California. He

MICHAEL JACKSON'S LAST DANCE

will rest in the Hollow Terrace section of the Mausoleum bearing Michelangelo-like Sistine Chapel depictions and Da Vinci's *Last Supper*. Michael himself had commissioned his own *Last Supper* which lay above his bed at Neverland. He was buried wearing a silver glove, according to his sister Janet. We are told further, Paris placed a crown upon his gold covered casket, adorned with white flowers, in another of those wonderfully moving tributes the young lady demonstrated in appreciation of the love and affection she held for her father.

As indicated in the beautiful invitation, this was a private ceremony hosted by the family with the media not permitted within the cemetery gates. Because of special considerations, the cemetery area is a no-fly zone prohibiting flyover for media coverage from the air. Yet, with powerful lens, they provided distance coverage from beyond the marker. Some 60 media outlets from around the world lined the adjacent vicinity while police kept fans and onlookers two blocks away. Still, from the air coverage CNN showed the 200-seat arrangement being filled up by arriving guests and tracked the 31-car motorcade bringing Michael's body, while CNN reporter Randi Kaye, from outside the front gate identified as many celebrities as possible as they alighted from their cars. Among celebrities identified as being in attendance Elizabeth Taylor who had stayed away, came out. So too did Quincy Jones, despite his not wanting to "attend any more funerals." Michael's friend Macaulay Caulking, Corey Feldman, Chris Tucker, Mila Kunis, and Barry Bonds, were among so many others who paid final respects to the musical genius

Slated to begin at 10:00 pm EST (7:00 PST) the funeral ceremony was late getting started. The family released their own regulated video portions of events on a delayed basis, which the networks aired in split screen coverage. Meanwhile Larry King Live hosted individuals who offered commentary before departing to be part of the ceremony laying Michael in his final place of rest. Others as Deepak Chopra and his son Gotham Chopra remained to provide commentary and recount their experiences with the fallen star.

It is interesting that at a private funeral such as this only select people were invited. Among those invited was Leonard Rowe who had appeared on Larry King and left to attend the funeral. When we consider what was said about Leonard Rowe, especially by Frank Dileo that Michael wanted him out of the picture, if so; the question becomes 'Why would Leonard be invited to the private funeral?' It is not clear if Frank was invited. Many others who expressed all kinds of wild thoughts about Michael, and since the guest list was not made public, we don't know if they were invited.

We were told by Janet Jackson, among the memorabilia Michael was buried with, his black Fedora and sequined glove were included as tools of his trade, that he probably wore as he "Moon walked" through Heaven's door on his way to become a member of the heavenly choir!

Michael Jackson's Last Dance Photo 198. Back outside, the Marquee sign has changed, advertising this day's event.

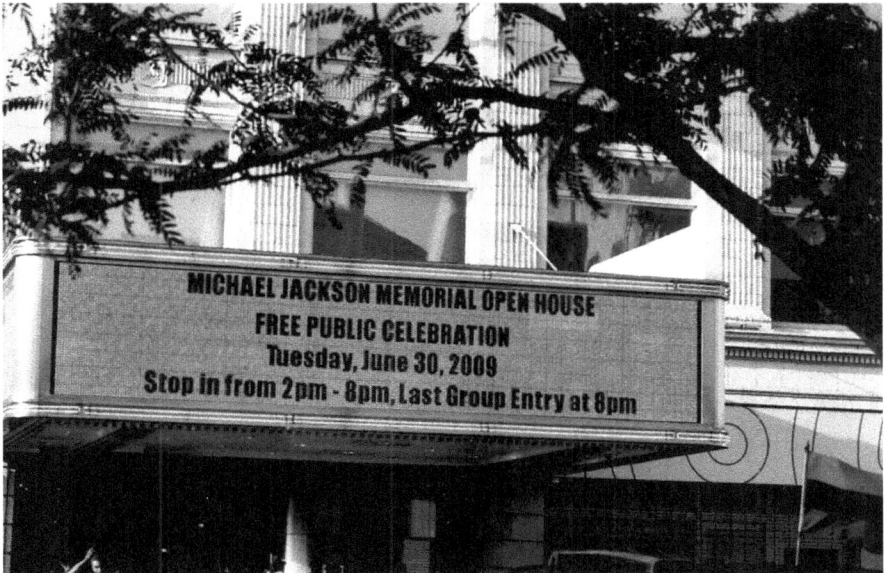

Michael Jackson's Last Dance Photo 199. Red, Black and Green and the new sign.

MICHAEL JACKSON'S LAST DANCE

Michael Jackson's Last Dance Photo 200. A view of the full name of the Theater.

FREDERICK MONDERSON

Michael Jackson's Last Dance Photo 201. There's that "Little Green Belt" again signing "The Great Wall."

20. PERIODICAL BIBLIOGRAPHICAL REFERENCE FOR FURTHER RESEARCH

The original intent of this section was to provide a database (partial) for researchers to be able to look into the life and work of Michael Jackson. That still holds. However, a number of observations have shed light on the complexity of the man, artist, musician, humanitarian, etc. It also underscores the Media's obsession with Michael Jackson and how, that obsession distorted their perception and portrayal of the phenomenon of the "King of Pop."

In his age, no entertainer/celebrity has had as extensive media coverage as Michael Jackson. Yet, one article seems to sum it all up: "Who's on his side?" Even more, the media has revealed contradictions in its coverage. For example, one article in *Ebony* detailed Michael Jackson's disdain for Africa on many counts. Yet, he was feted even though he did not agree to perform. He was made King and enthroned. He was also made a member of a South African tribe. These developments could not have happened if he behaved in any way inappropriate with Africans when he visited that continent.

Michael Jackson's Last Dance Photo 202. Another view from across the street.

FREDERICK MONDERSON

What is interesting, much of the negative press seems to have begun before Michael was accused of child molestation and that first accusation opened flood doors of the "hounding." Perhaps the signing of a contract with Sony for $600 million dollars when he did was an unimaginable development for a black man in America to be involved in. Later he had the audacity to name a small mountain on Neverland Ranch "Mount Katherine" and that too may have contributed to the animus that developed fed by the accusation. And so on and on! Well, it's all here and without a doubt Michael Jackson was an extraordinary person who brought fame not only to his person but to the people who fed off him. It is also interesting how many newspaper and magazine, even Journal covers he graced, in the feeding frenzy that followed his career.

1971

Jackson 5 - *Life* 71: 50-51 September 24, 1971.

1977

Michael Jackson: A Young bachelor married to Music. Ill. Bob Lucas *Jet* 52: 60-63 (March 31, 1977).

1978

Michael Jackson digs The Wiz! Interview, Ed by E. Miller. Pors. *Seventeen* 37: 270-01+ August 1978.
Blame it on the Boogie? T. White. Il. Pors. *Crawdaddy* p. 48-51 December, 1978.
Michael Jackson: Wiz kid. Por. *Teen* 23: 50+ January, 1979.
On the Move. R. Windeler. Il. Pors. *People* 10: 85-86+ November 27, 1978.

1979

Michael Jackson. Il. Robert Johnson. *Jet* 56: 30-33+ (August 16, 1979).

1980

Michael teams with Sister Latoya Jackson. Robert E. Johnson. *Jet* 15: 58-63, April 1980.
Michael Jackson: 'Wiz' Sweep Image Awards. *Jet* 15: 60-62, February 1980.

1981

MICHAEL JACKSON'S LAST DANCE

Michael Jackson: Most Popular Male Entertainer. Ill. *Jet* 61: 150-52 (November 5, 1981).

1982

Michael Jackson. Ill. Charles L. Sanders. *Ebony* 38: 126-30+ November 1892.

1983

Are Lady Di and Michael Jackson still soul mates? Il. Por. *People Weekly* 20: 28, August 8, 1983.
Diana and Michael. C.L. Sanders. Il. Pors. *Ebony* 39: 29-30+ November 1983.
Michael Jackson. G. Hirshey. Il. Pors. *Rolling Stone* pp. 120-11 + February 17, 1983.
The Peter Pan of Pop. J. Miller. Il. Pors. *Newsweek* 101: 52-4, January 10, 1983.
Thanks to a Thriller Album, the former small fry of the Jacksons become the biggest star in Pop music. Por. *People Weekly* 20: 73 December 26, 1983-January 2, 1984.

1984

All About Michael (Jackson). Il. Pors *People Weekly* 22 September issue 3-23+ November–December, 1984.
Anyone who wants a date with Michael Jackson can get 365 of them next year. Il. Por. *People Weekly* 22: 34 July 30, 1984.
The bizarre ways of Michael Jackson look-alikes. C. Krupp. Il. Por. *Glamour* 82: 61, July 1984.
Bringing back the magic. J. Cocks. Il. Por. *Time* 124: 6-65+ July 16, 1984.
A different kind of celebration. A. Haley. Por. *Ladies Home Journal* 101: 126+ December 1984.
The Glove comes off as Michael Jackson goes to work. J. McBride. Il. Por. *People's Weekly* 21: 151-2+ June 11, 1984.
Its coming, Michaelmania. Il. por. *Newsweek* 104: 26, July 2, 1984.
Jackson attempts to block Thriller film from stores. Il. Por. *Jet* 66: 16, May 28, 1984.
The Jackson Brothers grim. Por. *Esquire* 101: 88, January 1984.
The Jackson family talks about Michael. R.E. Johnson. Il. Pors. *Jet* 66: 56-60 March 26, 1984.
Jackson names Epic V.P. Frank Dileo, new manager. Disney world expands Michael Jackson Suite. Il. Por. *Jet* 66: 58-9 April 9, 1984.
Jackson Thriller gets MTV Video Music Awards. Por. *Jet* 67: 60 October 8, 1984.
Just One More Thriller. A. B. Block. Il. Por. *Forbes* 134; Spring Issue: 232 + October 1, 1984.

FREDERICK MONDERSON

Making Michael Jackson Thriller. M. Cohen. Il. *High Fidelity* 34: 57-8,

The Magic of Michael Jackson. S. Weller. Il. Pors. *McCall's* 111: 38+ May 1984.

Michael! G. Smith. Il. Pors. *People's Weekly* 22: 82-4+ August 27, 1984.

Michael Jackson and Brooke Shields: they share a special friendship. Il. Pors. *Jet* 65: 14-18 February 27, 1984.

Michael Jackson didn't steal song, court rules. Il. Pors. *Jet* 67: 53-57 December 31, 1984-January7, 1985.

Michael Jackson gives share of Victory Tour to UNCF, others. Il. Por. *Jet* 67: 56 October 15, 1984.

Michael Jackson Inc. K. Folitz. *Newsweek* 103: 66-67 February 27, 1984.

The Michael Jackson nobody knows [Interview] R. E. Johnson. Il. Pors. *Ebony* 40: 155-58 December 1984.

The Michael Jackson Syndrome. C. Rubenstein. Il. Por. *Discover* 5: 68-70, September 1984.

Michael Jackson: the world's greatest entertainer. R.E. Johnson. Il. Pors. *Ebony* 39: 163-65+ May 1984.

Michael Jackson's Money Machine. Por. *US News and World Report* 97: 14 July 16, 1984.

Michael Jackson live wire. Il. Por. Vogue 174: 450-1 March 1984.

Michael Jackson rests at home; healing of burns pleases medics. Il. Pors. *Jet* 67: 56 November 26, 1984.

Michael Jackson tells Ebony things he never talked about before; Jackson to write about his scalp operation while home. Il. Por. *Jet* 66: 55-6 May 7, 1984.

Michael weaves magic spell as he bounces back from burn bout. Il. Por. *Jet* 65: 54-56. February 20, 1984.

Michaelmania. Il. Por. *Ebony* 39: 120+ July 1984.

Michael's magic show. G. Hirshey. Il. Por. *Rolling Stone* p. 27-9+ August 16, 1984.

The new wizard of Opp. G. MacKay. Il. Por. *MacLean's* 97: 38-40+ July 23, 1984.

Singer Michael Jackson sweeps American Music Awards wins eight honors. Il. Por. Jet 65: 62 January 30, 1984.

Thriller Chiller. C. Arrington. Il. Pors. *People's Weekly* 21: 24-27 February 13, 1984.

The Tour, the Money, the Magic. J. Miller. Il. Por. *Newsweek* 104: 64-70July 16, 1984.

Why he's a Thriller. J. Cocks. Il. Pors. *Time* 123: 54-57+ March 19, 1984.

Why Michael hid out in a White House men's room and other tales of the day power played host to fame. Il. Por. *People's Weekly* 21: 75 May 28, 1984.

Bringing back the magic. J. Cocks. Il. Por. *Time* 12: 64-65 July 16, 1984.

The Jackson fireworks. W. Plummer. Il. Pors. *People's Weekly* 22: 44-47 July 23, 1984.

Jackson mania [Release of Victory]. J. Pareles. Il. *Mademoiselle* 90: 74+ November 1984.

MICHAEL JACKSON'S LAST DANCE

The Jacksons dazzle New York fans; Won't bow to death threats and cancel Knoxville. Il. *Jet* 66: 54-56+ August 20, 1984.

Jacksons complete control of Victory Tour to keep million$ in family. Il. *Jet* 66: 55-56 July 9, 1984.

The Jacksons score an appealingly modest, almost hollow Victory. V. Aletti. Il. *Rolling Stone* p. 35+ August 16, 1984.

Jacksons hit the jackpot on U.S. Tour. M. Goldberg. *Rolling Stone* p. 56 November 8, 1984.

Mother of the Jacksons hit press lies about family, upcoming tour. Il. *Jet* 66: 54-555 June 4, 1984.

Pepsi stages two days to premiere long-awaited TV ads with the Jacksons. Il. *Jet* 66: 14-15 March 19, 1984.

1985

Can Michael Jackson keep the faith? B.G. Harrison. *Mademoiselle* 91: 142 January 1985.

Jackson pays $47.5 million for Beatles songs. D. Fricke. Il. Por. *Rolling Stone* p. 22 September 26, 1985.

Jackson pens, produces new tune for holidays. Por. *Jet* 6 8: 58 June 10, 1985.

Living With Michael Jackson. T. Gold. Il. por. *McCall's* 112: 28+ February 1985.

Michael Jackson and Lionel Richie's song earns millions for Africa's famine victims. *Jet* 68: 60-64 April 8, 1985.

Michael Jackson is 'painfully' shy, says Brooke Shields on TV. Por. *Jet* 68: 61 July 15, 1985.

Michael Jackson named US teen's top hero. Il. Por. *Jet* 67: 57 January 14, 1985.

Michael Jackson pays $47.5m for Beatles hits. Il. Por. *Jet* 68: 55 September 2, 1985.

Michael Jackson undergoes airport search in London. Il. Por. *Jet* 68: 34 April 15, 1985.

Michael Testifies. M. Possley. Il. *Rolling Stones* p. 20 January, 1985.

Michael to Paul: beat it. Il. Por. *Newsweek* 106: 48 August 26, 1985.

Michaelmania grips London as superstar unveils his wax figure. Il. Pors. *Jet* 68: 55 April 15, 1 985.

The sound of one glove clapping. G. Hirshey. Il. *Rolling Stone* p. 11-12 December 19, 1985-January 2, 1986.

1986

25 Arts students awarded Jackson UNCF scholarships. Por. *Jet* 70: 22 April 7, 1986.

Jackson may keep giraffe at his Encino menagerie. *Jet* 70: 54 July 14, 1986.

Jackson's plans for own hyperbaric chamber nixed. Por. *Jet* 72: 38 October 20, 1986.

Michael Jackson inks a $15 million Pepsi pact. Il. Por. *Jet* 70: 56 May 26, 1986.

Michael Jackson inks multimillion-dollar deal with Pepsi. A. DeCurtis. *Rolling Stone*
p. 13 June 19, 1986.

Michael Jackson may sing at Moscow's Goodwill Games. For. *Jet* 70: 57 June 23, 1986.

Officials order Jackson to enlarge zoo for giraffe. *Jet* 70: 14 July 14, 1986.

When Disneyland debuted his 3-D movie marvel, Michael Jackson was in another dimension. S. Haller. Il. *People's Weekly* 26: 30-32 September 29, 1986.

1987

And in Ethiopia, the cult of the Gloved One. Por. *Newsweek* 109: 31 May 25, 1987.

'Bad' Michael Jackson thrills Tokyo audience during Japan tour debut. Il. Por. *Jet* 73: 4+ September 28, 1987.

The Badder they come. J. Cocks. Il. Pors. *Time* 130: 85 September 14, 1987.

For sale: the Gloved One's cast-off main squeeze. Il. Por. *People's Weekly* 27: 88 May 25, 21987.

Good news: 'Bad' news. D. Handelman. *Rolling Stone* p. 11 August 13, 1987.

Is Michael Jackson for real? [Cover story] M. Goldberg and D. Handelman. Il. Pors. *Rolling Stone* p 50-1+ September 24, 1987.

Jackson LP: early sales for 'Bad' are good. F. Goodman *Rolling Stone* p. 15 October 8, 1987.

Michael grows up. D. Sigerson. Il. Por. *Rolling Stone* p 87-88 October 22, 1987.

Michael Jackson: Bad; Prince: Sign of the times. D. Wolff. *Nation* 245: 728-9 December 12, 1987.

Michael Jackson comes back! [Cover story] R.E. Johnson. Il. Pors. *Ebony* 42: 142-44+ September, 1987.

Michael Jackson conquers Japan and continues his world tour. [Cover story] Il. Pors. *Jet* 73: 54-57 November 9, 1987.

Michael Jackson tells Ebony about his new sole career. Il. Por. *Jet* 72: 65 September 7, 1987.

Michael Jackson to get $10 million for Pepsi ads. *Jet* 71: 22 February 9, 1987.

Michael Jackson 'Bad' album released this month. Por. *Jet* 72: 56 August 10, 1987.

Michael Jackson's newest thriller. C. McGuigan. Por. *Newsweek* 110: 69 August 3, 1987.

Michael's first epistle [cover story] M. Small. Il. Pors. *People's Weekly* 28: 102-04+ October 12, 1987.

MICHAEL JACKSON'S LAST DANCE

The Peter Pan of songs and dances. V. Ross. Il. Pors. *MacLean's* 100: 57-58 September 14, 1987.

Richie talks about friend, fellow star Michael Jackson. Il. Pors. *Jet* 71: 62 February 16, 1987.

Simian star of a new toy line, Michael Jackson's pet Bubbles, plays second banana to no one. Il. *People's Weekly* 28: 189 November 16, 1987.

The trouble with Michael Jackson. J. Pareles. Il. *Mademoiselle* 93: 108+ March 1987.

Unlike anyone, even himself [cover story]. C. Durkee. Il. Pors. *People's Weekly* 28: 86-87+ September 14, 1987.

A way to play Michael. T. Jaffe. Por. *Forbes* 140: 221 September 21, 1987.

1988

"The 'Bad' boy and the Boss. C. McGuigan; B. Barol. Il. Pors. *Newsweek* 111: 71 March 7, 1988.

Big number. *The New Yor*ker 64: 31-32 March 14, 1988.

Bob Jones leaves Motown to handle PR for Jackson. Pors. *Jet* 73: 56 January 25, 1988.

The image culture: Michael Jackson, Cindy Sherman, and the art of self-manipulation. M. Jefferson. Il. Pors. *Vogue* 178: 122+ March, 1988.

The Invisible man returns. M. Gilmore. Il. Pors. *Rolling Stone* p. 35+ March 24, 1988.

Jackson boosting the Beatles. J. Ressner. *Rolling Stone* p. 35+ March 24, 1988.

Jackson is first to have 5 no. 1 hits on album; aids the Motown Museum. Il. Por. *Jet* 74: 54, July 25, 1988.

The man in the mirror. L. Black. Il. Por. MacLean's 101: 67 May 2, 1988.

Michael debuts his new show in Kansas City. M. Gilmore. Il. Por. *Rolling Stone* p 15+ April 7, 1988.

Michael Jackson: a new look at superstar and behind the scenes. R.E. Johnson. Il. Pors. *Jet* 73: 56-63 March 21, 1988.

Michael Jackson conquers Europe. [Cover story] Il. Pors. *Jet* 74: 62-64 August 8, 1988.

Michael Jackson donates $125,000 to Motown Museum. Il. Pors. *Jet* 75: 57-58 November 14, 1988.

Michael Jackson earns $97 million to become highest paid entertainer. Il. Por. *Jet* 75: 12 October 3, 1988.

Michael Jackson gives blacks a big piece of money action on his concert tour. Il. Pors. *Jet* 73: 52-58 March 28, 1988.

Michael Jackson plans to quit concert tours. Il. Por. *Jet* 74: 53 September 19, 1988.

Michael Jackson shares Chicago honor with his guest, Lola Falana, who is fighting MS disease. Il. Por. *Jet* 74: 54 May 9, 1988.

Michael Jackson to hit the road for limited American tour. A. De Curtis. Il. Por. *Rolling Stone* p 23 February 11, 1988.

FREDERICK MONDERSON

Michael Jackson turns 30! Il. Pors. *Jet* 74: 58-59 August 29, 1988.

Michael Jackson's book reveals secrets of his success [cover story] R.E. Johnson. Il. Pors. *Jet* 74: 36-39 May 16, 1988.

Michael turns 30! Q. Troupe. Il. Pors. *Essence* 19: 52-5 4+ July 1988.

A new and revealing look at Michael Jackson [cover story] R.E. Johnson. Il. Pors. *Ebony* 43: 176+ June 1988.

On tour, he's still 'Michael!' But his charity work has won him a new title: Dr. Jackson. T. Gold. Il. Pors. *People's Weekly* 29: 36-37 March 28, 1988.

The score on Michael Jackson. T. Gold. Il. Pors. *McCall's* 115: 66-68+ August 1988.

Turning Bad into good, Motown Michael sends some concert cash back to his musical roots. J. Young. Il. Pors. *People's Weekly* 30: 143-44 November 7, 1988.

Walking softly. Il. Pors. *Newsweek* 111: 77 May 2, 1988.

1989

All bad things must come to an end as a tearful Michael Jackson bids bye-bye to the highway. S. Dougherty. Por. *People's Weekly* 31: 52-53 February 13, 1989.

Magical tours. J. Cocks. Il. Por. *Time* 133: 59 January 23, 1989.

Michael Jackson. R. Lacayo. Por. *People's Weekly* 32 Special Issue: 68-69 Fall 1989.

Michael Jackson and his manager Frank Dileo go their separate ways. Il. Pors. *Jet* 75: 57 March 6, 1989.

Michael Jackson earns $125 million and remains highest paid entertainer. Il. Por. *Jet* 76: 26+ October 2, 1989.

Michael Jackson gets award from his sixth grade teacher in L.A. Il. Pors. *Jet* 77: 29 October 30, 1989.

Michael Jackson quits concert stage after world tour sets me records [cover story] R.E. Johnson. Il. Pors. *Jet* 75: 54-59 February 27, 1989.

Michael Jackson says good-bye. M. Hammer. Il. Pors. *Ladies Home Journal* 106: 116+ May, 1989.

Michael Jackson says his 18 month worldwide tour was an 'incredible journey.' Il. Por. *Jet* 75: 61 January 23, 1989.

Michael's last tour [Cover story]. Il. Por. *Ebony* 44: 142-44+ April 1989.

1990

Bush Lauds Michael Jackson as 'Entertainer of the Decade.' Il. Pors. *Jet* 78: 4-5 April 23, 1990.

Dumped by Jackson, former manager Frank Dileo bounces back as one of Hollywood's GoodFellas. T. Gold. Il. Pors. *People's Weekly* 34: 99-100 October 22, 1990.

MICHAEL JACKSON'S LAST DANCE

McCartney blames Yoko for Jackson's Beatles purchase. Il. Por. *Jet* 78: 38 May 7, 1990.

Michael Jackson feted as top artist of the decade after selling 110 million discs. Il. Por. *Jet* 77: 60 March 12, 1990.

Michael Jackson opens home to 45 Dream Street Campers. Il. Por. *Jet* 78: 55 August 13, 1990.

Michael Jackson rushed to hospital suffering from chest discomfort. Por. *Jet* 78: 54 June 18, 1990.

Not yet. P. Newcomb. Il. Por. *Forbes* 146 Special Issue 8 October 33, 1990.

Portrait of Michael Jackson sells for $2.1 million. Il. Pors. *Jet* 77: 14 February 12, 1990.

1991

The biggest brother-sister stars in show business history. Il. Pors. *Ebony* 46:40 August, 1991.

Books on Jackson, Springsteen due, J. Ressner. *Rolling Stone* p. 22 February 7, 1992.

Brooke Shields rebukes critics of 'Dangerous' album by Michael Jackson. Il. Pors. *Jet* 18: 54 December 9, 1991.

A first look at Michael's "Black or white" mega-video [Cover story] S. Galloway. Il. Pors. *TV Guide* 39: 4-6 November 2-8, 1991.

The great Michael make-over. Il. Por. *People's Weekly* 35: 120-01 June 10, 1991.

Jackson, Michael: Dangerous [sound recording] Reviews

       Jet – IL. Pors. 81: 58-62 December 2, 1991.

       Newsweek – IL. Por., 118: 72-73 December 9, 1991. J. Leland.

       Time – IL. Por. 138: 86 December 2, 1991. J. Cocks.

The Jacksons score big: Michael and Janet set new standards for artist deals. M. Goldberg. Il. Pors. *Rolling Stone* p. 15-16 May 2, 1991.

Jackson's "Thriller" glove is recovered in Detroit. Il. Por. *Jet* 81: 52 October 21, 1991.

Madonna and Michael [Cover story] S. Dougherty. Il. Pors. *People's Weekly* 35: 64-68, April 15, 1991.

Michael Jackson inks unprecedented multi-media deal with Sony. Il. Por. *Jet* 79: 56-57 April 8, 1991.

Michael Jackson to visit four African countries. Il. por. *Jet* 79: 29 January 28, 1991.

1992

Bringing up Michael [Cover] s. Pond. Il. Pors. *TV Guide* 40: 8-11+ November 14-20, 1992.

Ebony/Jet interview with Michael Jackson. Por. *Ebony* 48: 126+ November 19923.

FREDERICK MONDERSON

Eyewitness report on Michael Jackson's tour inside Africa [Cover story] R. E. Johnson. Il. Pors. *Jet* 81: 10-17+ March 16, 1992.

Fast start for 'Dangerous.' M. Goldberg. *Rolling Stone* 9+ January 23, 1992.

Jackson, Michael: Dangerous [sound recording] Reviews

       The Nation 254: 138-39 February 3, 1992. G. Santoro

       Rolling Stone IL. p. 49-51 January 9, 1992. A Light

Jackson, Michael. In the Closet [videotape] Reviews

       Jet IL. Pors. 82: 56-57 April 27, 1992.

Jackson pays for burial of boy killed by random shot. Por. *Jet* 82: 6 June 8, 1992.

Jacksons ends aid supplies to children in Sarajevo. Il. Pors. *Jet* 83: 58 December 14, 1992.

Michael Jackson. Il. Por. *People's Weekly* 38: 62-63 July 27, 1992.

Michael Jackson. G. Hirshey. Por. *Rolling Stone* p. 135-36 June 11, 1992.

Michael Jackson [concert at Wembley Stadium, London] A. Light. Il. Pors. *Rolling Stone* P. 38 September 17, 1992.

Michael Jackson: Crowned in Africa, pop music king tells real story of controversial trip [cover story; with interview] R.E. Johnson. Il. Pors. *Ebony* 47: 34-36+ May 1992.

Michael Jackson kicks off dangerous tour in Europe. Il. Pors. *Jet* 82: 58 July 6, 1992.

Michael Jackson receives NABOB top achievement award. Il. Por. *Jet* 81: 57 March 30, 1992.

Michael Jackson schedules his first-ever televised concert for $20 million. Por. *Jet* 82: 58-59 August 31, 1992.

Michael Jackson signs to head Super Bowl XXVII halftime TV spectacular. Por. *Jet* 82: 22 September 28, 1992.

Michael Jackson stops fan from suicide attempt; Meets Prince of Wales. Il. por. *Jet* 82: 65 August 127, 1992.

Michael Jackson: The making of the "King of Pop" [cover story] M. Goldberg. Il. Pors. *Rolling Stone* p. 3 2-37 January 9, 1992.

Michael Jackson thrills 70,000 at historic concert in Bucharest, Romania. Il. Por. *Jet* 82: 62 October 9, 1992.

Michael Jackson wins in court; judge halts publishing of his photo by London Daily mirror. Por. *Jet* 82: 34-35 August 17, 1992.

Michael Jackson's lawyers respond to charges of copyright infringement. *Jet* 82: 60 May 11, 1992.

1993

An abuse of trust? M. Goldberg. Il. Por. *Rolling Stone* p. 21 October 14, 1993.

Choosing sides in Michael Thriller. K. Hamilton. Il. Por. *Newsweek* v 122 p. 38 December 27, 1993.

Dangerous. M. Rosen. Il. Pors. *People's Weekly* 40 p. 40-42 September 6, 1993.

MICHAEL JACKSON'S LAST DANCE

Facing the music. R. Corliss. Il. Pors. *Time* 142: 67December 27, 1993.

Family and fans support Michael Jackson in child abuse investigation [cover story]. Il. Pors. *Jet* 84: 52-59 September 13, 1993.

Jackson hires black attorney Johnny Cochran to defend him against charges. Por. *Jet* 85: 61 December 20, 1993.

Jacksons's Dangerous game. A. Light. Il. *Rolling Stone* 17 April 1, 1993.

Jacksons refute Latoya's charge Michael kept boys with him at family home. Il. por. *Jet* 85: 52+ December 27, 1993-January 3, 1994.

Liz Taylor says she faced the same kind of addictions as Michael Jackson. Il. Pors. *Jet* 85: 12+ December 13, 1993.

Mega-Michael. R. Scheer. *The Nation* 257: 376-77 October 11, 1993.

Michael in Wonderland [Cover story]. D. Friend. Il. Pors. *Life* 16 52-58+ June 1993.

Michael is back, but is he bad? D. Brandy. Il. Por. *Maclean's* 106: 62 December 27, 1993.

Michael Jackson. Il. Por. *People's Weekly* 40: 48-49 December 27, 1993.

Michael Jackson and Little Richard awarded special Grammy honors. Il. Por. *Jet* 83: 52 March 15, 1993.

Michael Jackson ends world tour, blames addiction to painkillers. Il. Pors. *Jet* 83: 16-18, November 29, 1993.

Michael Jackson gives first live interview to Oprah Winfrey [cover story]. Il. Pors. *Jet* 83: 62-63 February 8, 1993.

Michael Jackson gives revealing record breaking interview to Oprah Winfrey. *Jet* IL. Pors. 83: 56-57 March 1, 1993.

Michael Jackson tries to keep career from crumbling as he fights addiction to painkiller drugs and charges of child molestation [cover story]. A. Collier. Il. Pors. *Jet* 85: 54-59 December 6, 1993.

Michael Jackson's album soars to the top of the charts. Il. Por. *Jet* 83: 60 March 8, 1993.

Michael Jackson's mother and brother Jermaine appear on television to defend superstar. Il. *Jet* 85: 59-61 December 20, 1993.

Michael Jackson's new hue. L. D. Peden. Il. Por. *American Health* 12: 28 May 1993.

Michael's malady [Interview]. Il. Por. *People's Weekly* 39: 46 March 1, 1993.

Michael's world [Cover story]. C. McGuigan. Il. Pors. *Newsweek* 122: 34-38 September 6, 1993.

Peter pan speaks. R. Corliss. Il. Pors. *Time* 141: 66-67 February 22, 1993.

The Risks of wishing upon a star. J. Giles *Newsweek* 122: 39 September 6, 1993.

The shield of vulnerability. J. Alter. Il. *Newsweek* 122: 38 September 6, 1993.

Superstar Michael Jackson is back and ready to fight back! Il. Por. *Jet* 85: 56-57 December 27, 1993-January 3, 1994.

Transatlantic hide and seek. J. Giles. Il. Pors. *Newsweek* 122: 70-71 November 29, 1993.

The vanishing [Cover story]. E. Gleick. Il. Pors. *People's Weekly* 40: 42-47 November 29, 1993.

251

We are the weird. E. Diamond. Il. Por. *New Yorker* 26: 28+ September 13, 1993.
Who's bad? R. Corliss. Il. Pors. *Time* 142: 54-56 September 6, 1993.

1994

The check is in the mail. J. Giles. Il. Por. *Newsweek* 123 p. 57 February 7, 1994.

Did Michael do it? [Cover story] M. A. Fischer. Il. Pors. *Gentleman's Quarterly* 64 pp. 214-21+ October 1994.

Dodging the bullet. [Cover story] B. Hewitt. Il. Pors. *Peop'e's Weekly* 41 pp. 64-68 February 7, 1994.

Fear of flying. P. D. Bauman. *Commonweal* 121 pp. 4-5 February 25, 1994.

Federal jury rules in favor of Michael Jackson, others charged with stealing songs. Il. Por. *Jet* 85 pp. 58-59 January 31, 1994.

Hungarian rhapsody. D. Santow. Il. Pors. *People's Weekly* 41 pp. 64-68 February 7, 1994.

A Message to Michael. P. Johnson. Il. *Essence* 24 p. 146 March 1994.

Michael and Lisa. Il. Pors. *Jet* 86 pp. 56-57, August 15, 1994.

Michael Jackson and Lisa Marie Presley 'look forward to raising a family and living happy...' [Cover story] R. E. Johnson. Il. Pors. *Jet* 86 Pp. 56-60 August 22, 1994.

Michael Jackson denies report that he wed Elvis Presley daughter. Il. Pors. *Jet* 86 p. 59 July 25, 1994.

Michael Jackson joins family during 'Jackson family honors' gala fundraiser in Las Vegas. IL Pors. *Jet* 85 p. 54+ March 7, 1994.

Michael Jackson makes surprise appearance at NAACP Image Awards. Il. Por. *Jet* 85 pp. 58-60 January 24, 1994.

Michael Jackson owns rights to Rose Bowl champs fight song, 'On Wisconsin'. Il. Por. *Jet* 85 p. 64 January 24, 1994.

Michael Jackson settles suit, maintains innocence and "gets on with his life" [cover story] IL. Pors. *Jet* 85 pp. 58-62 February 14, 1994.

Michael Jackson speaks: "I am totally innocent of any wrongdoing'. Por. *Jet* 85 pp. 60-61 January 10, 1994.

Michael Jackson 'thankful' child molestation probe over, no charges filed but case to stay open. Il. Por. *Jet* 86 pp. 46-47 October 10, 1994.

Michael Jackson's parents Joseph and Katherine say: "LaToya is still lying – there are people trying to destroy our son. We love him" [Cover story] R. E. Johnson. Il. Pors. *Jet* 85 pp. 54-59 January 10, 1994.

Michael tells 'where I met Lisa Marie and how I proposed' [cover story] R. E. Johnson. Il. Pors. *Ebony* 4 9 pp. 118-24+ October 1994.

Neverland meets Graceland [cover story] T. Giatto. Il. Pors. *People's Weekly* 42 pp. 30-35 August 15, 1994.

Nightmare in Neverland. M. Orth. IL. Pors. *Vanity Fair* 57 Pp. 70-77+ January 1994.

MICHAEL JACKSON'S LAST DANCE

The price is right. R. Corliss. Il. Por. *Time* 143 pp. 60-61 February 7, 1994.
Royal wedding. G. Belafonte. Il. Pors. *Time* 144 p. 63 August 15, 1994.
Vow? Wow! K.S. Schneider. Il. Pors. *People's Weekly* 42 pp. 160-62 July 25, 1994.

1995

Brownstone: new group makes debut on Michael Jackson's record label [cover story] IL. *Jet* 88 pp. 58-61 June 19, 1995.
Curiouser and curiouser. K. Schoemer. Il. Pors. *Newsweek* 125 p. 55 June 26, 1995.
Hooked. S. Crouch. Il. *The New Republic* 213 pp. 18-20 August 21-128, 1995.
The Jackson jive. M. Orth. IL. Pors. *Vanity Fair* No. 421 p. 114+ September 1995.
Jackson, Michael: HIStory [sound recording] Reviews
    Esquire IL. 124 p. 192 September 1995. M. Jacobson.
    Newsweek IL. 125 p. 75 June 5, 1995. J. Giles.
    Rolling Stone IL. p. 55+ August 10, 1995. J. Hunter.
    Stereo Review IL. Por. 60, p. 90 October 1995. R. Givens.
    Time IL. Por. 145 p. 58 June 19, 1995. C. J. Farley
Lazy, hazy, crazy days. J. Martin. Il. *America* 173 pp. 22-23 July 15-22, 1995.
Making HIStory? J. Wiederhorn. Il. Por. *Rolling Stone* p. 24 June 15, 1995.
Michael Jackson and Sony enter joint publishing venture valued at $600 million. Por. *Jet* 89 pp. 36-37 November 27, 1995.
Michael Jackson and wife Lisa Marie Presley reveal intimate side as lovers, parents and best friends [cover story] IL. Pors. *Jet* 88 pp. 12-16, July 3, 12995.
Michael Jackson files $100 million slander suit against TV show. Por. *Jet* 87 p. 54 January 30, 1995.
Michael Jackson hosts West African ruler who made him King of Sanwi. Il. Pors. *Jet* 87 pp. 32-33 February 13, 1995.
Michael Jackson recovers after collapsing in New York. Il. Por. *Jet* 89 p. 62 December 25, 1995-January1, 1996.
Michael Jackson tells HIStory [Primetime live interview with D. Sawyer] S. Pond. Il. Pors. *TV Guide* 43 pp. 20-22 June 10-16, 1995.
A Michael Jackson thriller for Sony. R. Grover. Il. *Business Week* p. 36 July 3, 1995.
Michael Jackson Wows MTV Video Awards with show stopping performance, wind three top awards. Il. Pors. *Jet* 88 pp. 22-25, September 22, 1995.
Moments of fright. Il. Por. *People's Weekly* 44 p. 50 December 18, 1995.
The trouble with celebrity worship. F. Bruning. Il. *Maclean's* 108 p. 11 July 1171, 1995.
What, me worry? J.L. Roberts. Il. Por. *Newsweek* 126 p. 60 November 13, 1995.

1996

FREDERICK MONDERSON

Citing irreconcilable differences, Lisa Marie Presley fies for divorce from Michael Jackson. Pors. *Jet* 89 p. 62+ February 5, 1996.

From here to paternity. K. S. Schneider. Il. Pors. *People's Weekly* 46 pp. 48-49 November 18, 1996.

HBO: Jacko will be backo! M. hammer. Por. *TV Guide* 44 pp. 5-6 January 6-12, 1996.

Jackson, Michael and Jackson, Janet: Scream [videotape] Reviews
   TCI IL. Pors. 29 pp. 52-53 November 1995.

A message to Michael. [Cover story] K. S. Schneider. Il. Pors. *People's Weekly* 45 pp. 52-56 February 5, 1996.

Michael Jackson recovering in France. Il. Por. *Jet* 89 p. 34 January 8, 1996.

Tanks for the memories: Michael Jackson imposes "HIStory" on the Czech Republic. M. Morrison. Il. Por. *Rolling Stone* p. 26 October 31, 1996.

Thinner gone bad. K. Schoemer. Il. Pors. *Newsweek* 127 pp. 48-49 January 29, 1996.

What friends are for [cover story]? K. S. Schneider. Il. Pors. *People's Weekly* 46 pp. 100-04, December 2, 1996.

When TV sold out to Michael Jackson. M. Orth. Pors. *Reader's Digest* 147 pp. 74-78 December 1995.

1997

Jacko's adventures in the Arabian Magic Kingdom. S. Macleod. Il. Por. *Time* 150 pp. 66-67 December 1, 1997.

Jackson, Michael: Blood on the Dance Floor: HIStory in the mix [sound recording] Reviews
   Rolling Stone IL. Pors. P. 118 July 10-24, 1997. N. Brackett.

The king as "pop" [Cover story] D. Friend. Il. Pors. *Life* 20 pp. 92-98+ December 1997.

Michael Jackson and Wife Debbie Rowe, expecting second child, a daughter. Il. Pors. *Jet* 93 p. 31 December 22, 1997.

Michael Jackson reveals that he feels imprisoned by the paparazzi. Por. *Jet* 92 pp. 34-35, October 6, 1997.

Michael Jackson sees concert promoter in German prison; had to show ID after look-alike tried to enter. Il. Por. *Jet* 92 p. 64 May 26, 1997.

1998

Man in the Mirror. R. La Franco. Por. *Forbes* 161 p. 43-44 March 23, 1998.

Royal budget cuts for the king of pop. Il. Pors. *People's Weekly* 49 No. 17 pp. 6-7 May 4, 1998.

MICHAEL JACKSON'S LAST DANCE

A Thriller on Wall Street [m. Jackson to issue bonds] J. L. Roberts Il. Por. *Newsweek* 132 No. 21 p. 87 November 23, 1998.

1999

The Gloved Wonder. Q. Jones. Il. Por. *Newsweek* 133 No. 26 p. 74 June 28, 1999.
Michael Jackson and wife, Debbie Rowe, agree to divorce in L.A. Il. Pors. *Jet* 97 [i.e. 96] No. 21 p. 62 October 25, 1999.
Michael Jackson talks about fame, plastic surgery and 'Thriller'. Por. *Jet* 97 No. 3 p. 57 December 20, 1999.
The once and future king [Cover story; interview] L. Bernhard. Il. Pors. *TV Guide* 47 No. 49 pp. 10-14+ December 4 -10, 1999.
Surprise! It's Over. S. Dougherty. Il. Pors *People's Weekly* 52 No. 16 pp. 73-74 October 25, 1999.

2000

Michael Jackson and Mariah Carey named best-selling artists of millennium at World Music Awards in Monaco. Por. *Jet* 97 No. 25 pp. 24-25 May 29, 2000.

2001

Children today robbed of childhood says Michael Jackson during Oxford Union address. Por. *Jet* 99 No. 15 pp. 30-31 March 26, 2001.
Michael Jackson gets all-star tribute in New York. Il. por. *Jet* 100 No. 16 pp. 56-59 October 1, 2001.
Jackson, Michael: Invincible [sound recording] Reviews
   New York Por. 34 No. 45 p. 118 November 26, 2001. E. Brown.
   The New Yorker IL. 77 No. 39 pp. 113-16 December 10. 2001. G. Greenman.
   Newsweek Por. 139 [i.e. 138] No. 19 p. 69 November 5, 2001
Jackson, Michael: Off the wall [sound recording] Reviews
   Rolling Stone Por. No. 861 p. 59 February 1, 2001.
Michael Jackson, Solomon Burke, the Flamingos inducted into Rock and Roll Hall of Fame. Por. *Jet* 99 No. 17 pp. 34-36 April 9, 2001.
Michael Jackson TV special draws 25 million viewers; 'Invincible' debuts No. 1. Por. *Jet* 100 No. 25 pp. 54-55 September 10, 2001.
The Man in the Mirror. M. Murphy and J. Graham. Por. *TV Guide* 49 No. 45 pp. 16-22, 51 November 10-16, 2001.
Higher yearning [M. Jackson's remarks before the Oxford Union Society] Por. *People's Weekly* 55 No. 11 p. 65 March 19, 2001.

2002

FREDERICK MONDERSON

Black Skin, White Mask. K. R. Good. Por. *Vibe* 10 No. 3, p. 114 March 2002.

Daydream nation [MTV and America] A. Mulrine. Por. *U.S. News and World Report* 133 No. 2 p. 64 July 8-15, 2002.

Jackson heights. B. M. Raftery. Por. *Entertainment Weekly* no. 642 p. 84 March 1, 2002.

Michael Jackson Calls Music Labels Racist. Por. *Jet* 102 No. 4, p. 10 July 22, 2002.

Michael Jackson's Meltdown [Singer battles Sony] F. Goodman. Por. *Rolling Stone* No. 902, pp. 19020 August 8, 2002.

Pop Goes the King? [KM. Jackson] S. Miller. Il. Por. *People* (New York, N.Y. 2002) 58 No. 6, pp. 54-57 August 2, 2002.

Scream gem. M. A. Lipton. Por. *People's Weekly* 57 No. pp. 109-10 March 11, 2002.

Sharpton, Cochran Form Group to Protect Recording Artists; Michael Jackson Named First Member. Por. *Jet* 102 No. 2, p. 6, July 1, 2002.

Unconditional Love [Editorial] E. Wilbekin. Por. *Vibe* 10, No 3 p. 50 March 2002.

MJ; unbreakable [Cover story] R. Jones. Por. *Vibe* 10 No. 3 106-08 March 2002.

Is the King of Pop going broke? P. Wilkinson. Graph. Il. Por. *Rolling Stone* 894 pp. 25-28, April 25, 2002.

Who's the Unfairest of Them All? B. Pulley. Por. *Forbes* 170 No. 3 p. 54 August 1`2, 2002.

2003

The 50 Most Intriguing Blacks of 2003. Il. *Ebony* 59 pp. 71-73, 76, 79-80, 84, 86, 88, 90, 92-94, 96-97, 101-02, 104, 106-08, 110, 112, 114, 116-17, 120, 122, 124, 126-28, 130, November 2003.

Losing His Grip [M. Jackson]. M. Orth. Por. *Vanity Fair* No. 512, p. 420-05, 443-48 April 2003.

Michael Jackson Honored In Hometown of Gary, IN; Receives Key To The City. Por. *Jet* 104 No. 1, 38-39 June 30, 2003.

Michael Jackson Honored with Germany's Bambi Award Following Baby Dangling Snafu. Por. *Jet* 102 No. 25, p. 16, 18, December 9, 2 002.

The President of Pop [Election of M. Jackson to presidency in a parallel universe] B. Handy and G. Sweeney. Il. Por. *Time* 161 No. 9, pp. 82 March 3, 2003.

Circus of the Star [Allegations Against M. Jackson] T Sinclair. Il. Por. *Entertainment Weekly* No. 740 p. 12-14 December 5, 2002.

Face the Nation [M. Bashir's controversial documentary on the singer, M. Jackson] S. Dumeneco. Por. *New York* 36 no. 7, p. 16 March 3, 2003.

The King of Pop's Media Mayhem. S. Halperin. Por. *Rolling Stone* No. 918 pp. 123-14 March 20, 2003.

MICHAEL JACKSON'S LAST DANCE

Michael on the Couch. D. Merkin. Por. *New York* 36, No. 43 pp. 38-39, 87 December 8, 2003.

Michael Jackson Exposed. J. Eliscu. Por. *Rolling Stone* No. 918 pp. 13-14, March 20, 2003.

The Cuffed one [Child molesting allegations against M. Jackson]. R. Corliss. Il. Por. *Time* 162 No. 22 p. 48, 50 December 1, 2003.

Fight of His Life [Child molesting allegations against M. Jackson; cover story] S. Schindehette and T. Gliatto. Il. Por. *People* (*New York, N. Y. 2002*) 60 No. 23, pp. 84-91 December 8, 2003.

From Moonwalk to Perp Walk [M. Jackson is accused of child molesting] D. J. Jefferson and A. Murr. Il. Por. *Newsweek* 142 No. 22, pp. 38-40 December 1, 2003.

Jackson's Legacy. M. Gilmore. Por. *Rolling Stone* 938-939 P. 18, December 25, 2003-January 8, 2004.

Michael Jackson Calls Child Molestation Charges 'Lies.' Por. *Jet* 104 No. 24, pp. 16-18, December 8, 2003.

Michael Jackson Ordered To Pay $5.3 million For Backing Out Of New Year's Eve Concerts. Por. *Jet* 103 No. 14 p. 20, March 31, 2003.

Our Great, Societal Neverland [Pedophilia responsibility] T. Dalrymple. *National Review* 55 No. 24, pp. 30-31, December 22, 2003.

Trouble in Neverland [Allegations against M. Jackson] J. Smolowe. Il. Por. *People* (*New York, N.Y. 2002*) 60 No. 22, pp. 58-61, December 1, 2003.

How 'Thriller' Lost Its Thrill [Coverage of M. Jackson] J. Alter. Por. *Newsweek* 142 No. 22 p. 41 December 1, 2003.

2004

Favorite Sons. E. West. Por. *Indianapolis Monthly* 28 No. 2 PP. 138-51, September, 2004.

Jackson Refutes Molestation Charges; maintains Views on Sleeping With Kids During '60 Minutes' Interview. Por. *Jet* 105 No. 3 p. 55 January 19, 2004.

Michael Jackson [50 most intriguing blacks of 2004] Por. *Ebony* 60 No. 4 P. 90 November, 2004.

Monitor [Brief news items and Obituaries] M. Kung. Il. *Entertainment Weekly* No. 764 pp. 22-23, May 7, 2004.

Passages [Short news items] O. Abel. Il. *People* (*New York, N.Y. 2002*) 62 No. 12 p. 199 September 20, 2004.

Unsolved Mysteries. Il. Por. *People* (*New York, N.Y. 2002)* 61 No. 14 pp. 141-4, 145-46 April 12, 2004.

Boswell's Life of Jackson. P. Marx. Il. *The New Yorker* 79 No. 45 pp. 34-35 February 2, 2004.

Michael Jackson [Interview] B. Rather. Por. Interview 34 no. 1 pp.92-93, 126, February, 2004.

The Truth about Michael Jackson's Money. P. Wilkinson. Por. *Rolling Stone* No.

FREDERICK MONDERSON

938/939 pp. 17-18 December 25, 2003/January 8, 2004.

Et. Tu. "Nightline"? [Celebrity press coverage] J. Rosen. Por. *American Journalism Review* 26 No. 1 pp. 18-23 February/March, 2004.

All the news that's fit. L. Dobbs. IL, *US News and World Report* 136 No. 7 p. 48 February 23/March 1, 2004.

You Don't Know Jackson. S. King. Il. *Entertainment Weekly* No. 751 p. 80 February 13, 2004.

Man in the Mirror. [M. Jackson] C. Ho. Coker. Por. *Essence* 34 No. 12 pp. 186-88, 190 April, 2004.

Dick Gregory Endures 40-Day Fast In Support Of Michael Jackson. Por. *Jet* 105 No. 4 p. 36, January 26, 2004.

And the verdict is …. Guilty! A. Goldman.il. *TV Guide* 52 No. 3 Pp. 51-52, 54 January 17-23, 2004.

Crime Watch. Il. Por. *People (New York, N.Y. 2002)* 61No. 18 p. 76 May 10, 2004.

Fired Gun. D. Dunne. Il. Por. *Vanity Fair* No. 531 pp. 178, 180, 182 November 2004.

His Story [M. Jackson] J. Smolowe. Il. Por. People (New York, N.Y. 2002) 61 No. 1 pp. 64-65, January 12, 2004.

Michael Jackson Charged in Case Stemming From Child Molestation Allegations. Por. *Jet* 105, No. 2 p. 64 January 12, 2004.

Monitor [Brief news items and obituaries] IL. *Entertainment Weekly* 770 pp. 28-29 June 18, 2004.

Monitor [Brief news items and obituaries] M. Kung. Il. *Entertainment Weekly* No. 762-763 pp., 28-29 April 30, 2004.

Monitor [Brief news items and obituaries] M. Kung. Il. *Entertainment Weekly* 768 pp. 26-27 June 4, 2004.

Monitor [Brief news items and obituaries] Mk. Kung. Il. Entertainment *Weekly* No. 769 pp. 30-31 June 11, 2004.

Monitor [Brief news items and obituaries] M. Kung and others. *Entertainment Weekly* No. 765 p. 23 May 14, 2004.

Monitor [Brief news items and obituaries] W. Pastorek. Por. *Entertainment Weekly* No. 790 p. 20 October 29, 2004.

Neverland's Lost Boys. M. Orth. Por. *Vanity Fair* 523 pp. 384-89, 415-21 March 2004.

Newsmakers [Short news items] IL. *Newsweek* 32 No. 18 p. 67 May 3, 2004.

Notebook [Short news items and obituaries] IL. *Time* 163 No. 19 pp. 19-21, 26 May 10, 2004.

Off the Wall. J. Spong. Il. Por. Texas Monthly 32 No. 2 pp. 38, 40, 45-46 February 2004.

Passages [Short news items] T. L. Redwood. Il. *People (New York, N.Y. 2002)* 61 No. 16 p. 71 April 16, 2004.

Prosecutor Tried To Get Michael Jackson On Child Molestation Charges Years ago. *Jet* 104 No. 24 p. 17 December 8, 2004.

MICHAEL JACKSON'S LAST DANCE

Scoop [Short news items] IL. *People* (*New York, N.Y. 2002*) 61 No. 25 pp. 19-20, 22, 24 June 28, 2004.

Star-Stricken. J. Durbin. Por. *Maclean's* 17 No. 25 56-57 June 21, 2004.

Who's in His Corner? [M. Jackson] IL. Por. People (*New York, N.Y. 2002*) 61 No. 4 pp. 44-45, February 2, 200.

Ya Heard? [Short news items] A. Woodson. Il. *Vibe* 12 No. 9 p 110 September 2004.

2005

Is Michael Jackson Getting a Reality Show? M. Murphy. Por. *TV Guide* 53 No. 28, p. 80 July 10-16, 2005.

The Beautiful Shall Inherit the Earth. J. M. Laskas. Il. Por. *Gentleman's Quarterly* 75 No. 5, 240-45 May 2005.

King of Pop Faces Grueling Nominations Process on Hill. Por. *Weekly Standard* 10 No. 20, p. 40 February 7, 2005.

The Fake Trial of Michael Jackson. [E! Entertainment Television presentation of M. Jackson Trial] G. Gumpert and S. J. Drucker. Por. *Television Quarterly* 35, No. 32/4 Spring/Summer 2005.

The True Believers [M. Jackson's fans] L. Ali. Il. Por. *Newsweek* 145: No. 10, 52-54, March 7, 2005.

Another Accuser's Explosive Charges. [M. Jackson trial] IL. Por. *People* (*New York, N.Y. 2002*) 64 No. 15 p. 72 April 18, 2005.

As End Nears. Who's Winning? [M. Jackson trial] J. Smolowe. Il. Por. *People* (*New York, N.Y. 2002*) 063, No. 22 p. 79-80 June 6, 2005.

Beating the Rap [M. Jackson trial] B. Hewitt. Il. Por. *People* (*New York, N.Y. 2002*) 63 No. 25, 58-61 June 27, 2005.

Beyond the Pale. P. J. Williams. Il. *The Nation* 280: No 20, p. 12 May 23, 2005.

C.S.I. Neverland [The Jackson trial] M. Orth. Por. *Vanity Fair* No. 539 p. 80-85, 134-37, July 2005.

The Case Against Michael Jackson [Child Molesting trial pending in California] P. Wilkinson. Il. Por. *Rolling Stone* No. 967, p. 13-14, February 10, 2005.

Celebrities Behaving Madly. D. Dunne. Il. Por. *Vanity Fair* 540, p. 86, 88, 90 August 2005.

The Gloves Come Off. [M. Jackson trial] B. Hewitt. Il. Por. *People* (*New York, N.Y. 2002*)

In the Grip of Predators. B. Amiel. Il. Por. *Maclean's* 118, No. 24, p. 4 2-4 6, June 13, 2005.

Inside the Michael Jackson Trial. M. Murphy. Il. *TV Guide* 53 No. 14, p. 13 April 3-9, 2005.

Inside the Strangest Trial on Earth [M. Jackson case] M. Taibbi. Il. Por. *Rolling Stone* 971, p. 35-36, 38, 65 April 7, 2005.

Jacko's Bad Day in Court. [Trial of M. Jackson] R. Corliss. Il. Por. *Time* 165: No. 2, p. 56-57 March 21, 2005.

Jackson vs. the State of California. Il. Por. People (*New York, N.Y. 2002*) 63: No. 6, pp. 66-67 February 14, 2005.

Jackson's Troubling Trial [Interview with J. Silberg] D. Cole. *U.S. News and World Report* 138 No. 10, p. 18, March 21, 2005.

King's Court [M. Jackson's Fans] J. Katz. Il. *Los Angeles Magazine* 50 No. 7 pp. 74-83, July 2005.

Looking for Boundaries. T. Dalrymple. Por. *National Review* 57 No. 11, pp. 26-27 June 20, 2005.

Michael Jackson Not Guilty in Molestation Trial. Il. Por. *Jet* 107, Nc. 26 pp. 61-65, June 27, 2005.

Monitor [Brief News Item] T. Stack. Por. *Entertainment Weekly* No. 844/845 p. 24, October 14, 2005.

The Nation in the Mirror. M. Taibbi. Il. Por. *Rolling Stone* No. 977/978 pp. 69-72 June 30-July 14, 2005.

Playing the Class Card [M. Jackson's trial] A. Murr. Por. *Newsweek145* No. 10, p. 54 March 7, 2005.

Star Witness: Victim or Liar? [M. Jackson trial] A. Tresniowski. Il. Por. *People* (New *York, N.Y.* 2002) 63, No. 12 pp. 89-90 March 28, 2005.

The True Believers [M. Jackson's fans] L. Ali. Il. Por. *Newsweek* 145 No. 10, pp. 52-54 March 7, 2005.

2006

Michael Jackson to sell Neverland Ranch. Famous Glittery Glove during Auction. Por. *Jet* 14, No. 25, p. 28 January 12, 2009.

One the Block [M. Jackson possessions up for auction] R. Dyball. Il. Por. *People* (New York, N. Y.

2007

'Can he be forgiven?' [M. Jackson] A. Wherry. Por. *McLean's* 120: No. 8, 76-78 March 5, 2007.

Michael Jackson breaks silence. Remembers Mime Marcel Marceau. J. T. Bennett. Por. *Jet* 112 No. 15 p. 32 October 15, 2007.

Michael: The Thrill is Back. [M. Jackson cover story] J.T. Bennett. Por. *Ebony* 63 No. 2 80-83, 86, 88, 90-93, December 2007.

Michael Jackson: In his own words. [Interview] B. Monroe. Por. *Ebony* 63: No. 2, 94. 96, 98-100, 104-106, 109, December 2007.

2008

MICHAEL JACKSON'S LAST DANCE

Scoop [Short news items]. Il. Por. *People* (*New York, N.Y. 2002*) 70 No. 4 p. 23, 25, 26, 28, 30 July 28, 2008.

OMG They're 50! C. Tapper. Por. *People* (*New York, N.Y. 2002*) 70 No. 9 pp. 94-95 September 1, 2008.

Neverland Lost? Il. Por. *People* (*New York, N.Y. 2002*) 69 No. 10 pp. 66-67 March 17, 2008.

Thrills to come [25th anniversary edition of Thriller produced by M. Jackson and featuring K. West, Akon and Will.i.am; cover story] J.T. Bennett. Por. *Jet* 112 No. 25 pp. 58-62, December 24-31, 2007.

Come Beat It. K. Tucker. Il. *Entertainment Weekly* No. 978 pp. 64-65 February 21, 2008.

2009

Michael Jackson to sell Neverland Ranch, Famous Glittery Gove During auction. Por. *Jet* 114 No. 25 p. 28 January 12, 2009.

On the Block [M. Jackson possessions up for auction] R. Dyball. Il. Por. *People* (New York, N.Y. 2002) 71 No. 8, pp. 68-69 March 2, 2009.

Monitor [Brief News Items and Obituaries] K. Ward. Il. Por. *Entertainment Weekly* No. 1024 p. 2-21 December 5, 2008.

Avoiding the Wreck. J. Muller. Por. *Forbes* 183 No. 5 pp. 34, 37, March 16, 2009.

NEW YORK TIMES

1984

Books - January 28; March 14

Music – January 14, 22; February 8, 29; April 3, 5, 6, 7, 8; June 27; July 5, 6, 7, 9, 15, 20, 21, 22, 24, 29, 30; August 3, 5, 6, 7, 8; September 2; Presidential Election 1984 – June 24,

Roads – May 15; South Africa – July 13; Television – Making of 'Thriller' The (TV Program) February 2

Singer Michael Jackson gives his mother red Rolls-Royce at her birthday party, Beverly Hills, Calif. (S), May 7, II 11: 4.

Police raid string of Toronto stores to end proliferation of counterfeit Michael Jackson paraphernalia (S), July 12, III, 13: 3.

1985

Movie – July 24; 28, 31.

FREDERICK MONDERSON

Music – February 27; June 12; July 17; August 16.

1986

Apparel – April 17.
Motion Pictures – Captain Eo (Movie), September 14.
Sex Crimes –July 14.

1987

Motion Pictures – Captain Eo (Movie) June 24
Music – May 17; July 22; August 29, 31; September 1, 2, 3, 10, 13, 14

1988

Book Reviews – Ken Tucker reviews Moonwalk by Michael Jackson, photo, June 5, VII, 51: 1
Dancing, March 6.
Music - January 14; February 9, 11, 24, 25; March 3, 5, 6, 23; June 29; September 12; October 11.
Scholarships and Fellowships - January 14.
Television – Motown on Showtime (TV Program), March 12;Michael Jackson Book Moonwalk, in which he discusses his show business friends, his plastic surgery, his girlfriends and his rise to musical superstardom, is about to be published by Doubleday (M), April 18: III, 22: 1.

1990

Acquired Immune Deficiency Syndrome (AIDS), April 12.
Children and Youth, April 6.
Music – November 21; December 14.

1991

Acquired Immune Deficiency Syndrome – September 21.
Music – March 21, 24, 28; November 6, 10, 17, 24, 28; December 1.
Taylor, Elizabeth – December 7.

1992

MICHAEL JACKSON'S LAST DANCE

Music – February 4; March 16; April 25; August 13.
Shoes and Boots – September 14; November 28.

1993

Advertising – February 18; November 16.
Music – November 25.
Soft Drinks – November 15, 16
Television – March 27.
United States Politics and Government – January 18.
Oprah Winfrey will talk with Michael Jackson in 90-minute special in February; ABC says it will be Jackson's first live interview (S) - January 11, B, 7: 3.
Oprah Winfrey's interview with Michael Jackson on ABC was highest rated entertainment show in six years, (S) - February 12, C, 32: 3.
Dermatologist Arnold Klein confirms that singer Michael Jackson, his patient, suffers from vitiligo, little-understood disease which causes loss of skin pigment; photo; other doctors comment on limited treatment available (S) - February 13, I, 7: 1.

1994

Children and Youth – April 27.
Music – February 21; September 9.
Photo of Michael Jackson accepting NAACP award for choreography, and proclaiming his innocence in face of child-molestation charges - January 7, A, 14: 4.
Los Angeles District Attorney's office reports that criminal investigation into allegations of extortion plot against Michael Jackson is completed and no action is planned (S) - January 25, A, 13: 1.

1995

Music – May 25; June 15, 16, 17, 18, 19, 22, 23, 25, 29; July 17, 20, 26, 27; September 4, 23; November 8; December 21.
Thomas L. Friedman Op-Ed column on the real economic powers in the world includes singer Michael Jackson because his personal GNP is so huge (S) - May 28, IV, 121: 5.

1996

Gary (Indiana) - November 29.

263

FREDERICK MONDERSON

King Entertainment - March 20.

Landmark Entertainment Group – October 30.

Music – February 11; May 9; October 7; November 25. Lisa Marie Presley and Michael Jackson are planning to divorce; their photos (M), January 19, B, 5: 1.

Lisa Marie Presley files for divorce from Michael Jackson; photo (S), January 21, IV, 2: 1.

Michael Jackson weds Debbie Rowe in Australia: Jackson says Rowe is six months pregnant with their child (S) November 15, B, 7: 1.

1997

Boxing – December 16.

Music – January 6; May 20; June 23; September 7.

Michael Jackson and Debbie Rowe have a baby girl – February 14, B: 6: 1.

Michael Jackson was made a Member of Bafokengka Bakwena (People of the Crocodile) Tribe of Phokeng, South Africa – October 14, B 12: 6.

1998

Africa – July 7.

Amusement Parks March - 19.

Apparel February - 27.

2000

Music – January 9; February 24; December 21.

2001

Art – April 20.

Blacks – September 2.

Israel – March 23.

Music – March 20; September7, 10, 13; October 28; November 1; December 20.

Terrorism – September 18.

2002

Music – June 6, 15; July 7, 8, 10, 11, 15, 16; October 7; November 22, 23.

264

MICHAEL JACKSON'S LAST DANCE

Michael Jackson's Last Dance Photo 203. Classic Michael Jackson pose and photo.

2004

Acquired Immune Deficiency Syndrome -, April 1.
Housing - May 7.
Motion Pictures – Miss Cast Away (Movie), May 31.
Music – January 4; February 12; October 24.
Sex Crimes – January 1, 3, 4, 5, 17, 21, 25; February 3, 12, 14; April 3, 14, 22, 23, 24, 26, 27; May 1, 6, 9, 29; June 26; July 15, 23, 28; August 15, 17; September 3, 4, 18; October 13, 24; December 6, 21.

FREDERICK MONDERSON

Television – Man in the Mirror: The Michael Jackson Story (TV Program), August 6.
Transit Systems, January 18.

Music - May 25; June 15, 16, 17, 18, 19, 22, 23, 25, 29; July 17, 20, 26, 27; September 4, 23; November 8; December 21.

2005

Housing - June 19.
Music - May 5, June 14, 15, July 12, September 14, November 25.
Sex Crimes - January 13, 14, 15, 29, 31; February 1, 6, 10, 15, 16, 29, 22, 23, 24, 25, 28; March 1, 2, 3, 4, 5, 8, 9, 10, 11, 12, 15, 16, 17, 18, 19, 22, 23, 24, 26, 27, 29, 30, 31; April 2, 5, 6, 8, 9, 11, 12, 13, 14, 17, 18, 20, 24, 25, 26, 27, 28, 29, 30; May 4, 5, 6, 7, 10, 11, 12, 13, 14, 17, 18, 20, 24, 25, 26, 27, 28; June 1, 2, 3, 4, 6, 7, 8, 9, 12, 14, 15, 16; August 9, 24, 31; December 11.

MICHAEL JACKSON'S LAST DANCE

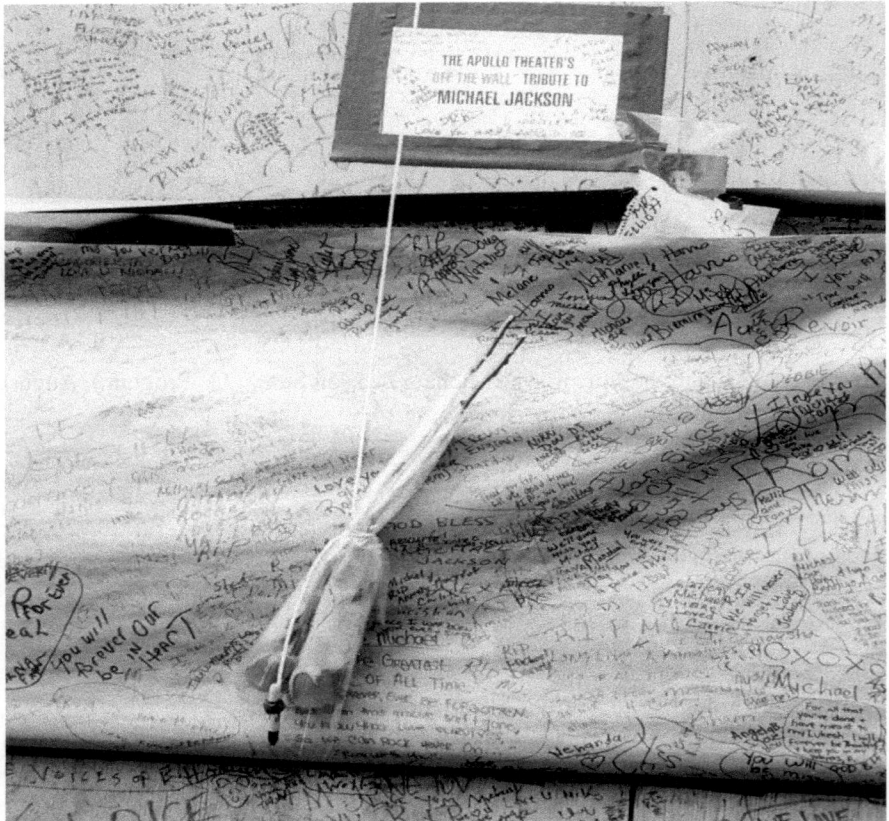

Michael Jackson's Last Dance Photo 204. Someone placed a rose over the tribute "Wall."

2006

Amusement and Theme Parks - March 11, 13, 18.
Art - December 4.
Books and Literature on Michael Jackson (Book) - January 15, 24.
Music - April 13, 14, 15; May 27, July 7, 17; August 3, November 9, 2 4, 25; December 26, 31.

FREDERICK MONDERSON

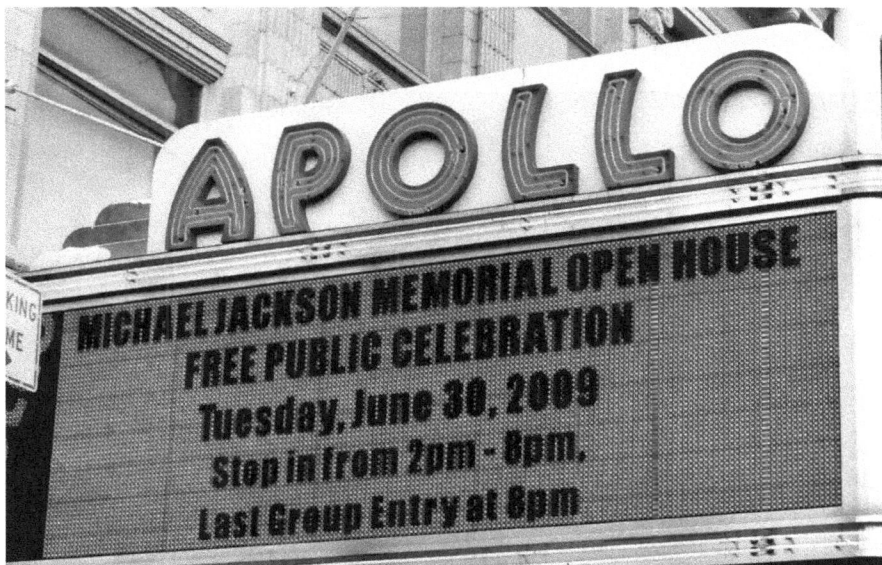

Michael Jackson's Last Dance Photo 205. More of the Marquee of the Apollo.

Michael Jackson's Last Dance Photo 206. Honoring Michael Jackson as an Apollo legend.

MICHAEL JACKSON'S LAST DANCE

Michael Jackson's Last Dance Photo 207. Teddy bears to hug Michael Jackson, Icon.

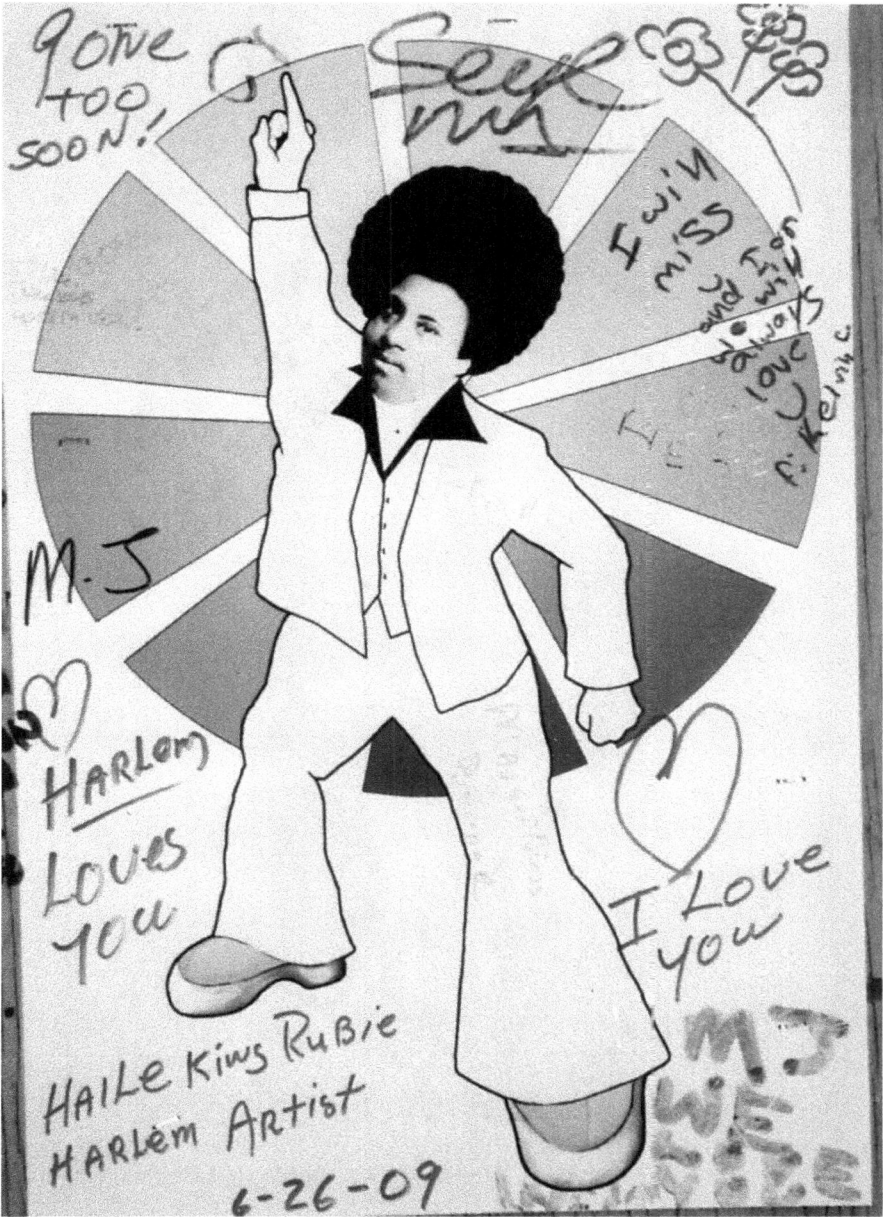

Michael Jackson's Last Dance Photo 208. Photo says MJ's "Working day and Night!"

MICHAEL JACKSON'S LAST DANCE

Michael Jackson's Last Dance Photo 209. Beauty holds classic photo of Michael J.

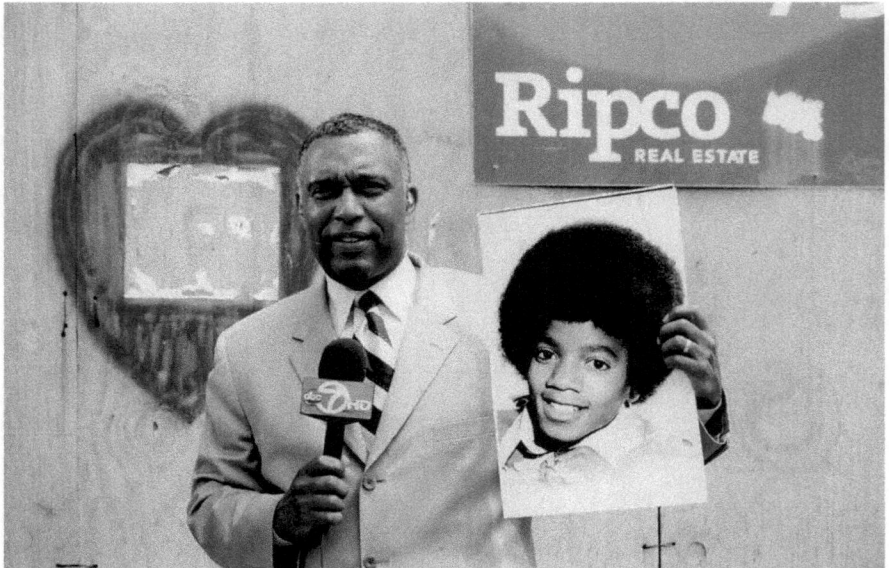

Michael Jackson's Last Dance Photo 210. Legendary Television newscaster holds photo of young Michael Jackson with his mice sporting Chanel 7, New York Logo.

Michael Jackson's Last Dance Photo 211. Fan holds differing images of Michael while wearing President Barack Obama shirt.

Michael Jackson's Last Dance Photo 212. Beautiful people gathered to salute Michael Jackson, the "King of Pop."

Michael Jackson's Last Dance Photo 213. On the upper level of the Apollo Theater news people gather to observe the Tribute below and on stage.

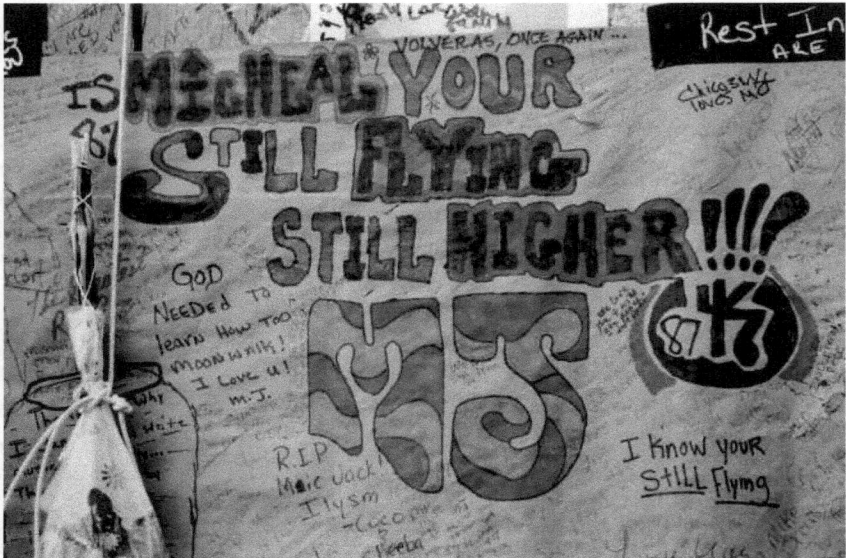

Michael Jackson's Last Dance Photo 214. The sign says it all.

FREDERICK MONDERSON

Michael Jackson's Last Dance Photo 215. Crowds gather to get a glimpse of the "Altar of Remembrance."

Michael Jackson's Last Dance Photo 216. More of the crowd with "The Wall" in rear as the excitement continues to build.

MICHAEL JACKSON'S LAST DANCE

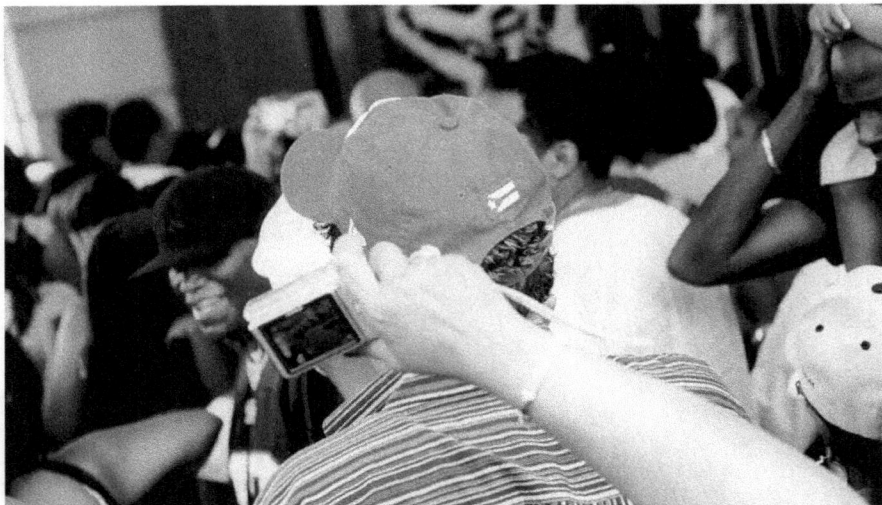

Michael Jackson's Last Dance Photo 217. Close up of the excitement.

Michael Jackson's Last Dance Photo 218. Even closer look as people try for photos.

FREDERICK MONDERSON

Michael Jackson's Last Dance Photo 219. Delivering the classic image of Michael J.

MICHAEL JACKSON'S LAST DANCE

Michael Jackson's Last Dance Photo 220. The quintessential Michael Jackson's pose and other memorabilia on the "Altar of Remembrance."